Dancing Black, Dancing White

T0355321

Dancing Black, Dancing White

Rock 'n' Roll, Race, and Youth Culture of the 1950s and Early 1960s

JULIE MALNIG

OXFORD
UNIVERSITY PRESS

OXFORD
UNIVERSITY PRESS

Oxford University Press is a department of the University of Oxford. It furthers
the University's objective of excellence in research, scholarship, and education
by publishing worldwide. Oxford is a registered trade mark of Oxford University
Press in the UK and certain other countries.

Published in the United States of America by Oxford University Press
198 Madison Avenue, New York, NY 10016, United States of America.

© Oxford University Press 2023

All rights reserved. No part of this publication may be reproduced, stored in
a retrieval system, or transmitted, in any form or by any means, without the
prior permission in writing of Oxford University Press, or as expressly permitted
by law, by license, or under terms agreed with the appropriate reproduction
rights organization. Inquiries concerning reproduction outside the scope of the
above should be sent to the Rights Department, Oxford University Press, at the
address above.

You must not circulate this work in any other form
and you must impose this same condition on any acquirer.

Library of Congress Cataloging-in-Publication Data
Names: Malnig, Julie, author.
Title: Dancing black, dancing white : rock 'n' roll, race, and youth
culture of the 1950s and early 1960s / Julie Malnig.
Description: New York : Oxford University Press, 2023. |
Includes bibliographical references and index.
Identifiers: LCCN 2022054550 (print) | LCCN 2022054551 (ebook) |
ISBN 9780197536261 (paperback)
ISBN 9780197536254 (hardback) | ISBN 9780197536285 (epub)
Subjects: LCSH: Television dance parties—United States—History—20th century. |
Rock and roll dancing—United States—History—20th century. |
Dance and race—United States—History—20th century. |
Music and race—United States—History—20th century. |
United States—Race relations—History—20th century.
Classification: LCC PN1992.8.D3 M35 2023 (print) | LCC PN1992.8.D3 (ebook) |
DDC 791.450973/09045—dc23/eng/20230126
LC record available at https://lccn.loc.gov/2022054550
LC ebook record available at https://lccn.loc.gov/2022054551

DOI: 10.1093/oso/9780197536254.001.0001

Paperback printed by Marquis Book Printing, Canada
Hardback printed by Bridgeport National Bindery, Inc., United States of America

For Ogden . . .

Contents

Illustrations

Illustrations

Foreword

Michael Dinwiddie

NOW THAT I CAN DANCE. . . .
In 1962 a Motown group called the Contours introduced a song that opened with a tender somewhat forlorn verse aimed at a teenage girl:

> You broke my heart
> 'Cause I couldn't dance
> You didn't even want me around
> And now I'm back
> To let you know
> I can really shake 'em down.

A raucous, raspy male voice then broke in with a demanding question, "Do you love me?," which after being repeated six times in a call-and-response pattern was answered by the selfsame singer with the lusty, arrogant boast, "Now that I can dance!" And then it repeated three times:

> Dance!
> Dance!
> Dance!

Learning to dance was a key to successful courtship, self-acceptance, and "true" love in the teen years. It was a rite of passage that eventually hurried one forward on the path to autonomous adulthood. Once the current dance steps were mastered, the confidence to strut out on the floor—hopefully with a partner—let everyone know how "cool" you had become. And pity the poor clumsy kids who papered the walls, unable to master the simple movements that were enumerated in so many lyrics of the era: the Twist, the Mashed Potatoes, the Cool Jerk, the Monkey, the Horse, the Watusi, the Swim, etc. Each dance evoked a tribal response of belonging, of fitting in, of knowing what to do next.

And where did we teens learn those intricate moves that put us on top of the world? Surely not in an Arthur Murray studio or a fancy white-glove dance salon filled with little lord and lady Fauntleroys. Even those of us lucky enough to have an older brother or sister could not rely on them for the latest moves. They were fickle teachers, more interested in hanging out with their own friends and making age a greater chasm than it turned out to be in later life. And nerdy older siblings were of little or no use; they were more content to open a book and do their math homework than to master a new dance. What was a desperate tweener to do?

For those of us who came of age during the Eisenhower/Kennedy years, the most reliable way to get in step was by tuning in to one of the dance shows that aired on our black-and-white Zenith televisions. Under various names—*Teen Dance Party, Teenage Frolics, Swingin' Time, Teenarama, The Buddy Deane Show*—these early programs served up a polyglot mix of entertainment to a vibrant youth culture hungry for community, celebrity, terpsichorean instruction, and just plain fun.

Male radio disc jockeys (never women) were the pioneers of these early experimental forays into TV Land. The deejays made it seem like the most natural progression in the universe—from spinning 45s in a sound booth to doing the same on-air in front of a live, gyrating audience. They were the logical "leaders" into this new world where rock, roll, and rhythm and blues ruled the airwaves.

Broadcast stations were eager to attract younger viewers, and the dance shows were easy and inexpensive to produce. They all followed a familiar format with slight regional variations: local high schools were tapped for unpaid dancers, new records were introduced for ratings, and a studio set, sometimes with bleachers for non-dancers, would finish out the space. The set decoration might consist of giant cardboard records and a chart to record dancers' responses. The deejay father figure, along with cameras that acted as chaperones, reassured parents that their young people were behaving: nicely coiffed, well-dressed, and safely interacting at a respectable distance from each other. Even with all the physical exertion and crowded spaces, no one was breaking a sweat. In this groundbreaking study, Julie Malnig frames the societal elements at play in what passed for a neutral safe zone for young people. She exposes the ways in which a repressive society enforced racial, sexual, and class tropes in plain sight.

What a surprise—to discover in this book that these teen dance shows reflected some of the most pernicious aspects of American culture. Racial segregation was practiced as a matter of course and crossing that line could have immediate consequences. When African American pop singer Frankie Lymon appeared on Alan Freed's 1957 *Big Beat* show, at the end of his performance Freed invited the audience to "come on stage and dance." Lymon took the hand of a young white girl, and the action was caught on camera. An uproar ensued from Southern affiliates of ABC-TV, and Freed was told that he could no longer host Black performers. Freed refused to accept such a condition and his show was summarily canceled. Other shows, to protect themselves, conducted screening interviews to ensure a "whites only" admission policy. A few would allow an occasional Black couple to participate on the dance floor, but that couple might never be seen by the viewing audience. And when the cameras were off, it was not uncommon for Black and whites to socialize and dance together, even though it was understood that "race mixing" was unacceptable to much of the white public. As Malnig chronicles, on Dick Clark's fabled *American Bandstand*, which ran for more than thirty years, a young white couple could not even admit in an on-air interview that they had learned a dance step from watching a Black couple create it. They understood, from the social pressure of the period, that it would be improper to admit their appropriation. Dick Clark claimed that the step had been invented on his show, but he issued an apology once he learned the truth. This type of appropriation was rampant in all aspects of entertainment for generations, with people of color receiving no credit or acknowledgment for their creative contributions.

Powerful examples punctuate the narrative of exclusion that Malnig describes. In Tulsa, Oklahoma, local KOTV Channel 6 allowed Black students from Booker T. Washington High School to appear on-air one day out of the entire year. It was the struggle to integrate *The Buddy Deane Show* in Baltimore that was immortalized in John Waters's film and later on the Broadway stage with *Hairspray*. The struggle to dismantle "Negro Day" and the bias against plus-size people is depicted in a tongue-in-cheek manner that belies the serious fissures caused by racial intolerance. Malnig demonstrates the complicated issues raised in terms of politics, economics, and social mediation when these issues were confronted.

There was, however, another angle to complicate the conversation. Black deejays were also able to make the transition to television and create programs tailored to their specific communities. *The Mitch Thomas Show*, which aired for three years from Wilmington, Delaware, was a popular destination for Black dancers who came from as far away as Philadelphia to perform. And in

Raleigh, North Carolina, J. D. Lewis, starting in 1958, hosted *Teenage Frolics* on WRAL-TV for more than two decades. These Black-hosted programs were heavily involved in providing services that improved young people's self-esteem and built a strong sense of community.

As a final note, I grew up in Detroit watching radio-TV personality Robin Seymour's after-school dance show *Swingin' Time*. Seymour, who was white, was delighted to attract and showcase dancers from all races. And his stance gained him a loyal ally in Motown founder Berry Gordy, who debuted all his young artists on *Swingin' Time*. Motown's motto, "The Sound of Young America," needed a space where all teenagers would be welcome. The Supremes, the Marvelettes, Martha and the Vandellas, the Temptations, Marvin Gaye, Smokey Robinson and the Miracles, and Stevie Wonder all made their first television appearance in a setting where teenagers could lose the false racial barriers that had been constructed around them. It was a sonic space where they could listen, gyrate, and mash all the potatoes they wanted. A longing for acceptance and love pulled listeners across all strata to celebrate the new music that was upbeat, positive, and (most important of all) danceable! This volume unwraps the nostalgia of this complicated time.

Acknowledgments

This book has been numerous years in the making, and many individuals and institutions have been involved in its creation. First and foremost, I wish to thank those former teenage dancers who graciously agreed to interviews with me. They include Calleen Anderegg, Tony Bonanno, Earlene Briggs, Peg Desonier, John Dew, Kathy Doty, Lana Drouillard, Robert Frye, Otis Givens, Gwen Horton, Ralph Irish, Joyce Jackson, Christine Liddell, Antoinette Matlins, Yvonne Mills, Elaine Oakes, Laverne Parks, James Preston, Linda Roman, James Ross, Leslie Tipton Russell, James Sator, Marvin Talley, Virginia Talley, Mickey Teague, Steve Vilarino, and Kay Wheeler.

I am indebted to those former teen dance hosts, directors, and producers whom I interviewed: Robin Seymour (*Swingin' Time*), Art Laboe (*The Art Laboe Show*), Dale Young (*Detroit Bandstand*), Steve Stephens (*The Steve Stephens Show*), Lee Woodward (*Oklahoma Bandstand*), Kerry Richards (*The Larry Kane Show*), Jim Rowley (*The!!!! Beat*), and Greg Stewart (*Uptight*). Bud Buschardt, the producer of *The Sump'n Else Show*, who sadly passed away during the course of this book, shared his contacts with me without hesitation and led me to several former teen dancers. Other interviewees I would like to thank include Sam Sauls (Bud Buschardt's coauthor of the book *The Sump'n Else Show*), Jim Hibbard, Alonzo Kittrels, Paul Pope, Brant Hart, Patrick Richards, Sandra Hubbard, and Leah Branstetter. Glenn Pitts, a former dancer on *The Larry Kane Show*, was a font of information on teen dance shows in Texas, and I thank him for kindly sharing images from his collection. Jonathan Prince, the showrunner for the TV series *American Dreams*, was particularly insightful about creating a program based on *American Bandstand*.

I am indebted to Beverly Lindsay-Johnson, filmmaker, producer, and executive director of the documentary *Dance Party: The Teenarama Story*, for numerous conversations, interviews, and follow-up emails. She also generously shared her contacts with me, which enabled interviews with many former *Teenarama Dance Party* dancers. I also thank Jiiko Azimba, who along with Beverly granted me an interview regarding their musical *Dancing on the Air: The Teenarama Story*.

I also owe special thanks to Yvonne Lewis Holley, who took time out from her hectic schedule as a candidate for lieutenant governor in North Carolina to speak with me about her father, teen dance host, deejay, and broadcasting executive J. D. Lewis. Clarence Williams, a former producer at WRAL and Raleigh, North Carolina's *Teenage Frolics*, was extremely enthusiastic about my project and put me in touch with former dancers Virginia Talley, Earlene Briggs, and Gwen Horton, who offered their personal stories and recollections of *Teenage Frolics* and life in Raleigh. Phyllis Stamz, the daughter of Richard Stamz—the host of *Richard's Open Door*—helped me fill in important details on the history of the show. I wish to thank former social dancer Steve Vilarino for his interview and for sharing images with me, and to Joanna Morones, for her help with acquiring photographs of Art Laboe and arranging an interview with him. I especially thank Toni Basil for her interview and follow-up correspondence and for her terrific Zoom social dance classes; she is a wealth of knowledge of 1960s popular dance.

Individuals who either lent sources or expertise include dance writer Debra Levine, a consistent supporter and cheerleader of this work, who offered many valuable contacts, among them Chris Nichols, senior editor at *Los Angeles* magazine, who provided excellent leads on 1960s dance shows and possesses a wealth of information on LA popular culture. Historian Eric Foner was particularly helpful in enabling me to think through the political and protest history of the 1960s and offered many helpful and incisive ideas. Rachel Devlin, the author of *A Girl Stands at the Door: The Generation of Young Women Who Desegregated America's Schools*, kindly corresponded with me about young women and girls in the civil rights movement. She also put me in touch with her former doctoral student Mia Carey, writing on Black girlhood in the interwar years, who steered me to appropriate and valuable research collections including the Moorland-Spingarn Research Center at Howard University and the Behind the Veil Project (African American Life in the Jim Crow South Records) at Duke University. I owe a debt of gratitude to Lynn Garafola for her ongoing support and for inviting me to speak at the Columbia University Dance Seminar where I received extremely valuable comments from the group's participants.

My work has been buttressed by several colleagues and friends at New York University's Gallatin School of Individualized Study; I can't thank them enough. In particular, I am grateful to Sharon Friedman for her always sage advice, her constant optimism about this project, and always seeing through ideas and issues with me; Leslie Satin for many inspired and enlightening conversations about this material and for her keen insights, and Michael Dinwiddie for his support and friendship and for connecting me with former *Oklahoma Bandstand* dancer Joyce Johnson. Hannah Gurman and Eugene Vydrin kindly shared their expertise regarding the decade of the 1950s and Cold War history, and John Castellano Kwami Coleman were vitally important to my understanding of the intricacies of rhythm and blues music. To former Gallatin Dean Susanne Wofford, I owe special thanks for her constant optimism regarding this project, her ideas, and several Faculty Enrichment Fund grants to see the book through to its completion. I also want to thank Jennifer Homans, director of NYU's Center for Ballet and the Arts, for her support during my tenure at the Center as a Faculty Fellow, as well as Associate Director Andrea Salvatore for helping make my stay there extremely pleasant.

Other individuals I wish to thank include Janice Ross, my colleague at the Center for Ballet and the Arts, for her encouragement and enthusiasm for this project. Stephen Steinberg was a wellspring of information concerning matters of race and ethnicity and offered many illuminating suggestions and sources. Sally Sommer has been a most valued colleague and friend over many years and inspired my interest in popular and social dance in the first place. My longtime colleague Barbara Stratyner also offered vital assistance at several points during the course of the book. Former dance professor and professional dancer Karen W. Hubbard lent her expertise regarding jazz dance over the course of several conversations, and I am most grateful to her. Matthew F. Delmont, professor of history at Dartmouth College and the author of *The Nicest Kids in Town: American Bandstand, Rock 'n' Roll, and the Struggle for Civil Rights in 1950s Philadelphia*, graciously shared many valuable sources and contacts. His work was an inspiration to my own. I also thank Carla Walter for helpful conversations about the intersections between Black dance and advertising practices.

Several former students and research assistants were tremendously helpful, including Kate Enright, Lillian Rafson, Elspeth Walker, and Claudia Vera. My final assistant, Emilia Litwak, was an excellent and enterprising researcher and devised a superb organizational database of my research materials.

I owe a special measure of thanks to my editor Norm Hirschy, who consistently supported this book project from its initial proposal to the final manuscript and offered much helpful advice and counsel along the way. I also thank Oxford University Press project editors Lauralee Yeary and Zara Cannon-Mohammed.

Finally, I owe some of my greatest thanks to Anita Malnig—*mia sorella*— for her unflinching support and love and for reading numerous drafts of my manuscript with her scrupulous editorial eye; she is an editor par excellence. And to my husband, Ogden Goelet, for standing by me all the way, through the ups and downs of writing, and for his determination to help me see the book through to its completion.

Introduction

One of the most iconic rock 'n' roll dances of the late 1950s, the Madison, sparked a national dance craze after its introduction on the Baltimore-based televised teen dance program *The Buddy Deane Show*. This classic line dance, performed to the hit music single "The Madison Time," by noted jazz pianist Ray Bryant (with the Ray Bryant Combo), featured Baltimore disk jockey Eddie Morrison doing "calls," or shout-outs, of current dance steps that teenagers might follow. The record sold 10,000 copies in its first week. In the dance, teenagers line up in a series of parallel rows and to the jazzy, medium-tempo rock 'n' roll number employ a series of quick shifts of weight from one hip to the other, take small forward, backward, and side steps, and enact the popular-culture references shouted out by the caller ("Give me a Wilt Chamberlain hook!" "Do a strong Jackie Gleason shuffle!"), all in a kind of smooth, calculated "cool." The dance became a sensation in Europe after filmmaker Jean-Luc Godard included an altered rendition of it in his film *Bande à part*, in 1964. And then the dance became immortalized in John Waters's 1998 film *Hairspray*.[1]

The dance in some ways epitomizes the teenage years. Kids moving in unison, keeping in step with one another, and literally and metaphorically afraid of falling out of line with the group. At the same time, the dance offered the possibility to show off, to create one's own variation, to improvise during the caller's commands. Such was the seeming contradiction of the push and pull of teenage life. The origins of the dance—as is true for most social dances—are obscure. While the dance took off once it aired on *The Buddy Deane Show* in 1959 (and inspired all manner of regional variations), it didn't originate there, but rather in Black social clubs at least a year earlier. Black teenagers had gotten there first.[2] The Black composer of the song, Ray Bryant, had a large following of both adults and teenagers, which helped spark the craze in the Black community. A 1960 issue of *Ebony* magazine explained that the dance "has already brought new life to sagging night club business," and named Baltimore Uptown Club as "The Home of the Madison." As *Ebony* made clear about the dance, "like most of its predecessors, it has been taken

Dancing Black, Dancing White. Julie Malnig, Oxford University Press. © Oxford University Press 2023.
DOI: 10.1093/oso/9780197536254.003.0001

over by white enthusiasts, who today constitute the majority of the Madison-dancing population."[3]

The Madison—the dance, its creation, its popularization on television, and its variations created by Black and white teenagers—embodies various elements of this book: a study of rock 'n' roll dance during the 1950s and early 1960s and its dissemination on the televised teen dance program, that phenomenon of early television that captivated teenagers around the country. While not every teenager participated in or even watched these programs, the shows were nonetheless an important vehicle for the transmission of rock 'n' roll social dances during this era. While Dick Clark's *American Bandstand* may immediately come to mind, there were literally hundreds of such programs that aired on local TV stations between approximately 1955 and 1964. This book emphasizes both the *practice* of dance and what these practices meant to the lives of these teenagers and young adults that are often neglected or glossed over in the history of rock 'n' roll music.

As a historian of social dance and so-called social dance crazes, I have always been interested in the cultural phenomena underpinning those crazes and what inspires people to devote significant amounts of time and often considerable expense in pursuing these dance passions. While my earlier work focused on the "social dance revolution" of early twentieth-century America, I turn here to the mid-twentieth century, and a time of enormous cultural turbulence despite the conservatism that we associate with the era. My interests are not purely intellectual, though, as I always like to "dress up" when I teach my Popular Dance and American Cultural Identity seminar— vintage poodle skirt, button-down cardigan, and Mary Janes—to experience for myself, and convey to my students, something of the feeling and atmospherics of these dance events.[4] (For our unit on disco dance, I've been known to come to class with a fringed jacket and a disco bag.) The combination of clothing, dancing, and affecting a pose no doubt helps me truly embody these dances so that I am better able to understand them. Clearly, social dance has many functions, as my book *Ballroom, Boogie, Shimmy Sham, Shake* teased out: it is at once a means of self-expression, identity formation, group cohesiveness, resistance to societal values, and, not least, a source of physical and emotional pleasure.

That all of these elements are at play in teenage dancing drew me to this particular occurrence as it speaks to the power of social dance to galvanize individuals in communal connection. Rooted in the materiality of their everyday lives, rock 'n' roll dancing became, for many teenagers, synonymous with adolescent desires, feelings, hopes, beliefs. And the televised teen dance shows—the centerpiece of my cultural history—exemplify the way in which social dance expression can develop into a cultural and media phenomenon. But the story, I felt, and the way it has been told, was incomplete. Because of the social conditions of the era—the 1950s were some of the darkest years of Jim Crow and white supremacist racism—it became crucial to explore how that communal connection got thwarted *between* Black and white youth and how the racial politics of the time created the conditions in which essentially Black dance got filtered and diluted through young, white bodies. While I tread on what may be familiar rock 'n' roll history to some readers, my intention is to bring together in one place a book that focuses on several interconnected occurrences: the ascendancy of rock 'n' roll and recorded music, the rise of the "teenager" as a distinct cultural subset, the beginning of television, and the effects of segregation and the country's struggle with race. I am telling two stories here, of the different experiences of Black and white adolescents. It became important to me to illustrate how social dance—and rock 'n' roll dance in particular—was an important means of heightened visceral and creative possibilities for both.

* * *

Rock 'n' roll dance, which at its inception was greeted with consternation by cultural commentators and the press, took place in many venues, including social clubs, school dances, rent and house parties, and rock 'n' roll concerts. The prominence of the televised teen dance program suggests that these shows were not only incubators of new styles of social and popular dance but products of a mass-mediated technology that both reflected and reinstantiated the racial politics of the time. Often referred to as "dance parties," the shows helped cultivate a nascent youth culture in the post–World War II era. As I will show, they also helped assuage some of the criticisms of rock and roll music and dance as they presented basically clean-cut kids and an adult host. The youth culture depicted on the shows, however, was primarily white. Black teenagers had a youth culture, too, of course, but the injustice was glaring: Black culture and expressivity was not always in evident display on the airwaves, as television of the era, like the nation at large, was deeply segregated and appealed to what it *perceived* as a primarily white, homogeneous audience.

The history that informs the televised teen dance program was the nascent years of the civil rights movement. In the early 1950s, after the war, the

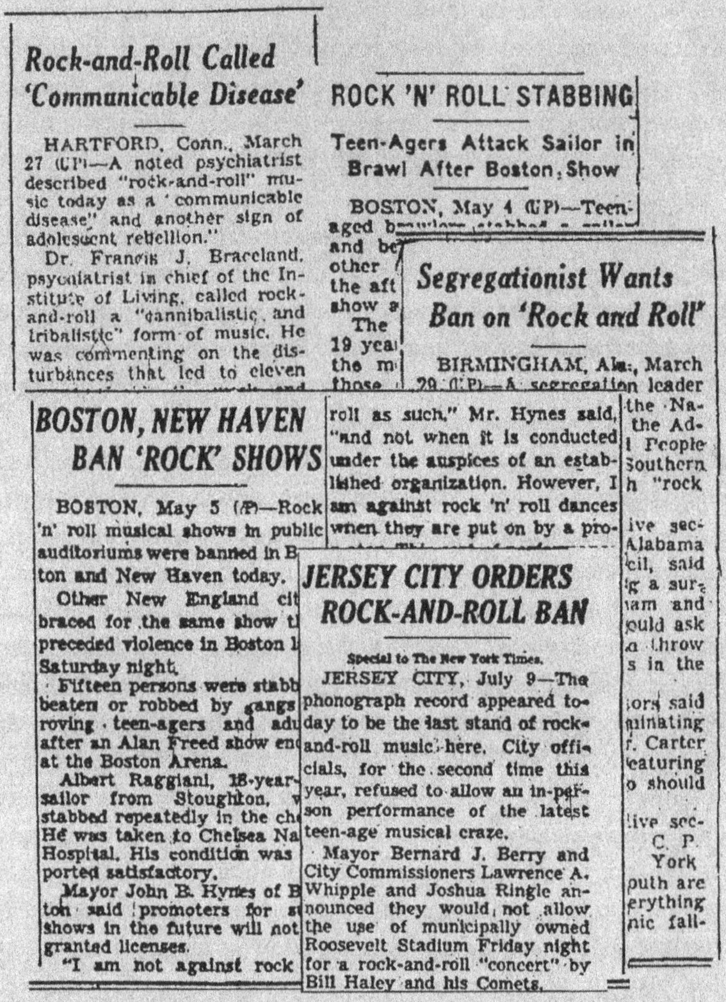

Rock-and-Roll Called 'Communicable Disease'

HARTFORD, Conn., March 27 (UP)—A noted psychiatrist described "rock-and-roll" music today as a 'communicable disease" and another sign of adolescent rebellion."

Dr. Francis J. Braceland, psychiatrist in chief of the Institute of Living, called rock-and-roll a "cannibalistic and tribalistic" form of music. He was commenting on the disturbances that led to eleven

ROCK 'N' ROLL STABBING

Teen-Agers Attack Sailor in Brawl After Boston Show

BOSTON, May 4 (UP)—Teen-aged b... and be... other ... the aft... show a... The ... 19 yea... the m... those

Segregationist Wants Ban on 'Rock and Roll'

BIRMINGHAM, Ala., March 29 (UP)—A segregation leader ... the Na- ... the Ad- ... People ... Southern ... "rock ... ive sec- ... Alabama ... cil, said ... a sur- ... am and ... ould ask ... throw ... s in the ... ors said ... minating ... r. Carter ... featuring ... o should ... ive sec- ... C. P. York ... outh are ... erything ... nic fall-

BOSTON, NEW HAVEN BAN 'ROCK' SHOWS

BOSTON, May 5 (AP)—Rock 'n' roll musical shows in public auditoriums were banned in B...ton and New Haven today.

Other New England cit... braced for the same show t... preceded violence in Boston l... Saturday night.

Fifteen persons were stabb... beaten or robbed by gangs ... roving teen-agers and adu... after an Alan Freed show en... at the Boston Arena.

Albert Raggiani, 18-year-... sailor from Stoughton, w... stabbed repeatedly in the ch... He was taken to Chelsea Na... Hospital. His condition was ... ported satisfactory.

Mayor John B. Hynes of B...ton said promoters for s... shows in the future will not ... granted licenses.

"I am not against rock roll as such," Mr. Hynes said, "and not when it is conducted under the auspices of an established organization. However, I am against rock 'n' roll dances when they are put on by a pro-

JERSEY CITY ORDERS ROCK-AND-ROLL BAN

Special to The New York Times.

JERSEY CITY, July 9—The phonograph record appeared today to be the last stand of rock-and-roll music here. City officials, for the second time this year, refused to allow an in-person performance of the latest teen-age musical craze.

Mayor Bernard J. Berry and City Commissioners Lawrence A. Whipple and Joshua Ringle announced they would not allow the use of municipally owned Roosevelt Stadium Friday night for a rock-and-roll "concert" by Bill Haley and his Comets.

The mass media spread the alarm about the dangers of rock 'n' roll, as in these newspaper headlines from the mid-1950s.

Figure I.1 Outcries over rock 'n' roll music and dance are illustrated in these newspaper headlines from the mid-1950s. From Glenn C. Altschuler, *All Shook Up: How Rock 'N' Roll Changed America* (New York: Oxford University Press, 2003).

United States experienced a glow of might and superiority along with a burst of economic expansion. This affluence affected large numbers of Americans, particularly in the suburbs, but, as historian Eric Foner notes, "it left Blacks in the declining rural areas of the South and the urban ghettos of the North."[5] The modern civil rights movement, which had begun during World War II as a result of the exclusion of Black workers in the expanded war industries, gathered steam in the 1950s. Most notable was the Montgomery bus boycott, led by Martin Luther King Jr. in 1956, which had been precipitated by Rosa Parks, the veteran civil rights activist, who, on December 1, 1955, refused to relinquish her seat on a city bus to a white rider, an act for which she was arrested.[6] On November 13, 1956, the Supreme Court shut down segregation, in this case on public transportation, but as white supremacists' actions of "massive resistance" continued, King and other leaders of the Montgomery boycott in 1957 founded the Southern Christian Leadership Conference (SCLC), which organized political actions by Black churches.[7] The news of the *Brown v. Board of Education of Topeka* decision, in 1954, banning segregation in public schools, had heartened many in the US Department of Justice, in part because of the hope that it would assuage criticisms by the Soviet Union that the United States was nothing if not hypocritical for its stance on racial segregation. Those hopes were dashed, though, when on September 2, 1957, Arkansas's governor, Orval Faubus, called in the state's National Guard to block students from entering Little Rock Central High School.[8] Although President Dwight Eisenhower had been a reluctant proponent of major civil rights legislation, ultimately, on September 24, he federalized the National Guard and sent US Army troops to Central High School to enforce the court order (Figures I.2 and I.3). According to legal historian Mary L. Dudziak, "School desegregation in Little Rock was no longer a local or state issue, but a critical national problem."[9]

It was against this backdrop that televised teen dance unfolded. The story of televised teen dance that I tell in this book is about Black and white teenagers wanting to dance to rock 'n' roll music despite the barriers placed on their ability to do so. It is also a story that weaves together issues of race, morality, and sexuality. The teenagers are the protagonists here, and the clash is between their desires and wishes and those of both the cultural guardians of morality (parents, teachers, conservative cultural critics) and the decision makers (TV owners, network executives, sponsors, and advertisers) who dictated policy and protocols. Some of the barriers had to do with network concerns about TV's role as a "family" entertainment medium and decency

Figure I.2 Troops of the 327th Airborne Battle Group, 101st Airborne Division, escorting the Little Rock Nine to Little Rock High School on September 23, 1957. Courtesy of Pictorial Press, Ltd./Alamy Stock Photo.

issues; the other had to do with concerns about race (although the two are related, as will be discussed) and the networks' intractability in allowing Black and white mixing on TV. So much about television in the 1950s, and into the 1960s, was about appeasing the Southern TV affiliates and bending to the will of the prevailing segregationists. The desire of the teenagers was to have a space of their own where they could be seen, heard, appreciated, and understood, and in many ways the teen dance shows fulfilled these aims. At this moment in history, when the country was racially divided, Black teenagers took pleasure and satisfaction in forming their own programs, with the help of enterprising and supportive deejay-hosts, when the white-based shows proved inhospitable or when protesting to gain admittance to these shows proved futile. As my interviews revealed, in the face of such resistance, many were overwhelmingly intent on seeking out places to dance and to exhibit and demonstrate their proficiency and skill. And it was on these shows, as I will illustrate, that the somatic power of social dance reigned. In Chapter 3, I explore a handful of all-Black teen dance programs that took shape in the late 1950s and early 1960s. While Don Cornelius's famed *Soul Train*, which emerged in 1970, is considered the first all-Black televised teen show, these other shows had actually gotten there first.

Figure I.3 The weight of the world suddenly upon a courageous young woman being escorted to Little Rock High School. Larry Obsitnik Photo Archives, Box 8, Series 2, courtesy of Special Collections, University of Arkansas Libraries, Fayetteville.

It is important to remember that at its inception, television was considered revolutionary, and as media historian Alan Nadel has written, it "monopolized the nation's vision."[10] Like the Internet technology of today, it ushered in new entertainment genres and redefined the ways that individuals related to their families, friends, and social environment. Throughout the book, I use the term "mediatization," which takes on particular resonance when considering social and popular dance because, unlike other forms of dance, it is constantly shifting, changing, borrowing, and reinventing to create the next new sensation. But that same characteristic—that "borrowing"—presents a problem when Black forms are appropriated by white dancers and performers, when the racial roots of the dances are ignored or unaccounted for, and when Black performers are denied compensation. Mediatization here refers essentially to a process of transmitting, disseminating, and popularizing social dance styles. Moving from their place of origin, whether the street, a club, or a church basement, to the television airwaves by necessity involved a process of changing/simplifying/negating/degrading and all manner of "whitening" of social dance styles, most of which were of Black origin. How a cultural object, then, such as dance, becomes a product of the mass media or technology is one of my central concerns. Mediatization is not a neutral term to describe these products of the mass media but rather one that suggests they are part of a larger, fluid, socio-political process. Media, generally fueled by advertising, creates demand and need for products, services, and trends, which, in turn, convey prevailing social values and ideologies regarding gender, race, or class. Media forms, such as the teen dance shows, it was clear, were not simply reflections of reality, but, rather, as cultural theorist Raymond Williams has explained, "a major way in which reality is continually formed and changed."[11]

A "mediated" reality that early television communicated was that of the domestic landscape that supposedly united family members and communities. The family unit assumed great significance in the postwar years. If the Cold War was meant to "contain" communism and promote democracy, a similar kind of "containment" was occurring on the home front. It was a national closing of ranks, a postwar return to "normalcy" symbolized by a mass exodus to suburbia, which came to serve as a united front against outsiders bent on the destruction of the American way of life. This same kind of thinking permeated TV, which had become a crucial component of the domestic landscape uniting family members and communities. The teen shows were a part of this cultural fixation. TV both appealed to a substantial demographic—white middle-class suburbanites—but attempted to also create and construct such viewers by instructing them in 1950s values of "home and hearth." As media critic Lynn Spigel writes, television "was seen as a kind of household cement that promised to reassemble the splintered lives of families who had been separated during the war. It was also meant to reinforce the new suburban unit, which had left most of its extended family and friends behind in the city."[12]

While this book will not focus on the contemporary social-media scene, I hope the reader will keep in mind the parallels between then and now and consider how the 1950s televisual world set the *blueprint* for how media facilitates the transmission of social dance within gendered and racial frameworks. As illustrated above, in the discussion about its appeals to family, TV projected what was safe, "normal," familiar. And white. As Nadel states, "The imaginary America that television represented, in other words, was one particularly distrustful of diversity."[13] It is fair to say that history seems to be repeating itself. In September of 2014, for instance, fourteen-year-old Jalaiah Harmon, a Black girl from suburban Atlanta, created an Internet dance with a twelve-year-old friend, Kaliyah Davis, that became a runaway sensation. The Renegade, a fusion of hip-hop, jazz, ballet, and tumbling (all of which Harmon had studied), accompanied the chorus of the song "Lottery" by Atlanta rapper E-Camp and incorporated viral moves including the wave and the whoa.[14] Harmon posted the dance number to the video editing livestreaming app Funimate and then to her more than 20,000 followers on Instagram. By October, though, the dance appeared on the popular video app TikTok, where the white, fifteen-year-old TikTok star Charli D'Amelio performed it and was dubbed the dance's "C.E.O." for popularizing it. A firestorm erupted on social media when Harmon wasn't given due credit. Eventually D'Amelio apologized publicly (after major media outlets such as the *New York Times* and NBC's *Today Show* picked up the story) and indicated that she would like to collaborate with Harmon in the future.

That this process of mediatization still occurs is disturbing, but it has a long history. As will be discussed in Chapter 2, the dance known as the Stroll developed on an all-Black teen dance show airing out of Baltimore (*The Mitch Thomas Show*) but ultimately became known as a white dance, especially when it was popularized on the nationally syndicated *American Bandstand* by the white rock 'n' roll group. The Diamonds. The idea that the Stroll was born on *American Bandstand* was fueled in several ways: by the machinery of advertising and promotion of the dance (which credited *American Bandstand* and Dick Clark); types of filming practices (how the dance was shown by white dance couples); and advertising for the dance (in mass-market magazines). Social dancers on *The Mitch Thomas Show* were aggrieved upon learning that the Stroll was first associated with *American*

Bandstand. When Thomas himself called Clark and presented the problem, Clark apparently graciously agreed to make an announcement on his show to correct this misconception.[15] But as sociologist Matthew Delmont so astutely points out, the Black dancers could not achieve the full recognition they deserved: "The dance style perfected by Black teenagers on *The Mitch Thomas Show* did reach a national audience, but the teens themselves were not depicted as part of the national youth culture *American Bandstand* broadcast to viewers."[16]

* * *

In many ways, this book is a study in "crossovers." Traditionally, musicologists and music historians employ that term to refer to the process of African American songs that crossed over from the Black R&B charts to the mainstream that was white pop music and "top 40" charts as indicative of their ability to reach mass popularity with white as well as Black listeners. The term also applies to ways in which white singers and songwriters covered the musical compositions of Black artists in a manner and style deemed more acceptable and palatable for a white audience. There did exist Black cover versions of white artists, too, on the R&B market; as music historian Brian Ward points out, the wildly popular R&B song "Sh-Boom," recorded by the Chords, was actually a B-side song of the Patti Page hit "Cross over the Bridge."[17] But this was the 1950s, a time of entrenched structural racism and racial segregation in the music industry (and, of course, the culture at large). In this era, in which racial segregation was in place both by custom and by law, particularly in the South, all too often Black artists were robbed of income and royalties as the major record labels turned to white covers to capitalize on the growing popularity of R&B among white listeners.

There existed other crossovers, too, as I will describe in Chapter 1, between and among white and Black listeners of R&B and what would eventually become rock 'n' roll. One of the main reasons for the burgeoning of rock 'n' roll in the mid-1950s was the desegregation of the radio airwaves. The rise of the independent record labels helped carry what was previously known as "race music" to a wider Black and white market, and the opening up of greater radio frequencies meant that white teenagers began listening to Black radio in droves. Here were the beginnings of what was to become "a national crossover phenomenon among white teenagers."[18] Contemporary journalist and music critic Wesley Morris, in his 2019 essay "Why Is Everyone Always Stealing Black Music?," makes a point about the "elaborate tangle" of American popular music, invested as it is in a myth of racial separateness, "the idea that art forms can be either 'white' or 'black' in character." As he writes, "This country's music is an advertisement for 400 years of the opposite: centuries of 'amalgamation' and 'miscegenation' as they long ago called it, of all manner of interracial collaboration conducted with dismaying ranges of consent."[19] This issue of consent is important and troubling and is as true for social dance forms (as the Jalaiah Harmon story indicates) as for music. The majority of the dances explored in this book that were essentially sold, marketed, and mediatized to an integrated youth culture mostly derived from the Black dance tradition, as I will discuss in Chapter 4. What is gained and what is lost in this process? How are the dances adapted, changed, borrowed, and sold within a culture that was inherently unequal? What challenges did Black dancers, dances, and Blackness itself pose to young white social dancers, especially when Black dancers were relegated to the margins of the TV frame? Conversely, how did young Black dancers challenge what was often the usurpation of their dance styles for a white audience? These, too, are some of the questions this study asks.

One of my primary aims was to collect stories from the teenage participants themselves. Both Black and white informants—many of them in their late seventies and early-to-mid-eighties—helped piece the story together to create the fullest picture of what rock 'n' roll music and dance meant to them and why the shows were important. Black and white teenagers, of course, reacted differently to this question because of deeply rooted prejudice and racism. As a result, my study also includes the documentation and analysis of Black subjectivity and resistance. I illustrate how despite the racist underpinnings of many of the shows, Black youth were able to use the shows to self-identify during a racially segregated era and create alternative cultures. In part, then, this is also a story of Black institution-building in the face of Jim Crowism, and the need to develop separate communities free of the corrosive structures of racism.[20] Although there were only a handful of Black teen dance shows in the 1950s, they were extremely important in creating local community. They provided another venue or institution where Black youth could congregate on their own, learn dances and cultural mores from one another, and demonstrate their inventiveness, creativity, and dance prowess.

As many scholars have pointed out, popular culture is often the place where Black and white racial identities are most often tested and contested. Many reasons account for why any particular form gains popularity and why white youth were attracted to Black culture.[21] But, as we know from cultural historian Eric Lott, in his well-known formulation of Black minstrelsy, white racial desire and fantasy were coupled with a mixture of envy and disdain, with expropriation of elements of Black culture, in an attempt to create a "fascinating imaginary space of fun and license" seemingly existing outside of "Victorian bourgeois norms."[22] As Toni Morrison has also explained, in her discussion of late nineteenth-century and early twentieth-century white writers' fascination with Black characters, these stories more often than not served the white writer's own unserved longings and desires than any authentic attempt to understand or inhabit Black culture.[23] Morrison's idea is certainly at work in Norman Mailer's 1957 essay "The White Negro: Superficial Reflections on the Hipster," often cited during the late 1950s and early 1960s to explain teenagers' fascination with R&B music and rock 'n' roll dance. Mailer attributes to Black men (and it is men and boys specifically whom he speaks of) over-determined qualities of hedonism, sensuality, and a kind of willed recklessness (because of their outsider status) that white hipsters needed to borrow in order to inhabit their role as "urban adventurers."[24]

As I will discuss in Chapter 2, many white youth, in their rebellion against mainstream culture, derived from Black R&B music a means of identifying an expressive, creative part of themselves either denied, repressed, or deemed inadmissible due to middle-class proscriptions on behavior. What Mailer did get right (perhaps unbeknownst to him) was that "racial symbolic capital," a later formulation of Lott's, accrued to the white hipster; in the adoption of hip, Black argot, dress, and dance style he becomes an oppositional figure prized within his community and by his peers.[25] And, yet, as I discuss in Chapter 5, which focuses on girls and rock 'n' roll music and dance, the intense attraction to R&B music and rock 'n' roll dance was not solely about exploitative desires and racial voyeurism; for some, the music and dance was a transformative experience. As sociologist Wini Breines explains, in the context of the 1950s, "racial difference was of interest to white teenagers because excluded cultures and behaviors encompassed so much that was off-limits."[26] The post–World War II era saw a middle-class exodus to the suburbs and with it an inward-looking focus that exalted family and home although, as Foner points out, there were actually many "suburbias": "upper-class suburbs, working-class suburbs, industrial suburbs, and 'suburban' neighborhoods."[27] What they all had in common was racial division and racial uniformity. Breines argues that many white youth, in their disdain for a suburban, homogeneous culture, were rejecting the racist values of their parents. As historian George Lipsitz notes, "at least part of the motivation for the middle-class white youth adoption of Afro-American and working-class music as their own in the 1950s stemmed from a collective judgment about the demise of the urban industrial city and the rise of the suburb."[28]

One more crossover category of this book is the combination of historical and scholarly analysis with interviews and oral histories of white and Black former social dancers and hosts. This crisscrossing between methodological styles has enabled me to fill in important gaps in the literature and history of the dancing of the period, in that very few recordings or kinescopes (an early method of television recording) of the televised programs have been saved. It was the most unfortunate practice during these early years of television to either tape over existing programs or destroy them with no thought to their value for posterity. Some do exist, of course, along with photographic images, and other primary texts, which have enabled my research. In what music theorist Guthrie Ramsey calls "practice theory," the interviews and oral histories have provided an invaluable ethnographic perspective that has helped deepen an understanding of what these social dance communities meant in the lives of those who inhabited them. These memories and reminiscences provide what Ramsey calls "living photographs,"[29] which clarify the experiences of individuals during a very specific cultural time and place.

Despite the segregation of the shows, there were still many instances of inter-racial association. While I don't subscribe to the idea, shared by some music historians, that a mutual love for rock 'n' roll music and dance *necessarily* brought Black and white youth together, it is nonetheless the case that they shared certain associations that promoted similar sensibilities.[30] Both Black and white teenagers, for instance, were copying from one another in schools, at dance hops, and even on the teen dance programs themselves, when the cameras weren't looking. While for sure, these associations, or collaborations, were not necessarily productive of social or cultural change, they do point to the ways that Black and white youth were accessing each other's cultures, unavoidably learning from one another, and in the process creating new cultural forms. We do know that these associations did not result in greater equality for the Black population at the time or, in the case of television, any sort of real racial parity until perhaps the 1970s and 1980s. However, what I focus on here is what was happening in the "seams"; that is, what constituted the interstitial moments when white youth was introduced to Black music and dance via television and where there might have been productive interchanges between white and Black cultures. While today it may strain our vision to see where these interchanges occurred, they were often happening at the margins—not, for instance, on primetime television, but in local broadcasting, which could often take chances that the major networks would not. The two stories here that I hope to illuminate are what it means for white youth to "borrow" attributes of Black culture in their practice of rock 'n' roll dance, and, in turn, how Black youth propelled the emergence of rock 'n' roll dance styles despite blatant discrimination by white culture. Both sets of youth were driven by their inventive and expressive capabilities and ambitions.

1

Rock 'n' Roll, Dance, and
the TV Experiment

The rise of the televised teen dance show went hand-in-hand with the rise of rock 'n' roll and rhythm and blues (or R&B) music; TV, like the recording and radio industries, got swept up in promoting rock 'n' roll in order to satisfy the demands for white teen audiences, in particular. However, what were essentially Black-derived social dances were transformed into a viewing experience made palatable for (mostly) white teen audiences. The recording, radio, and television industries eagerly capitalized on this teen culture, now a bona fide "market." The ranks of students in high schools across the country swelled; while in 1920, for instance, 51 percent of American sixteen-year-olds were in high school, by 1950 that number had grown to 81 percent.[1] This growing population with more disposable income than their Depression-era parents could have dreamed of now had the ability to purchase transistor radios and record players on which to listen to the music. RCA manufactured "a plastic phonograph that sold for $12.95 and played the 45-rpm disks."[2] And, of course, most important, this was *dance* music, which, in turn, created the need by teenagers (and the media industries that catered to them) for spaces in which to let loose.

Music historian Reebee Garofalo has remarked that by 1947, "a musical era in the United States had come to an end."[3] In part, he was referring to the postwar economy that could no longer sustain twenty-piece big-band orchestras and large ballrooms. Record sales, in turn, had diminished by more than $50 million, "which at the time represented more than 20 percent of the dollar volume of the industry."[4] But something else was taking place—the rise of a national audience for R&B music that was limited mostly to regional markets. Several reasons, cultural and technological, accounted for this development. One was the large migration of Black people moving northward and relocating in urban markets with easily accessible radio receivers. Another was the lessening cost of making records after the war, which was a boon for the independent labels that swelled in number during

Dancing Black, Dancing White. Julie Malnig, Oxford University Press. © Oxford University Press 2023.
DOI: 10.1093/oso/9780197536254.003.0002

this time including Chess in Chicago, Atlantic in New York, Peacock in Houston, and Modern, Imperial, and Specialty in Los Angeles.[5] Interestingly, as Garofalo explains, even by the late forties, TV had swooped up most of the major national advertising, thus leaving network radio stations in the lurch. This turned out to be a boon, though, for local radio stations who could attract local advertisers and then experiment with new programs and the new sounds of rhythm and blues and, eventually, rock 'n' roll.[6]

Radio, as media historian William Barlow has written, "was the match that ignited this sudden musical prairie fire."[7] While the music industry, like the country as a whole during this time, was deeply segregated (the fact that "race" records were designated as a separate category is just one indication), as many writers on rock 'n' roll history point out, the airwaves themselves were *not*.[8] With the rise of local R&B stations around the country, hundreds of white teenagers, along with Black teenagers, were now tuning in, making record requests, and purchasing R&B songs at Black record shops. Black teenagers, of course, had been there first; they had been listening in to Black radio as far back as the 1930s, and then it was they who discovered R&B.[9] By the late 1940s, Black-oriented programming mushroomed to meet the needs of the changing Black demographics. As musicologist Brian Ward notes, the postwar Black "radio boom" was fueled by an expanded Black consumer market, which while "still severely disadvantaged compared with their white counterparts," represented about $15 billion in 1953. Ward cites some relevant statistics: Atlanta, for instance, had an average of 1.8 sets per Black household in the early 1950s; just a few years later about 93 percent of all Black households in Memphis had radios. In the rural South, too, by the late 1950s Black radio ownership averaged between about 73 and 85 percent.[10] The success of the stations and broadcasts enabled "eavesdropping young whites" throughout the country to become devoted followers of R&B.[11]

Rock 'n' roll music possesses a rich and complex history with many roots and tributaries. At its core, rock 'n' roll grew out of a combination of Black-derived music including jazz, blues, and gospel along with white working-class styles of country and western, sometimes referred to as "hillbilly boogie."[12] After World War II, as swing music declined, musicians in black urban communities across the country began experimenting with new sounds, based on big-band arrangements, that came to be known as R&B. Louis Jordan, the saxophonist and swing-band leader, was a transitional figure who with his group the Tympani Five decreased the size of the former big-band configuration consisting of a smaller horn section, saxophone solos, a steady 2/4 drum pattern, and a driving boogie-woogie bassline.[13] This style of "jump blues" rhythm, also characterized by the guitarist T. Bone Walker, saxophonist Eddie "Cleanhead" Vincent, and blues shouter Big Joe Turner is considered a precursor to that of rock 'n' roll.[14]

"R&B," similar to "race music" in earlier decades, was in part a marketing term by record labels to designate Black musicians mainly for a Black audience. R&B itself had a range of styles from "good time blues" with a strong backbeat, electric blues that employed amplified guitar and a rhythm section, church and gospel singing and arrangements, as well as the incorporation of Latin rhythms.[15] As Ward explains, these "stylistic crosscurrents" moved some R&B forms "away from the blues and closer to the musical and lyrical orthodoxies of post-war 'white' popular musics, especially Tin Pan Alley pop and country which was itself undergoing a process of urban gentrification at this time."[16] These musical "transformations" were, as Ward notes, the result of various technological changes in the production of records, for instance, as well as the "widespread availability of radios and record players."[17]

R&B had an Afro-Cuban stream of influence as well, which also filtered into the music of various rock 'n' roll proponents. "This 'Latin tinge' can be traced to 1949 in the work of New Orleans boogie pianist Roy Byrd, also known as 'Professor Longhair.'"[18] Byrd's innovation was to blend Afro-Cuban rhythms and the clave rhythm with R&B. As Garofalo notes, Byrd described his playing as a '"combination of offbeat Spanish beats and calypso downbeats' and 'a mixture of rumba, mambo and calypso.'"[19] This style would become a major influence on R&B musician Fats Domino, who with hits such as "Ain't That a Shame" and "Blueberry Hill" became a rock 'n' roll star.[20] By the mid-1950s, Los Angeles emerged as a major center for Chicano-inspired rock 'n' roll music such as that of Frankie "Cannibal" Garcia and the Headhunters, who were fusing cultural styles.[21]

Rock 'n' roll, as its own full-fledged style, would emerge by the early-to-mid-1950s and feature both Black and white musicians and singers. In the transition, though, from R&B to rock 'n' roll, Black performers ushered in the new style. Garofalo names some of them and points out their diversity and range:

On the vocal front, the assertiveness of r&b performers such as Joe Turner, Ruth Brown, and LaVern Baker helped to create the rock 'n' roll style. The emotional intensity of Roy Brown ("Good Rockin' Tonight"), for example, was carried to an extreme in the outrageous antics of archetypal screamer

Little Richard ("Tutti-Frutti," "Long Tall Sally," "Rip It Up"). The jazz/gospel fusions of Ray Charles ("Hallelujah, I Love Her So," "I Got a Woman") and the more pop-oriented gospel stylings of vocalists Clyde McPhatter ("Treasure of Love," "A Lover's Question") and Sam Cooke ("You Send Me") brought the traditions of the black church into the secular world of rock 'n' roll. The elegant harmonies of urban vocal harmony groups like the Orioles ("Crying in the Chapel"), the Crows ("Gee"), the Chords ("Sh'Boom"), and the Penguins ("Earth Angel") ushered in a whole subgenre of rock 'n' roll known as *doo wop*.[22]

Although some controversy surrounds what constituted the "first" real rock 'n' roll hit—Bill Haley and His Comets' 1953 "Crazy Man Crazy," which was the first to reach the *Billboard's* national chart or the group's "Rock around the Clock," which achieved fame in the iconic 1955 film *Blackboard Jungle*; the Chords' 1954 "Sh-Boom," one of the first Black R&B songs to cross over into the white pop charts; or Elvis Presley's 1954 Sun Records hit "That's All Mama," the cover of the blues artist Arthur Crudup's "That's All Right"— the moniker "rock 'n' roll" stuck and by the mid-1950s came to designate Black R&B and its white equivalents. As Ward notes, this was the term essentially "given by the white media and marketplace in order to attract a mass, multi-racial audience."[23]

The Rise of the Radio Disk Jockey

One of the major reasons for the success of R&B, and eventually rock 'n' roll, was the radio deejays who would actually go on to become pivotal figures in televised teen dance shows. Both Black and white disk jockeys were key in capturing the imagination of a youthful following by introducing them to R&B music and Black expressive culture.[24] The deejays—spirited, enthusiastic, and often inspirational individuals—came to replace the live entertainers featured on radio of the 1930s and 1940s.[25] It was Black deejays, though, who first initiated and pioneered the introduction of R&B music in the late 1940s. William Barlow explains that many of these deejays were emblematic of the postwar urban migration, "and they gave voice to an apparent generational shift taking place in Black culture as whole."[26] Clearly, they paved the way for the popularization of R&B music despite a racist industry that was that run almost entirely by white businessmen, and although many

Black deejays controlled the content of their programs, they rarely held management positions, had no contracts or health insurance, and were required to solicit their own advertising in order to maintain their shows.[27]

Some of the most influential Black "postwar radio revolutionaries,"[28] as Barlow refers to them, were Al Benson, a former preacher from Mississippi who starred on WGES in Chicago in the late 1940s. Barlow, and others, credit Benson with "almost single-handedly" introducing R&B music to the Chicago airways.[29] Known as "The Old Swingmaster," Benson was particularly popular with rural, Southern Black individuals migrating North. Richard E. Stamz, also of WGES, picked up after Benson and attracted a teenage audience on his popular program "Open the Door Richard" named for the hit eponymous Dusty Fletcher number. Stamz would go on to host his own TV show in 1956 (discussed in Chapter 3).[30] Others, located in the South, included Nat D. Williams (aka "Nat Dee"), a former history teacher and the first Black deejay on WDIA in Memphis, which eventually became an all-Black oriented station. Williams, who had had prior experience as an emcee for a local talent concern, hosted two shows, *Tan Town Jamboree* and *Tan Town Coffee*. Hattie Leeper (known as "Chattie Hattie") was one of the few Black women deejays who hosted R&B programs at the integrated station WGIV in Charlotte, North Carolina. Up North, in Philadelphia and New York City, Douglas "Jocko" Henderson, became a major celebrity with his *Jocko's Rocket Ship Show* that aired on Philadelphia (WHAT and WDAS) and in New York (WOV) from 1954 to 1964.[31] They were the "trendsetters and salesmen,"[32] according to Nelson George, and they were pitching R&B music as well as the products of their commercial sponsors who made their shows possible. Despite the overwhelming success of Black-oriented radio, during these early years "few of the station owners, managers, or even technical staff, were black."[33] But the stations were structured in such a way that the deejays had considerable clout as long as the market for Black music thrived.[34] Black deejays were particularly influential within the Black communities in which their stations were located and served, in some instances, as unofficial "mayors," community leaders, and cultural arbiters promoting local businesses and charities on air as well as informing their audiences about local civic matters and civil rights issues (a practice that would carry over into the TV shows that they hosted). As Barlow explains, Black deejays were instrumental in "setting up the radio 'grapevine' on which civil rights information circulated in the black community."[35] One particularly activist deejay was Georgie Woods, of Philadelphia's WDAS and WHAT-AM radio in Philadelphia; Woods was known for using his record hops and dances as means of community building and, among other civil rights–oriented activities, produced benefit concerts (called "Freedom Shows") for the local NAACP.[36]

The dissemination of R&B and rock 'n' roll music, though, was also greatly facilitated by white deejays across the country who were genuine aficionados and students of R&B. This "integration of the airwaves," as several scholars describe it, actually suggested to some commentators of the time that racial tolerance might be within reach in a context where music was becoming a cross-racial phenomenon. Of course, though, there were economic reasons for the surge in interest on the part of the radio industry. As Barlow has pointed out, "During the postwar boom in black appeal radio, numerous stations in the South initially tried to capture the newly discovered Negro market without desegregating their on-air staffs."[37] While there were certainly many instances of white deejays simply jumping onto the bandwagon of the commercialization of R&B, many, too, were propelled in their mission by their love of the music and appreciation of Black musical styles. It is fair to say, then, that both Black and white deejays popularized the music with Black and white teenage audiences and helped propel the music into the pop mainstream.

The many white deejays to adopt R&B music actually began in the late 1930s and early 1940s in the South with "Jitterbug" Johnny Poorhall who on his late-night show on WHBQ in Memphis endeared himself to white and Black listeners with his preference for Black swing bands.[38] Some of the most popular of the postwar white deejays to move into the Black radio market were the "trio" of Gene Nobles, John "R" Richbourg, and William "Hoss" Allen at WLAC, in Nashville, Tennessee, credited with introducing their Black and white listeners to major Black popular artists of the day, including Little Richard (Penniman), Aretha Franklin, James Brown, Fats Domino, and many others. who first recorded on radio in 1951 at WLAC.[39] In Atlanta, on WATL and WGST, was Zenas "Daddy" Sears, an ex-GI and civil rights activist whose desegregation efforts won the support of the local Black community.[40] In Los Angeles, there were Hunter Hancock, who at KFVD (and later KGEJ) broke into the R&B format in 1948 with his show *Harlem Matinee*, which appealed to African American and Chicano teenagers;[41] and beloved LA-based deejay Art Laboe, who started playing R&B on WRKD in 1950 and was the first to catch the "big wave," as he referred to it, of rock 'n' roll from Bo Diddley to Jerry Lee Lewis to Elvis

Figure 1.1 Host and deejay Art Laboe, of *The Art Laboe Show* (Los Angeles), with Jerry Lee Lewis at the El Monte Legion Stadium, in East Los Angeles, which circumvented a city ordinance restricting admittance of young people under eighteen years of age. Ca. 1958. Laboe's concerts drew upward of 2,000 teenagers. Courtesy of the Art Laboe Archives.

Presley (Figure 1.1).[42] Laboe is well known for his rock 'n' roll concerts at the El Monte Legion Stadium in Los Angeles County, a working-class enclave in the San Gabriel Valley, which drew crowds of over 2,000 white, Black, and Chicano teenagers.[43]

The deejay who is generally given the most credit for breaking open the R&B/rock 'n' roll market for white youth is Alan Freed, a deejay, concert promoter, and eventual teen TV host, whose "Moondog" broadcast on WJW in Cleveland, Ohio, and then at WINS in New York City attracted a large mixed-race following. Historical legend has it that Freed coined the term "rock 'n' roll"; the term, however, had been used well before 1952, but Freed took up the rock 'n' roll moniker to help make Black R&B more acceptable to a white audience. Freed was a controversial figure then and, in some ways, remains so today. Though several critics and historians view him as a total opportunist, a voracious exploiter of the "Negro market," others credit him with championing Black R&B performers and paving the way for mass acceptance of what would become rock 'n' roll music and dance. There is no question that Freed was a popularizer of R&B music and rode the wave of rock 'n' roll's association with white, teenage youth.[44]

The televised teen dance program that emerged in the late 1940s was integrally tied to rock 'n' roll, its rise on the radio, and the rise of the 1950s youth culture. These interlocking elements coincided with the rise of television, which, in turn, became a primary vehicle—both lauded and reviled—for the mushrooming of rock 'n' roll music and dance. Ironically, even though it was the rise of TV that the network radio industry feared, the televised teen dance programs turned out to be a boon to *local* radio stations featuring R&B music since it was those very recordings that TV producers wanted to feature on their programs. (Of course, the record industry stood to gain substantially, as well.) There is some irony here in that the songs were lip-synced even though the shows were live; this gave the record industry a boost as teenagers wanted to hear those songs exactly as they were sung and performed on records and broadcast over radio.[45] The vehicle for the shows, of course, was the music— top hit recordings easy to reproduce on air. A good deal of the novelty of the teen dance shows lay in the idea that hit songs heard on the radio could now at the same time be made visible by the accompanying dances (similar to the experience of MTV).

As television historian Murray Forman explains, any type of musical programming was popular in these early years as it sold TV sets.[46] Television, in the early 1950s, as Forman notes, "rather than Broadway, nightclubs and ballrooms," became the most coveted vehicle for music and musicians hoping to continue or in many cases revive careers that had languished in the late 1940s with the limitations posed on them by the ballroom tax.[47] A popular genre between 1948 and 1956 were the big-band shows, or "cavalcades," as they were known, many of which were broadcast remotely from actual ballrooms (i.e., *The Guy Lombardo Show*).[48] Other musical programming included the various variety shows, such as *The Dinah Shore Show*, *The Perry Como Show*, and *The Tony Martin Show*; amateur talent shows; hit parade shows; musical quiz shows; and "educational entertainment" shows, such as the *Omnibus* or *Star of the Family* series.[49] But the main precursors of the teen TV dance shows were the so-called DJ shows, alternately called platter shows, and dance parties, which completely capitalized on the rock 'n' roll craze and pulled from the design of the R&B and rock 'n' roll radio programs.

The idea to "spin records" on TV, rather than hire studio orchestras or pay for remote broadcast locations, was far more desirable economically.[50] And, of course, the hope was that a radio deejay's star power would transfer to television.

The first glimmers that TV might serve both Black and white rock 'n' roll–hungry teenagers occurred at radio station studios. It was not uncommon, for instance, for the stations to open their studios for dancing during the broadcast's airing. The popular Philadelphia platter show *The 950 Club*, in 1946, was one of the earliest to invite students to the station's studio to dance to the records and attend special performances featuring some of the performers.[51] Former deejay and eventual teen-TV host Robin Seymour, one of the first white deejays to play R&B on local radio in the Detroit area, said this of his radio show on WJIL in Dearborn:

> I'll tell you, what really caught on, being in Dearborn it was a small day time [show] and then of course it got to be full time. Next door to us was oh— Our Lady—I can't even think of it, the Catholic church, the Sacred Heart School—and the reason I say that is it started where the kids would walk over next door after school, walk upstairs, and sit in the studio to do their homework and listen to my show and dance.[52]

The same was true, for instance, of the R&B program of beloved Black female deejay Hattie Leeper ("Chattie Hattie") whose late-night R&B program aired on the integrated radio station WGIV in Charlotte, North Carolina. Reminiscing years later, well-known "Rockin' Ray" Gooding, Leeper's fellow WGIV-AM deejay whose program preceded hers, recalls finding Black and white teenaged couples dancing to the music on Leeper's show (piped in through loudspeakers) in the radio station's lobby.[53] In an interview conducted in 2006, Leeper said that by the mid-1950s, Black and white teenagers' desire to hear rock 'n' roll music was irrepressible; she notes how broad the listenership was for WGIV:

> We were considered, you know, the urban station, meaning the black station. But gosh, we had so many listeners from Myers Park High School, you know, predominantly white schools because we had an integrated staff." She continued that "we really found out that we were more than just beaming into the urban areas. . . we would have events, concerts, and they would be almost 50/50 in race.[54]

The fact that radio deejays became the primary hosts of the teen dance shows, then, comes as no surprise. Through radio, they had already become important figures in the lives of teenagers who looked to them as role models. Just as many of them developed a devoted following on the radio for R&B music, so too did they spur enthusiasm and win teenaged fans for rock 'n' roll music and dance on television. Importantly, as Murray Forman notes, "the television DJ emerged as an additional cog in the music promotion apparatus."[55] Record promoters and distributors, of course, hoped that the hosts would promote their records, and for this reason, many a teen dance host got swept up in the infamous payola scandal of the 1950s that helped bring about the downfall of Alan Freed.[56] Many teen dance show hosts, who had recently returned from the war, were looking to jumpstart their careers, and the newly burgeoning field of television held out a lot of promise. Some were new to the radio business, but others had careers in radio before the war, and most of them were R&B aficionados.

The shows, in many respects, were modeled on the 1950s sock hop, which were essentially informal teenage dances usually held in schools, churches, or community centers. It had long been a practice for radio deejays to host special events, dance contests, or local concerts in the city in which their broadcasts aired, but many of the deejays-turned-teen TV hosts arranged such dances at local schools in order to recruit students for their television shows. Former teen host Milt Grant, of *The Milt Grant Show*, on WTTG-TV in Washington, DC, for instance, regularly held sock hops or "record hops" at various locations around the area including local high schools, arenas, and armories.[57] More often, the hosts produced and staged the sock hops with featured musicians and local bands. What were initially created as advertising venues for the TV station and the teen dance show often turned into concerts—with dancing—that drew up to 1,000 teenagers. Around 1957, Milt Grant, for instance, became known for his record hops and concerts at Silver Spring, Maryland's Glen Echo Park that eventually featured named performers such as Link Wray, Roy Orbison, and Johnny Cash.[58] A sometimes overlooked figure who pioneered playing R&B on the West Coast was LA-based deejay and teen-show host Art Laboe, popular on WTLA-radio. He initiated what essentially became record hops at Scrivner's Drive-In (at the corner of Sunset and Cahuenga) from which he broadcast his late-night radio show on KRLA (originally KXLA). Laboe, who in the mid-to-late 1950s was one of the first LA-based deejays to feature rock 'n' roll, said of the music that it "came like a tidal wave," as it caught on with high school–aged kids and those early on in college. The drive-in became so successful that KTLA installed a small portable dance floor right outside the entrance of the drive-in replete with klieg lights and two or three cameras. Remarked Laboe:

> We had traffic jams—we were friendly with the police—they used to come out there every afternoon and try to direct traffic. It finally got so bad that it was holding up everything. They finally said, well Scrivners has three drive-ins, and so I'll move around to the different ones in the afternoon. I named myself the [Scrivner's] Roving Disk Jockey.[59]

The Early Teen Dance Shows

The stage was set, then, for the explosion of the televised teen dance genre with a mass-appeal musical form, a burgeoning and enthusiastic teen culture for that music, eager and willing deejays, and, of course, the new medium of television that was willing to gamble on the new and unproven. The TV networks embraced the shows in part because they were easy to produce. The shows required little or no rehearsal, a minimum of production crews, one or two cameramen (initially), and, as Murray Foreman points out, were "perfectly suited for a multiplicity of spot commercials."[60] Essentially, station owners and network executives would try almost anything if would sell TV sets and advertising time. The limits of the technology had not been determined, and genres had not yet been established, so there was a sense, too, that TV was fertile ground for experimentation. For many producers, as Forman writes, the attitude was one of "anything is possible."[61] Of course, the teen dance shows won the support of music industry personnel who hoped that these programs would help promote their records.[62]

According to several scholars, the earliest so-called teen show was *Teen Canteen*, in 1946, airing from WRGB in Schenectady and then after two years moving to WPIX in New York City. *Teen Canteen*, and other programs of this ilk (known as "teen canteen shows") were patterned after canteens of the late 1930s that provided recreation for teenagers and places to congregate.[63] These were not strictly dancing shows, though; some were more like amateur talent shows featuring teenage baritone vocalists and tap-dancing violinists. By 1949, this type of show paved the way for Paul Whiteman's *TV Teen Club* that aired out WFIL-TV of Philadelphia. Whiteman—the former famous bandleader, the so-called King of Jazz of the 1940s—was an unlikely contender for teen dance host. Then a vice president of music at the ABC radio network, which owned WFIL, Whiteman decided to hold Saturday night dances in his hometown of Lambertville, New Jersey, mostly as a means of helping stem the tide against rising juvenile delinquency. These "hops," held just before the rage for rock 'n' roll, were popular with the "swingsters," as the *Herald Tribune* referred to them. The reporter quoted a fifteen-year-old farmer who drove in fifteen miles from Rosemont "for a good jitterbug session." The young man noted that "We get everything free and we like the way the dances are run—just like big-time parties, with good bands and entertainers."[64] Whiteman's entreaties to ABC management paid off, and on April 2, 1949, the show went on the air. Not yet a true "dance party" propelled by recorded music, as those of the 1950s, Whiteman's telecast was more of an amateur talent night featuring various acts and bands. According to author Jeff Martin, the teenage audience consisted of both Black and white teens watching the show together.[65]

Another strand of early teenage-driven TV programs was essentially radio deejay shows transferred to television. In 1950, *Billboard* writer June Bundy, in her survey of televised "spinners," described the shows as consisting of record playing, live talent, contest gimmicks, and a teenage studio audience; some of these programs included George Skinner's *The Whirligig Show* on WPTZ-Philadelphia; *The Alan Freed Show* on WXEL-Cleveland; Bud Abbott's *The Abbott Show* in Louisville, Kentucky; and *Peter Potter's Party* also in LA, at KNXT. According to Bundy: "Most platter pilots are past masters in the art of the gentle pitch, and the spiel has proved to be the most effective sales argument on TV."[66] These were all precursors, though, to the televised teen dance shows or "dance parties" that would crop up in most major cities in the early to mid-1950s in which rock 'n' roll music and dance had a starring role. A kind of combination of both the deejay genre and the amateur talent show, the teen dance shows featured known radio deejays serving as hosts and playing the latest top-40 recordings. Bob Horn's Philadelphia-based *Bandstand* (the precursor to *American Bandstand*), which debuted in 1952, is typically considered to be the very first televised teen dance show in the nation, although from the number of similar shows that cropped up around the same time, it seems that the concept was very much "in the air." *Jack's Corner Drug Store*, hosted by future NBC radio president Jack G. Thayer, for instance, debuted on WTCN-TV, Minneapolis, on September 7, 1953. The stage design was a replica of a drug store, described as a "jivey teen-age dance get-together."[67] By 1954, some of these shows included *Teen Bandstand*, on WOR-TV in New York City, hosted by former bandleader Ted Steele; *Bandstand Matinee*, hosted by Jim Lounsbury, on WGN-TV,[68] Chicago; *Dance Party* with Joe Grady and Ed Hurst at WPTZ-TV, Philadelphia; *Jack's Corner Drug Store*, on WTCN-TV in Minneapolis; *Ed McKenzie's Saturday Party* at WXYZ-TV, Detroit; *Top Ten Dance Party* with John Stewart on WCDA-TV, Albany; *Let's Dance* on KLAC-TV, Los Angeles, and the list goes on. Of course, it was also the case that as *American Bandstand* caught on in Philadelphia, other broadcasters wanted to follow suit. Dale Young, host of *Detroit Bandstand*, recalls how as while he was hosting a show he described as "a *Today Show* for kids," from 7 to 8:30 A.M., he was asked by management to host *Detroit Bandstand*: "They called me over because Dick Clark at *American Bandstand* had become popular out of Philadelphia. So they wanted to do something in Detroit as the same kind of thing."[69] (See Figure 1.2.) By the time that *American Bandstand*, with host Dick Clark, went national, in 1957, rock 'n' roll was in full swing, and there were close to a hundred such teen dance shows.[70]

Figure 1.2 Teenage dancers performing the Stroll on *Detroit Bandstand*, hosted by Dale Young, ca. 1957. Courtesy of Dale and Deborah Young.

By the early 1950s, four network stations ruled the airways: ABC, CBS, NBC, and Dumont (which ceased operations in 1956). Most TV viewing took place on the VHF channels, but when the Federal Communications Commissions (FCC) in the early 1950s lifted its restrictions on TV licenses, and opened up the UHF channels, it created the space for close to seventy new alternative channels in a many urban areas.[71] However, the major networks didn't invest in the UHF channels; instead "they rivaled each other for supremacy" and "programmed to the largest possible audiences."[72] The years 1955 to 1958 saw exponential growth in the number of television stations, from 108 in 1952 to 458 in 1955. Using statistics from the 1955 FCC Annual Report, sociologist (and *American Bandstand* chronicler) Matthew F. Delmont notes that "By 1955, the most populous cities each had between three and seven stations, and the FCC believed that 90 percent of the nation's population lived in the broadcast range of at least two stations."[73] Local stations, of course, were more apt to program a teen dance show knowing that they could support the shows through local advertising. Practically speaking, these shows had a built-in audience and could feature local musicians and bands and advertise local businesses. The local and independent stations, always looking for a financial boost, felt the teen shows might prove profitable.

TV in Black and White

Where, then, were the Black teen dance TV hosts? The vast majority of the local teen dance shows were hosted by white deejays leading groups of primarily white teenagers with Black (and white) performers as guests. There were some exceptions to this rule, however (as will be discussed in Chapter 3). As J. Fred MacDonald has indicated, Black performers were always a part of television, and they were there from the start. But the limited and often stereotypical manner in which they were represented sadly mirrored the larger culture's race divide. On the teen dance shows, similar to the raft of musical variety shows and amateur-oriented shows, Black singers, musicians, and band members were routinely featured performers but were rarely cast as hosts.[74] This seemed all the more astonishing since Black deejays, who had come to occupy such a vital role in American life, and *teenage* life, were ruling the airwaves. But, of course, one's identity on radio, unlike TV, is still hidden. To have had audiences see an Black man leading a teen dance TV show, overseeing Black and white teenagers as an authoritative father figure, and on national television, was simply unthinkable even in the supposedly liberal and reform-minded years of the mid-twentieth century.

For white and Black Americans as a whole, television's arrival was generally greeted with optimism; to many it seemed to be the next best hope for racial equity and integration. *Ebony* magazine, in 1950, extolled the virtues of television and felt it held out the promise for richer roles for Black Americans than any other medium.[75] TV in the late 1940s and early 1950s actually held out the promise of a more democratic future in its perceived ability to bring together people of different beliefs and backgrounds. There was a very ecumenical spirit about the potential of television in its early stages, particularly in TV's ability to connect people, in real time, within the space of one's living room. Media historian and theorist Lynn Spigel writes that television technology "offered the possibility of an intellectual neighborhood, purified of social unrest and human misunderstanding."[76] As Murray Forman points out, how was it possible, then, to square the seeming "tolerance, good will, and opportunity" that TV represented with network executive's narrowmindedness and inability to challenge societal norms?[77] One answer, not surprisingly, was the "bottom line" and the insidious effects of advertising sponsorship. Like radio, TV was financed by advertisers, and therefore its content was subject to commercial pressures. Because advertisers' goals were to appeal to as vast an audience as possible, as a rule they were ideologically inclined to conform to national norms and avoid creating any controversy or dissent. Network television had to consider what would be appropriate for each "market"; looming over television of the 1950s was the issue of not wanting to offend regional viewers, particularly in the South. Fred MacDonald offers the example of Georgia's governor Herman Talmadge, in 1952, of reprimanding network TV for any type of integrated programming that he felt promoted "'complete abolition of segregation customs' in the South." He objected to Black and white youngsters shown dancing together, and to Black teenagers talking together "on a purely equal social status."[78]

The Black teen dance shows that did exist aired in local markets, in Delaware, Washington, DC, North Carolina, Chicago, and Los Angeles, containing significant Black populations and strong community support. To a degree, the local teen dance shows—Black- or white-based—faced somewhat less pressure from advertisers who knew they had built-in communities and so the shows did not have to muster the same mass appeal. As will be explored in the next chapter, one of the reasons Dick Clark's *American Bandstand* maintained such sustained popular appeal, without any opposition from advertisers, was its rather generic rock 'n' roll dance style (with white, clean-cut looking dancers), whereas on the local shows one was apt to see the many regional variations on the basic rock 'n' roll dances, often more expressive and distinct. Clark's own persona, too, with his youthful, straight-up disposition (looking like one of the executives described in the 1956 *The Organization Man*), endeared him to adult viewers when *Bandstand* aired nationally;[79] it is difficult to imagine the manic, "motor-mouthed" Dewey Phillips, for instance, host of the local Memphis teen show *Phillips' Pop Shop* (and Elvis Presley champion), or even the loud, boisterous, rock 'n' roll impresario Alan Freed of New York City's *Big Beat* becoming national broadcast-TV material.[80] Clearly, Clark was the right man at the right moment to present rock 'n' roll in a form that would resonate with the conservative side of 1950s America.

The local shows could, and often did, take more chances and sometimes cross the color line. When this was the case, it didn't always go unnoticed or unpunished. On an episode of *Dance Party* that aired out of WGR-TV in Buffalo, New York, in 1954, a Black teenage boy was "ordered off the floor" because he was dancing with a young white girl. The host of the show "gave his refusal following phone calls of protest from viewers."[81] The host no doubt feared reprisals by the show's advertisers. This event, though, unlike others of its kind, had an interesting denouement: The WGR-TV station manager sent a letter of apology to the young man when he learned of the incident. In it, he wrote:

> I have been informed of and have read certain statements made by one of
> our employees that are not in keeping with this station's policy. I personally
> regret the hasty action on the part of this individual and want you to know
> that the action he took was done on his own initiative and did not reflect the
> policy of management.[82]

One would be hard-pressed to see this kind of admission occur for a nationally broadcast show; renowned Los Angeles deejay and rock 'n' roll promoter Al Jarvis apparently rejected an offer to host a national teen dance show when told that the show would be segregated.[83]

Many of the local shows, in particular the few Black-based shows, often faced difficulties when ratings dropped—however insignificant those ratings may have been. And while not being with an affiliated network provided a measure of freedom from commercial pressures, it also meant that the shows were subject to the financial dilemmas of the parent company. *The Mitch Thomas Show*, for instance, hosted by former deejay Mitch Thomas and broadcast on WPFH-TV in Wilmington, was owned by the Storer Broadcasting Company, whose acquisitive buying practices of multiple stations led to its ultimate downfall; Mitch Thomas's show was one of the earliest casualties. Matthew Delmont quotes a manager of WVUE broadcasting telling historian Gerry Wilkerson that "No one can make a profit with a TV station unless affiliated with NBC, CBS, or ABC."[84] That fact, coupled with the inherent racism of the era and TV practices generally, increased the precarity of the Black-based shows.

Although television production in the 1950s was still in a rather rudimentary state, without zoom lenses, sophisticated sound systems, or elaborate equipment, the shows did as much as they could with limited resources. Recording devices were available (i.e., the kinescope), but these could be prohibitively expensive, which in part explains why so many of the shows were not saved.[85] The studios were generally small, and although they could pack in up to 200 teenagers, the dance floor itself usually accommodated only about forty of them. Generally, no more than three cameras were used for any one show; the former unit manager for Dallas–Fort Worth's *Sump'n Else Show*, Bud Buschardt, explained how "through the magic of television," it was possible to make thirty dancers look like many more: "The way the dance floor was marked, and three cameras positioned, it looked like there were more dancers, because the cameras were cross-shooting the crowd. One camera showed the back of a couple while another camera covered the front."[86] All of the activities, including names of guests and songs, were printed up on large blank cards and mounted on boards. Lee Woodward, former host of *Tulsa Dance Party*, says that a lot of the shows were ad-libbed, and that if he got an idea on the spot, he would literally improvise by running to the director's booth (during a dance number). As he explained, "we would work something out verbally; I'd just go back out on the floor, and we'd do it; of course, he'd [the director] talk to the cameramen through the headsets and told them what was going on."[87] Steve Stephens, former host of *The Steve Stephens Show* that aired out of Little Rock, Arkansas, on KTHV-TV, said that "I didn't realize it at the time, but I not only was the host, but I was the producer. I would tell the director what we're going to do or what to zoom in on; I said every now and then, zoom in on a face because that gives more, you know, warmth and humanity for the show."[88] And, the shows being live, things could go awry. Gene Brendler, the host of *High Time*, a dance party that aired on KPYV-TV in Portland, Oregon, writes that "Of course, little things were always going on that would spark up the program, like the 7-Up machine would explode or flats—part of the sets—falling down, or the wrong cue cards getting put up, things like that. Today, of course, you'd stop, regroup, and go at it again."[89]

Television, at its inception, was touted for bringing the home viewer close to the event; in fact, it was often described as an extension of live theater. But TV occurred in the privacy of one's home where its intimacy is a product of its immediacy—it enables "the close proximity of viewer to event."[90] Early TV was characterized as "a performance in the present."[91] In many respects, the teen dance shows were the perfect vehicle for 1950s television with its associations of family and familiarity. Lynn Spigel perhaps describes this phenomenon best in suggesting that in the postwar years, television came to represent "a unifying agent" that brought together couples and families separated by the war. It also connected to postwar values that deemed the new suburbia as a haven for domestic serenity.[92] "Togetherness," in fact, had become a catch phrase of the postwar era, and the analogy of TV as the "electronic hearth" served to harness this new technology to traditional American values associated with family and home.[93] The networks' appeal to "family" also helped close the gap among television audience viewers strewn across different parts of the country. Cultural critic Raymond Williams has referred to this phenomenon as one of "mobile privatisation," in which the activities of the outside world are transmitted as dramas that join together groups despite their geographic distance.[94] Teen home audiences might view the programs alone or with their peers in their home but the familiar content and structure of the shows drew them into a "virtual" community of dancers with whom they might take vicarious pleasure.[95]

Media theorist Alan Nadel has remarked that throughout the late 1940s and early-to-mid-1950s, television promoted itself as a vehicle of "the real." "It was," writes Nadel, "the instrument that would connect every household with real life in real time."[96] Of a popular Louisville, Kentucky, teen dance show, *Variety* noted that "*Teen Time Dance Party* impressed as a 45-minutes stanza, at which the viewer is permitted to look-in and enjoy a group of wholesome youngsters have a good time."[97] The sense of the TV audience "looking in on" the shows, as if witnessing an intimate, everyday scene, conveys the idea that the teenage dancers were not actually entertaining the television audience but simply living life, and audiences were offered the chance to tune in (in real time). Carl Belz seems to agree with this assessment.

In an intriguing thesis, he asserts that the televised teen dance shows were a kind of "folk" theater. "The dance," he wrote "was a living drama," "a life situation which anyone was allowed to observe."[98] He likens the teenagers (on *American Bandstand*—his example) to "the folk," "anonymous," untrained dancers moving spontaneously to the music.

The folk analogy, while intriguing, goes only so far, though; what Belz fails to take into account is the constructedness of the TV show (and of TV itself) "fusing its images into a carefully controlled stream of visual statements."[99] More than simply a window into everyday life, the dance shows were mediated by the manipulation of electronic technology, the ideology of the home, and biases concerning race. So, while the dances may have derived from the "ordinary" worlds of school dances and dance hops, and casual exchanges with Black friends, they developed in a commercial *context*, and in another instance of cultural "borrowing" becoming appropriation, the dances were copied by other teenagers around the country, and codified in newspaper and magazine articles, dance instruction books, and sheet music. Moreover, that many of the dancers morphed into teen "stars," and were featured in teen and fan magazines, attests to their consciousness as arbiters of teenage styles of music, dance, and dress.[100] As the shows progressed, and the teenagers became more screen-savvy, many of them engaged in a process of deliberate self-presentation, playing to and for the camera, to home viewers, and to their friends.

Despite its great hopes for becoming a common space that united individuals around the country (and indeed the world), early TV was content to accept the cultural status quo and perpetuate the Jim Crow practices of the era.[101] Even though Black Americans, like their white counterparts, were "sold" the dream of the united postwar family—Spigel notes how *Ebony* magazine continually ran advertisements that displayed African Americans in middle-class living rooms, enjoying an evening of television—they were clearly not welcomed into the fold.[102] Media theorist John Fiske has observed that TV "serves to communicate to the members of [its] culture, a reinforcing version of themselves."[103] If that is indeed the case, then what was reinforced and communicated in the shows was an ideal of racial homogeneity. Despite the passage of legislation outlawing segregated schools in the wake of the Supreme Court's *Brown v. Board of Education* ruling in 1954, TV continued to promote the acceptability and desirability of this televisual segregation.[104] Of course, the shows (and TV as a whole) featured many Black entertainers, but that was not where the problem lay; it was with the possibility of Black and white male and female teenagers congregating and dancing with *one another*.

Television, as Fiske maintains, carries meanings that are multiple and conflicting.[105] The television "text," as such, may "read" differently by individuals and groups depending on their race, gender, age, sexuality, and geographic location. While one "reading" of the teen dance show was as a "toned down" version of rock 'n' roll dance performed by well-dressed mostly white girls and boys for a mass audience (that appealed to parents), another was as a form of adolescent rebellion—a subdued one, perhaps, but a rebellion nonetheless—that appealed to teenagers. The ritual activity around the show itself—cutting class to get to the studio in time; discussing parental problems with the host on live TV; and not least, dancing unimpeded to the sounds and rhythms of rock 'n' roll—all of this constituted teenagers' break from the music of their parents and an expression of teenagers' own preferences within an increasingly conformist and consumerist culture. A major part of that rebellion, as I will elaborate on in the next chapter, involved partaking in dances derived from the Black tradition and engaging in a cultural style and way of life that was seemingly "forbidden." Historian George Lipsitz explains these desires as arising from, in part, the concomitant decline of the industrial city and the emergence of the suburb. As he notes, "At the very moment that residential suburbs increased class and racial segregation, young people found 'prestige from below' by celebrating the ethnic and class interactions of the urban street."[106]

For Black teenagers, the teen dance shows read entirely differently. While viewers' experience of watching and participating in TV can reproduce the status quo and reinforce regressive behaviors or ideologies, viewers can also resist the dominant ideologies and bring their own meanings to bear on the television text. In a mass medium such as television, which has to appeal to a wide swath of viewers, there is often a slippage between what the shows purported to do and what they actually conveyed. Fiske, again, has pointed out how television audiences are not passive consumers; they may reinterpret, reframe, or, indeed, reject what is presented to them.[107] For Black citizens during this period, participation in popular culture was always a double-edged sword; Black TV viewers often "made choices under circumstances not of their own choosing."[108] Many Black teenagers, for instance, watched and liked Dick Clark's *American Bandstand*; many didn't. For those Black teenagers who did watch *American Bandstand*, or any of the local white teen dance shows, the viewing exchange was a complex one, which involved recognizing the egregious segregation of the shows, at the same time "using" or adopting the shows for their own purposes and pleasures. Although he is writing primarily about Black protest and freedom movements, historian Robin Kelley, in *Freedom Dreams: The Black Radical Imagination*, asks how Black consumers of culture have found satisfactions and pleasures even within systems that strove to exclude them.[109] As Chapter 3 will describe, many Black teenage viewers delighted in watching the stream of Black singers and musicians that appeared on the show, whose music they danced to in clubs, schools, and at parties; others, not wanting to deprive themselves of an opportunity to dance, were often able to get into the studios to dance before the cameras were turned on. And others, still, protested the shows' policies until they changed their practices.[110] There were obviously no such accommodations to make with the all-Black teen dance shows. For Black dancers who could now take center stage, there was pleasure to be had in unencumbered dancing and seeing oneself as the subject of these televised "living dramas." For both audiences and participants, as will be described in subsequent chapters, fun and fellowship merged as the social dancers reveled in a sense of community and took pride in their creativity and innovation. Bonds of social camaraderie developed now, too, between the on-screen social dancers and their viewing public as their experiences were validated and extolled. The existence and role of the all-Black teen dance shows, and what they meant for Black teenagers, will be explored in Chapter 3; the following chapter will explore how several, primarily white, mainstream teen dance shows proliferated and worked to create a widespread national teen culture that was a response to R&B and rock 'n' roll music. The chapter will expose the tension between the shows as places of conformity versus sites of rebellion for white youth, which took the form of adaptation of Black cultural and aesthetic styles.

2

Transgressing Boundaries

Restraint and Rebellion in the Teen Dance Shows

> Rock and roll had suddenly become interesting and exciting to
> you. Chuck Berry, Buddy Holly, and the Everly Brothers were the
> musicians you liked best, and you started collecting their records so
> you could listen to them alone in your upstairs bedroom . . . you
> would rush home to watch *American Bandstand*, that spectacle of
> the new rock-and-roll universe injected daily into the country's
> living rooms, but it was more than music that attracted you to the
> show, it was the sight of a roomful of teenagers dancing to the music
> that kept you watching, for that was what you aspired to most now,
> to become a teenager, and you studied those kids on the screen as a
> way to learn something about the next, impending step of your life.
>   —Paul Auster, *Report from the Interior*

The years 1952 through 1959 can be considered televised teen dance's
"golden years," when the shows proliferated at an astonishing rate. Television
was still gaining traction, and producers and network executives were willing
to gamble on the new and unproven. While *American Bandstand* has become the best known—largely as a result of its national reach—it was actually just one of many teen-oriented dance shows that sprang up in most
major cities across the country. There was at least one bandstand-type show
in most urban areas in the United States and parts of Canada. Broadcast from
Providence, Rhode Island, to Los Angeles, California, these local shows were
in some ways more popular than Dick Clark's national broadcast, since they
featured youth from the city and surrounding region whom studio and home
audiences knew or could at least identify with. Different styles of dance and
behavior were projected by teenagers nationwide, and as a result, the shows
came to reflect and create teen life.

Dancing Black, Dancing White. Julie Malnig, Oxford University Press. © Oxford University Press 2023.
DOI: 10.1093/oso/9780197536254.003.0003

In addition to the shows explored in this chapter—Dick Clark's *American Bandstand*, Alan Freed's *The Big Beat*, *The Buddy Deane Show*, and *The Milt Grant Show*—were many others that took root by the late 1950s; several of these were outgrowths of some of the earliest teen dance shows mentioned in Chapter 1, yet others were new. From a very large pool of shows that existed, these are a few: *Cleveland Bandstand* (WJW-TV, Cleveland), *The Al Jarvis Show* (KLAC-TV, Hollywood), *The Art Laboe Show* (KPOP, KTLA; Los Angeles), *Phillips' Pop Shop* (WHBQ-TV, Memphis), *Studio Party* (WABD, Dumont), *Seattle Bandstand* (KING-TV, Seattle), and *Portland Bandstand* (KGW-TV, Oregon).[1] Overall, this book's focus on the many local shows recognizes their importance in capturing regional mores and dance styles. It was in these smaller venues that hundreds of variations of major social dance and dance steps were born. The shows, in which teenagers learned steps and moves from each other, became a meeting ground for youth to experiment with all things "teenage"—from dating practices and social graces to rock 'n' roll dance. It was not any one show that was responsible for the teen dance phenomenon (as many commentators contended of *American Bandstand*), but rather a constellation of shows that drew youth audiences from around the country and helped to create and sustain a national youth culture.

Deceptively simple, the teen dance shows featured amateur and un-scripted teenagers dancing to the recorded music of R&B and rock 'n' roll music, guided by male hosts (most of them former radio disk jockeys), and performing before a studio audience of other teenagers. Many of the shows aired daily, after school hours, or on Saturdays. True to television's basic aes-thetic form, the shows, typically a half hour or hour in length, were organ-ized in relatively short, discrete segments. These included (and not always in this exact order) the host's introduction to and promotion of the latest hit recording, a dance by the teenagers, interviews with guest performers, patter and conversation between host and performers or host and teenagers, introductions of selected teenagers who named their schools, the "rate-a-record" section in which selected studio participants judged a new release, awarding of prizes for contests or fashion shows, and, of course, numerous product endorsements usually done live by the host (sometimes involving the teenagers).

But clearly there was more. As Paul Auster suggests, teenagers (as well as many adults) were enthralled by watching kids like themselves move, en masse, to the new strains of rock 'n' roll music. It was part spectacle, part communal catharsis, part reality show. Many critics seemed to agree that this verisimilitude made for engaging TV. As a *Variety* critic of the mid-1950s noted, "There's something about watching people being themselves whether adolescents or mature, that is intriguing-looking TV."[2] For many former dancers and viewers (and as many of my interviews bear out), the teen shows have enormous nostalgic value and signify a rite-of-passage from childhood to pre-adulthood. In his riveting memoir, *This Boy's Life*, Tobias Wolff describes a tumultuous and peripatetic childhood grounded in his remembrances of watching *Seattle Bandstand* while living in Washington State. It was the one thing that connected him to his estranged half-sister, Pearl, even while they lived in different locations: "She watched them at home. I watched them at the houses of kids along my [newspaper] route, staying for the length of a song and then tearing down the street to my next outpost, hooking papers over my head as I ran."[3] They were each alone yet united in the simultaneous experience of the show.

This chapter will look at some of the best documented, local teen shows (along with *American Bandstand*, which started out locally), to explore how they drew on 1950s ideologies of race, domesticity, and middle-class values to promote a primarily white-teenage culture. It will look, too, at the racial dynamics on the shows and how those played out within the restrictive parameters of 1950s television. The shows were in many ways bundles of contradictions. On one hand, they played to teenagers' need for belonging in the form of adherence to the group and quelled adolescent impulses in, for example, the exacting dress codes and the "rules" of engagement (described below). On the other hand, they fed teenagers' natural sense of rebellion and dismissiveness of authority. There is something intrinsically and especially subversive about being a teenager, and for many of them during this time, rock 'n' roll was a perfect means to voice their independence from the mores and manners of their parents. For sure, not all the music played on the shows was R&B-based; some of it was of the variety that music historian Reebee Garofalo describes as "schlock rock," pop music that, as he explains, was only a pale imitation of the best of rock 'n' roll.[4] But there was enough rock 'n' roll music and appearances by Black R&B-based artists on the shows to enable what historian Alan Matusow called "the teen breakout from jailhouse America."[5] It was the rawness and implicit sexuality of R&B, and much of rock 'n' roll, of course, that served this rebelliousness.

At one and the same time, the shows embodied the values of white, middle-class morality yet served as symbols of youthful liberation. The "liberation" was in part from the mores and values of their parents (symbolized

in part by what many of them felt was blandness of 1950s popular music—
e.g., Pat Boone). As the pioneering Sun Records producer Sam Phillips (and
promoter of Elvis Presley) remarked, "You could sell a half-million copies of
rhythm and blues records. . . . To city-born white children, it was something
new."[6] But the rebellion, too, for many, was against a culture of conservatism
that excluded different races and ethnicities. As cultural historian George
Lipsitz has observed, "Facing a choice between the sterile and homogenous
suburban cultures of their parents, or the dynamic street culture alive among
groups excluded from the middle-class consensus, a large body of youths
found themselves captivated and persuaded by the voices of difference."[7]
The consensus ideology that Lipsitz refers to, born of the sense of America's
power after World War II, was a means of uniting citizens against foreign and
domestic unrest and promoting adherence to the "group." A strong family
unit, agreed on its beliefs, was the starting place to develop a strong and fit
nation. But as cultural critic Gay Morris has noted of consensus thought, it
"admitted few racial, class, or ethnic differences to disturb the flow of postwar
American life."[8]

But racial segregation and racial discrimination did indeed "disturb" life
in the 1950s. Despite the *perception* of stability, enormous conflicts wracked
the United States. While the nation touted its status as the harbinger of the
free world, racial segregation and class conflict tore at its roots.[9] The petition
written by W. E. B. Du Bois and filed by the NAACP to the United Nations,
in 1947, denounced the treatment of Black people in the United States and
claimed that "It is not Russia that threatens the United States so much as
Mississippi . . . internal injustice done to one's brothers is far more dangerous
than the aggression of strangers from abroad."[10] Clearly, the country's racism
was both an internal problem as well as an external one regarding its image
and status on the world stage. The idea of Cold War containment, central to
this period, aided by the rise of McCarthyism, seeped into American cultural
life (as well as political life) and referred to a variety of practices in both private and public life in which people generally drew inward, became wary of
outsiders, and looked to family, hearth, and home to find support and com-
fort. The country witnessed a national closing of ranks, and domesticity and
the family unit, symbolized by a mass exodus to suburbia, came to serve as
a deterrent to outsiders bent on the destruction of the American way of life.
The "consensus" was that in light of communist threats, Americans would
come together and unify around an idea of America's "greatness." And the
consensus cast a pall on those considered "outsiders."

Nowhere was the concept of containment, tied as it was to the notion of togetherness, more prevalent than on television: the new mass-media form that created and distributed these narratives of belonging. Networks were eager to jump on the rock 'n' roll bandwagon to boost ratings to placate audiences and "package" rock 'n' roll for a popular (and mostly white) audience. As media historian Alan Nadel argues:

> If television was a guest, it was a very knowledgeable and instructive guest visiting a compliant and amenable host, one who was receptive to a national agenda and in touch with national norms and mores. Dedicated to normalizing and affirming the values and lifestyles of its audience, the television broadcasting system aimed, one could argue, at becoming a seamless extension of the television set, the piece of living room furniture that made those projections part of the flow of everyday life.[11]

Nadel points out how " 'togetherness,' in such a context, connoted the merger of national solidarity with individual resolve, of domestic security with the cult of domesticity."[12]

Seemingly paradoxically, at the same time that youth expressed their rebelliousness in the form of rock 'n' roll, they were drawn into this conservative domestic ideology of the 1950s, and, hence, of the shows.[13] As cultural critic Andrea Carosso notes, youth of the era were implicitly critical of the Cold War consensus, yet inextricably linked to it as well.[14] The teen dance shows, in their format and content, clearly replicated this sense of family and togetherness. One method was in their depiction of the life stages of the adolescent as he or she struggled to break free of parental control. The shows were essentially predicated on peer pressure, a key element in the teen maturation process. The off-screen teens identified with the on-screen teens, copying one another, "trying on" the latest dance styles and behaviors as well as outfits. What gave cohesion to the show were the internal workings of the "committee": those fifty or so teenagers selected as "regulars" who encouraged the participants to dance, opened and sorted fan mail, and generally served as role models for correct TV behavior.

In the same ritual structure characteristic of high school cliques, the teen dance regulars were the envy of their peers. As a prominent educator of the period, James S. Coleman, noted in *The Adolescent Society*, to gain an understanding of the adolescent mind, we should consider "those members that boys and girls most esteem—the ones they want to be like, the ones they would like to be friends with, the ones they see as members of the leading crowd."[15] The committee process, in fact, eventually became a means of self-policing where the larger threat was of *not* conforming enough to one's peers. To become a committee member, one had to be at least fourteen years old (many, of course, lied to get in), undergo an audition, and generally serve as a parental figure to the fifty or so other dancers on the set. The presence of the avuncular, affable host also helped to smooth the rougher edges of rock 'n' roll and promote a sense of family cohesion. As Carl Belz notes, the un-assuming manner of the host (typically a former disk jockey) was designed, in part, to let the music and dancing of the teens speak for itself.[16] It was a curious position that the host inhabited. He served as a "father figure," a pro-tective yet also amiable one who *licensed* the dancing (he introduced them to R&B music, after all) and supported various activities that fostered the kids' autonomy—allowing them to choose their favorite songs, dance couple, guest performers. In the process, the hosts helped to foster an emerging teenage population as a serious market for R&B-based music and dancing and teen products and paraphernalia.

Just as the culture of the 1950s struggled to come to terms with race and racial integration, so did the teen dance programs. In *Blacks and White TV*, J. Fred MacDonald has pointed out how network television's atmos-phere for Black performers during this time was an "ambivalent" one; since the late 1940s, Black singers, dancers, and comedians appeared, if inter-mittently, on TV variety shows. As MacDonald states, "Such utilization of Blacks was a conscious effort on the part of a new medium in an at-mosphere of postwar liberality."[17] The teen dance shows, in this spirit of "liberality," most always featured Black performers and musicians. But any seeming move toward greater inclusion was undercut by the fact that on the shows the *studio dancers* themselves were segregated. However, some did indeed include young Black dancers as studio participants. And some Black dancers might be among the mix, either on camera or in the studio audience, particularly in cities such as New York, Memphis, and Detroit, which contained significant Black populations. But there were few of them. The era's racism led to a state of affairs in which primarily white teenagers were dancing to R&B, copying Black dance and expressive styles, and "standing in," in a sense, for Black dancers who were not allowed on the shows. The teen "breakout" referred to earlier was accomplished by white teenagers adopting and adapting Black-inspired music and engaging in a cultural style deemed "forbidden."

One of the most glaring examples of the effects of this segregation occurred on only the second airing of rock 'n' roll impresario Alan Freed's teen TV show *Big Beat*, which debuted on New York City's ABC-TV on July 12, 1957. The episode in question featured Black teenage rock 'n' roll star Frankie Lymon (of Frankie Lymon and the Teenagers). Freed, it is important to note, unlike other deejays, had an enormous teenage following and, as explained in Chapter 1, was known for his zealous promotion of R&B music and Black musicians. He had established himself on the WJW-Cleveland-based radio program "Moondog Rock 'n' Roll Party," so named after the instrumental piece by the street performer Louis T. Hardin (aka "Moondog"), which debuted in July 1951. *Big Beat* was Freed's first foray into TV and designed to "show everyone in the family that this [rock 'n' roll] is a healthy, normal music."[18] At the end of the show, when Freed had invited kids in the audience to come on stage and dance, Lymon grabbed the hand of a young white girl, and the action was caught on TV. Freed paid dearly for this "infraction"; ABC's affiliates, particularly those in the South, were in an uproar. The show's sponsored warned Freed that from that point on he could only feature all-white acts. Freed refused, and the show ended its short run.[19]

American Bandstand

One of the most famous hosts was Dick Clark of *American Bandstand*. While the history of *American Bandstand* has already been well documented, it bears some scrutiny here because it was the first of the teen dance programs to air nationally and thus cement the pairing of teenagers and dance.[20] While many assume that *American Bandstand* was the prototype from which other bandstand-shows emerged, the historical record proves otherwise. *American Bandstand* (or *Bandstand*, as it was known in its earliest incarnation) didn't emerge *sui generis* but was actually a result of the confluence of several national trends, both cultural and industry-wide. As music historian Murray Forman explains, discussions in the press about TV as one of the best methods of selling records via the so-called deejay shows occurred as early as 1948.[21] What made Philadelphia unique, and especially ripe for a teen dance show, was that by the early 1950s it was considered a major destination spot for rock 'n' roll music, a "breakout" city where "pop records were tested before being distributed nationally."[22] According to sociologist Matthew F. Delmont, the major promotional circuit for records, in fact, consisted of

Baltimore-Washington, Cleveland, Pittsburgh, and Philadelphia. At that time, Philadelphia was the third largest city in the United States, and, of course, near to New York City, which made it enticing for music producers.[23]

American Bandstand debuted (as *Bandstand*) on September 9, 1952, hosted by former deejay Robert Horn, The show, broadcast on WFIL-TV, a fledgling affiliate of ABC TV, reached millions of regional viewers as it broadcast to parts of Pennsylvania, New Jersey, Delaware, and Maryland, becoming known as a four-state region called "WFIL-adelphia." *Bandstand* became *American Bandstand* in 1956, when Horn was arrested on drunk driving charges, and worse, brought up on statutory charges involving a fourteen-year-old girl. Dick Clark, though, who had hosted the popular radio show *Caravan of Music*, also on WFIL, had been waiting in the wings. He debuted as host on July 9, 1956. *Bandstand* then became *American Bandstand* on August 5, 1957, when the show went national with Clark still firmly at the helm.[24]

The new name signaled the show's reach to most parts of the country and the desire to use the show to foster a national youth culture. In fact, though, that white youth culture was *already* in formation and mirrored in teenagers' shared excitement for R&B music and dance, their attraction to the music on Black radio stations, and their purchase of transistor radios and record players, But *American Bandstand*, like other teen dance shows, deployed various strategies to tame and contain that energy and enthusiasm, which many commentators still feared as adolescent anarchy and loss of control. The way in which *American Bandstand* managed this contradiction can be seen in its various policies, protocols, and structural mechanisms to create a friendly and benign youth culture. That it was mostly white was not an accident. As Delmont points out, *Bandstand* tended to play "watered down," and more conservative white cover versions of R&B numbers that teens had heard on the Black radio stations; radio, unlike TV, could afford this exposure of more Black artists since the shows generally broadcast late at night and were, of course, not visual.[25]

Bob Horn had left Dick Clark a winning formula for the show. As *American Bandstand* chronicler John Jackson points out, *Bandstand* contained many of the ingredients that would eventually become staples of the teen dance programs. It aired after school, from 3:30 to 4:45 P.M. weekdays (another half-hour version of *Bandstand* was recorded in New York City on Saturdays from 7:30 to 8 P.M.) and featured a teenage-appropriate set: a canvas backdrop simulating the inside of a record store, rows of banners that named each of the local high schools represented on the show, and bleachers for the studio audience replicating a high-school gym.[26] All of the shows exuded a clean-cut image in part to assuage parental and network concerns, in part to contain the frenzy over the new and suggestive music and dance. In Clark's case, too, of course, the network feared having the show tainted by Horn's sex scandal. Clark was the ever steady, calm, suited-and-tied host with a benevolent, if bland, demeanor. All the shows had dress codes and specified what were acceptable televised behaviors. As Lilla Anderson, writing for the *TV Radio-Mirror* noted, Clark specified these rules in an internal WFIL memo: "For girls, that means any dress suitable to wear in the afternoon. Boys must wear a jacket and tie. Quality of clothes doesn't matter, but we want no jeans, no leather jackets, no toreador pants, no shorts."[27] Chewing gum was out of the question.

In *The Nicest Kids in Town*, Delmont, drawing on theorist Benedict Anderson, explains how *American Bandstand* essentially created ritual practices that drew teenagers together into their own "imagined community" that reinforced their sense of belonging and togetherness. Anderson discusses how while the mass consumption of newspapers once served as a "mass ceremony," which bound unseen readers to one another, now the televised teen shows now united teenagers "with little face-to-face knowledge of the millions of other viewers watching the shows."[28] *American Bandstand* went to great lengths to illustrate how the teens were part of a national youth culture linked by advertising potential. On the show, Clark often referred to a large map of the United States while sitting at his podium indicating the names of each TV station that carried the show; not only did the map illustrate the program's reach, it served as a reminder to sponsors that each affiliate station represented a new teenage market ready to be mined.

The strategies for drawing studio viewers and participants to the shows, too, mirror this type of community building. Like other teen shows, *American Bandstand* generally admitted teenagers on a first-come, first-served basis. The recruitment practices ensured teenagers' identification with the on-screen participants, as many of them were friends or peers from their own schools. Central to the teen shows were the appeals made to local high schools and community centers, churches, and civic organizations where sock hops might take place. The response to these appeals was overwhelming. For the opening broadcast of *Bandstand*, in 1952, 1,300 teenagers lined up to gain admission to a 200-person studio; by 1955, it was estimated that over 250,000 teenagers had entered the WFIL studio.[29]

Mirroring the consensus ideology of the time, though (the attempt to keep things safe, contained, and strife-free), the internal workings and mechanisms of the show ensured that audiences were predominantly white. As the show became more popular, prospective participants now needed some sort of official letter of admittance, the absence of which was often used as a way to deny the entry of Black youth. And although the *American Bandstand* studio, located on 46th and Market Street, in West Philadelphia, was literally next door to the racially mixed West Philadelphia High, by the mid-1950s—at the same moment that the landmark Supreme Court decision *Brown v. Board of Education*, outlawing segregated schools, was passed— *Bandstand* was primarily recruiting from the area's two parochial schools. West Catholic High for Girls and West Catholic High for Boys, unlike West Philadelphia High and John Bertram High, were *not* racially mixed. Matthew Delmont reports how Black and white teenagers fought outside the WFIL studio as a result of these exclusionary entry practices. In a sign of the insidious racial segregation and racism of the time, advertisers were reluctant to support a show where Black and white teens might have been dancing together or where audiences might witness any type of racial strife. As Delmont points out, WFIL and its advertisers were keen to draw on Philadelphia's "interracial music scene to create an entertaining and profitable television show while refusing to allow the city's Black teenagers into the studio audience for fear of alienating viewers and advertisers."[30] That alienation, of course, lay in the idea of social integration among white and Black teenagers and, by extension, fears of miscegenation.

In the earliest days of *American Bandstand*, when it was still broadcast locally, Black teens *were* allowed on the show. This was in 1952, when teenagers simply entered on a first-come, first-served basis and before the setup of the committee and the membership system. Delmont interviewed former dancer Weldon McDougal who attended West Philadelphia High School, near the *Bandstand* studios, who performed on the show:

West Philly [High School] was so close to *Bandstand*. *Bandstand* used to start at 2:45. West Philadelphia at the time, we used to get out at 2:15. When Bob Horn was there, I'd rush over there and it was first-come first-served. So I'd go in there and dance, until they started playing all of this corny music. Then there weren't many Black guys who would go over there. I was considered corny going over there. I was just seeing what was happening.[31]

The policy changed after 1953. Once the committee came into existence, many kids who were "invited" to the show were of the same social set as the committee members, who were white. (Many of them came from West Catholic High, which was mainly Irish and Italian.) Everyone but the committee members and the regulars, though, now had to send a letter to the station to request an appearance on the show for a specific day. What this meant practically was that the show attracted many teenagers who lived in the outskirts of Philadelphia, including Allentown, Reading, and other suburban towns, that had very small Black populations. As Delmont notes, "For Black teens who lived only a few blocks from the studio, the advance notice aspect of the admissions policy further marginalized them from the show."[32] By 1954, then, *Bandstand* had practically become an all-white show. As former Philadelphia social dancer Moe Booker recalls of the difficulties of getting on the show:

> Now the first host of *Bandstand* was a guy by the name of Bob Horn.... When he was host all the kids could go on.... When Dick Clark came on, a whole new policy was instilled, and Black kids were not allowed to go on at all. So I don't have great memories of Dick Clark. A lot of people do; I don't.[33]

Other Black teens, though, had a different reaction, and their experiences reveal how despite the segregated nature of the shows, they often found ways of circumventing the official racist policies. According to former social dancer Claudia Hall, *Bandstand* was worth watching since it introduced a lot of R&B performers at a time when Blacks were a rarity on TV: "A lot of home-grown music and a lot of Blacks got a start on there, too."[34] Most important, though, Hall recalls a practice that may have been true for other local shows in which Blacks were allowed to dance in the studio until the show actually went on the air. Other dancers confirm this point. Social dancers Mary Richardson and Regina Lyons, for instance, explain how after many failed attempts, they actually managed an appearance on *American Bandstand*. Lyons told Roberts that when she finally got on the show, "nobody ever saw us on camera, because the cameras never focused on any of us. We were there dancing. And I bet you any amount of money Dick Clark and Bob Horn would tell you that didn't go on, but it did. It did."[35]

What these kinds of crossovers meant, even when the acts of appearing on the shows were carried out surreptitiously and covertly, was that Black and white teens were indeed learning from one another, borrowing from one another, and involved in, as dance historian Brenda Dixon Gottschild calls it, "the merry-go round of appropriation."[36] Despite the official barriers, however, Black and white youth continued to associate with one another, and learn from each other, through a variety of channels. We know, of course, that both Black and white youth were copying dance moves and dress styles from one another in schools—at school dances, for instance—and in their neighborhoods, at local dance hops. Many Black youth still watched *Bandstand* and other primarily segregated teen dance shows and saw what white teens were dancing on television; in other cases, Black youth participated in the Blacks-only days where white teens watched them. It was also the case that Black youth were sometimes a part of the studio audience, and even danced side by side with white teenagers, during the commercial breaks, before the cameras were on. And, white teens got to view black teens dancing on the (few) all black-teen dance shows that aired local (as described in Chapter 3). Former *Buddy Deane Show* dancer Yvonne Moten recalls how these days were actually the best of the week.[37]

To paraphrase Gottschild, this borrowing could become "outright theft," though, particularly in a context where one group is denied the same resources, access, and status afforded the other and when, of course, the borrowing is not acknowledged.[38] An instance of how the racial politics played out on the shows in the late 1950s can be illustrated in the following scene from Ron Mann's 1992 rock 'n' roll documentary *Twist*, in which two former *American Bandstand* regulars (and stars) are interviewed many years later. The clip is worth describing in its entirety. In answer to a question about how they originated their dances, Joan Buck and Jimmy Peatross first explained how kids would pick up a new type of dance or style and bring it to the show where it would hopefully get "approved" by Dick Clark.

BUCK: Sometimes you would go to a different neighborhood and you'd pick up a new move or a new type of dance or style, and you would bring it to the show, and if Dick liked it, and it was approved, he'd put you in a spotlight dance. Jimmy and I went to the same high school together, and one day he asked me if I wanted to go on the show because they were having a jitterbug contest and Jimmy was a good dancer, so I said sure, and that's how we got on the show. Later on, we introduced a dance they had never seen called the Strand, and Dick gave us several spotlights doing the dance, and it became popular.

After a slight pause, she added,

The Strand, I think, was done before we brought it out, maybe not by white
people, but it was definitely done by Black people.
PEATROSS: And we used to see it in high school. We introduced it. . . .
BUCK: . . . as the Strand, not a Black dance, as a dance.
PEATROSS: And we made it up. We had to say we made it up on the air. If we
said . . . we weren't allowed to say Black people taught us.

After the interviewer asks why, Peatross is evasive; he goes on to say that
the day after they introduced the dance, about fifty or a hundred Black kids
were supposedly waiting outside the studio ready to beat them up, and Clark
called up for protection. "They beat you up?," asks the interviewer.

BUCK: Actually it was kind of a surprise when he [Clark] asked us on air
where you learned the dance; we didn't know quite how to handle it. It
wasn't that he said "you can't say Black people." He didn't say that. It's
just . . . We knew at the time he asked that question we didn't really want to
say that "oh, Black people taught it to us."

At this point, the film cuts to former *Bandstand* couple Carole Scaldeferri
and Joe Fusco:

FUSCO: We always thought, of course, that they [Black kids] definitely did it
better. But of course, we received all the fan mail, and we got the credit for
it in our letters and from our fans.
SCALDEFERRI: It wasn't fair. (softly)
FUSCO: No. It wasn't fair, really; if you think about it. Cause at that time you
didn't think you were stealing anything, but we were.[39]

What is striking here, of course, is the dancers' acknowledgment and
coming to consciousness—as well as embarrassment and shame—of their
own complicity in upholding the racist strictures of the time. The fact that
Buck and Peatross felt they could not tell Dick Clark where they learned
the dances is also indicative of the perniciousness of the racial system that
white and Black teenagers had internalized. We don't know for sure whether
or where Buck and Peatross had actually seen their Black counterparts,
but clearly the dance—a slow, close couple-dance peppered with turns

and intricate footwork—had originated within the Black community and initiated by dancers on all-Black teen dance show *The Mitch Thomas Show* that aired in the Philadelphia (and which will be discussed in the next chapter).[40]

The Milt Grant Show

Not far from Philadelphia, in Washington, DC, another popular teen dance show was moving up in the ratings—*The Milt Grant Show*. The show debuted on September 22, 1956, as *The Milt Grant Record Hop*, and after a year ran as *The Milt Grant Show* through 1961 on WTTG-Ch. 5. The show initially aired on Saturday nights from 4 to 5 P.M. at the run-down studio located in the ballroom of the Raleigh Hotel at 11th and E Streets, NW, and then weekdays from 4:30 to 5:30 P.M., while also retaining its Saturday slot.[41]

Significantly, *The Milt Grant Show* aired a year before Clark's *American Bandstand* went national, by which time Grant (who was referred to as "Washington's Dick Clark") had already become an institution with loyal fans and dedicated viewers not likely to switch allegiance to *Bandstand*. In fact, many stations nationwide refused to air *American Bandstand* for fear that it would upstage their network's local bandstand-type show.[42] The list of musicians and stars who performed on the show—considered a must stop for musicians to get significant airplay—included major figures from both the Black R&B and white rock 'n' roll and rockabilly worlds, such as Little Richard, Buddy Holly, Chubby Checker, Bo Diddley, the Everly Brothers, Bobby Darin, and many more.

Milt Grant, like every teen show host, hoped to make his program distinctive and use it to promote the emerging national youth culture. Grant himself was a highly popular and beloved figure in the DC area; like Dick Clark, he emerged from the radio business. After receiving a degree in engineering from New York University and serving as news director of WNYC in New York City, he hopped on the rock 'n' roll music bandwagon. While his teen show hewed to the same formula, it developed a dedicated following in part through the live sock hops Grant featured on the weekends near the city's schools. At stadiums, such as Glen Echo Park, the Fredericksburg Arena, and the Silver Spring Armory, Grant featured major guest bands and hired local musicians as backup musicians. Not only did the sock hops provide audiences for his daily televised show, they gave local teen musicians the chance to test their wings before a live audience on a major show.[43] According to Antoinette Matlins, a former dancer on *The Milt Grant Show*, Grant "loved the music of the era, and he loved helping promote the interests of his 'regulars.'"[44] She also describes how her participation on Grant's show enabled her to consider developing a musical career; two songs she composed were recorded by Teresa Brewer, a very well known female jazz and pop music singer of the 1950s.[45]

Many parents, pundits, and even sociologists perceived the teen dance shows as a balm to adolescent rebelliousness and rambunctiousness and as a way of warding off juvenile delinquency. As one *Variety* commentator noted of another local DC program, *Bandstand Matinee*, "All in all, this makes for an unusually lively afternoon show, with the possibilities of a public service angle—keeping juves off the street—tossed in."[46] In fact, television generally during this time, as Lynn Spigel notes, "was particularly hailed for its ability to keep youngsters out of sinful public spaces, away from the countless contaminations of everyday life."[47] In 1954, Estes Kefauver, the liberal senator from Tennessee, followed up on his famed organized crime hearings with another set of hearings that became known as the "comic-book inquisition," to investigate the causes of juvenile delinquency.[48] The investigation had actually earmarked rock 'n' roll, and especially the movie *Rock around the Clock*, that anthem to errant American youth featuring rock 'n' roll icon Bill Haley, as a possible link to the juvenile delinquency problem.[49]

Attempts to contain and quell these concerns are palpable in the interactions between Grant and his young studio dancers. In an appeal to home viewers, the host would typically ask the studio teenagers to name the schools they attended and what grades they were in. But it was Grant's "chats" about dating, curfews, homework, and home life that fostered a particular solidarity between himself and the teens, as in the following exchange from a 1958 broadcast. Grant asked the studio dancers, huddled around him, if they had experienced any "parental problems" lately:

GRANT: Anyone have any of those?

STUDIO DANCERS: Oh, yes! [in unison]

GRANT: All right, then. Let's get them. Ok. What's your name? [Turns to a young girl, Dee]

GRANT: Hi Dee. What's your problem?

DEE: Well, what happens when your mother doesn't trust you? [giggling]

GRANT: What do you mean she doesn't trust you?

DEE: Well, I don't know. [shrugs and more giggling]

GRANT: Doesn't trust you with what?

DEE: I don't know—anything!! [she dissolves into laughter]

GRANT: Anyone have a solution for that"?

["Kill her" is heard from a voice in the crowd.]

GRANT: Any other parental problems? Come on over here. And your name is
  Dick. All right, Dick; what's your problem?

DICK: Well, my problem is trying to get out Friday nights—how to ask your
  father.

GRANT: You mean Dad doesn't like you to go out Friday nights?

DICK: Well. . . .

GRANT: Does he have a curfew or what?

DICK: No, he lets me go out; the hard problem is asking him. You've gotta get
  enough nerve.

GRANT: Does he give you a lot of opposition to that?

DICK: Yes. . . .[50]

This scene is worth describing as it illustrates the show's ability both to represent teenage angst and convey it to home-viewing teens who might identify
with them, yet also to absorb those concerns into the ideological framework
of the white, suburban family. The subtle aggression and frustration exhibited
here on the part of the teenagers (despite all of the nervous laughter) is
double-coded. The teens at once present "themselves," airing their anxieties
and grievances, but their images get transmitted as *versions* of themselves by
the ideological codes at work on the shows. Media theorist Dick Hebdige, in
Subculture: The Meaning of Style, explains how this social process occurs. The
media conveys "a picture of their own lives which is 'contained' or 'framed'
by the ideological discourses which surround and situate it."[51] Here they are,
clean-cut, well-dressed looking kids, contesting their parents' values and
corralled into a picture of domestic charm.

A similar process of social-cohesion-building is at work in the teenagers'
trendsetting regarding clothing and hairstyle, what Hebdige refers to as "subcultural style." On one hand the styles that became popular were those urged
by the producers and considered "safe," "proper," and conservative; on *The
Milt Grant Show*, sweaters with so-called Peter Pan collars (flat with rounded
corners) became popular with the young girls and box-toed loafers, white
bucks, or saddle shoes with the boys.[52] Yet other stylistic affects, according
to Hebdige, can be read as "symbolic forms of resistance," as "symptoms of

a wider and more generally submerged dissent," characteristic of the entire postwar period itself.[53] While the teen dancers were largely from white,
middle-class backgrounds, they weren't *entirely* so; many of the shows drew a
distinctly urban and often working-class teen audience, such as on *American
Bandstand*, which featured many dancers from urban areas. According to
youth historian Thomas Hine, the city kids were in some ways a welcome
sight—they gave off a whiff of urban chic that was new to viewers: "After
more than a decade of parents moving to the suburbs for the sake of the children, the look and style of the city kid was becoming romantic. This was a
minor rebellion in itself."[54]

Former *Milt Grant Show* dancer and "regular" Tony Bonanno explains:

> I grew up in the city, in DC. Not in suburban Maryland, not in suburban
> Virginia. I was a city boy. And I think most of us on *The Milt Grant Show*
> were city kids. We tended to dress a little differently than, say, the suburbs
> of North Virginia, which were all the children of the generals and the
> politicians and all of that. Not that there weren't a lot of those people living
> in the city also, . . . but back at that age I really didn't have too much clarity
> about social classes, socioeconomic neighborhoods, all that stuff. I sort of
> thought we were all just kids.

Bonanno continues:

> You have to envision me as sort of a skinny kid, with curly hair, and sort
> of like a ducktail in back, and this thing that hung down in the front—peg
> pants—and . . . these shoes with pearl buttons on the sides, and a gold collar
> pin, with my skinny tie—I mean this was a whole different cultural look.[55]

What Bonanno describes is actually a replica of a zoot suit, the 1940s
outfit—consisting of flowing trousers, a draped coat, large lapels, and over-
sized shoulder pads—made popular by Black and Mexican street gangs. As
discussed earlier, youth were attempting to set their own standards but doing
so through the adaptation of Black and working-class styles of clothing,
speech idioms, and dance styles. Social cohesion, then, was, in Hebdige's
words, "maintained through the appropriation and redefinition of cultures
of resistance."[56] The media, in this case TV, took these stylistic and sartorial redefinitions and formulated them in ways that could be read by a mass

audience. Just as we see of the dances themselves, Black cultural expressions get filtered, or mediated, through young, white bodies.

The Buddy Deane Show

Like Philadelphia and New York City, Baltimore was a crucial testing ground for rock 'n' roll music. Highly popular musicians such as Ray Charles, Chuck Berry, and Chubby Checker graced *The Buddy Deane Show* studio. Originally airing out of WJZ-TV, from 1957 to 1964, *The Buddy Deane Show* was immortalized in the 1988 John Waters film *Hairspray* (and the subsequent musical in 2003). *Hairspray*'s *Corny Collins Show* was based on the real-life *Buddy Deane Show* and filmmaker John Waters's affectionate remembrance of growing up and becoming a teenager with the so-called Buddy Deaners whom he emulated.[57]

The Buddy Deane Show debuted on September 9, 1957, on WJZ-TV in Baltimore—only a little over a month after *American Bandstand* first broadcast nationally—and aired Mondays through Saturdays, from 3 to 5 P.M. As on *American Bandstand* and *The Milt Grant Show*, *The Buddy Deane Show* featured a particular school or teen club as well as Deane's "top 20" recorded songs each Saturday. The network actually saw to it that *American Bandstand* never, in fact, came to Baltimore. For a while, *The Buddy Deane Show* was the top-ranked local production in the nation, drawing hundreds of young people to its studio doors, many of them hoping for a shot at becoming members of the coveted committee. Thousands wrote to the station requesting the free tickets to perform on the show.[58]

The mastermind behind the show—Winston J. ("Buddy") Deane himself—hailed from Arizona but set himself up as a pioneering R&B-playing deejay on WITH-AM radio in Baltimore. (See Figure 2.1.) As a radio producer and announcer, Deane recalled:

> I was playing on-the-air records by people like Eddie Fisher and Dick Haines, and people like that. I noticed that that wasn't what the kids were asking for. They were asking for records by people like Fats Domino and Little Richard. I noticed a lot of the kids were listening to Black radio stations, they liked that music. After a while they wanted to hear Little Richard, and not a cover version of Little Richard, they wanted to hear Little Richard.

Figure 2.1 Buddy Deane, host of *The Buddy Deane Show* (Baltimore) on the set for his popular afternoon teen dance show, ca. 1957. From *The Buddy Deane Show 1950s & 1960s*, www.videobeat.com.

It wasn't long before Deane brought the music to the TV screen:

> We tried, we experimented with different things on the television show. As I said, we were just trying to play this music on television, looking for a way to play it, and a way to present it. The thing that obviously clicked was the youngsters dancing to the music.[59]

But it was the *combination* of the music, the dancing, the interactions among the kids, and the homegrown nature of the show that made it distinctive. It beat out the afternoon soap operas in ratings. In "The Last Dance," journalist Laura Wexler quotes Arlene Kozak, Buddy Deane's trusted assistant, who remarked: "Do you know what it takes to beat out soap operas?"[60]

It was *The Buddy Deane Show* committee that provided this serial drama. The very structure and framing apparatus of the shows was such that home audiences could "read into" and create narratives around these coveted teen dancers, become enamored of certain couples, and project romantic scenarios. As Antoinette Matlins remembers, "There was a certain attractiveness they were looking for, they wanted the regulars to be attractive, so there was a physical element; not that you had to be beautiful, but you had to have a certain look."[61] To ensure these elements, according to Buddy Deane himself, "We were very careful about the kids we got on there. You also had to have a recommendation from your priest, rabbi, or minister to be on the program, and, of course, some of them didn't want to give a recommendation for the kids to go dancing."[62] And in addition to creating general order in the studio, coaxing wallflowers to dance, and dealing with the flow of daily fan mail, *The Buddy Deane Show* committee members held auditions. According to Kozak, the dances the potential committee members auditioned for were "the jitterbug, cha-cha, slow dance and whatever dance was popular at the time. You picked people on their dancing ability and also on their personalities—the way they handled themselves."[63] The regulars, too, were responsible for creating a particular regional "look" copied by their viewers. The Buddy Deaner girls, for instance, popularized a teased, bouffant-style hairdo, known as "beehives," and what were called "cha-cha heels" (what are known today as kitten heels)[64].

Although a committee member's term was supposed to last for three months only, what really happened was that as TV viewing audiences became attached to the dancers and the dance couples, they were allowed to stay on in their committee member roles longer, sometimes indefinitely. The Buddy Deane dancers (like other teen-show dancers, particularly on *American Bandstand*) developed a rich rapport with their audience members who treated them like celebrities. Many of them were featured in teen magazines and local newspapers and recognized on the street. It was a heady experience, for sure, for fourteen- and fifteen-year-olds. Former Buddy Deane dancer Frani Hahn has written that

> Honestly, I was on the show for, I'd say about six months before my father even found out, and he found out quite by accident. My father was very strict. And my mother would pack a little paper bag with my cha-cha heels and my pastel pink lipstick. My father's boss came into work one day and said, "My daughter and my wife just love your daughter, and we can't believe that she's a TV star and you work for me!"[65]

The way that the televised teen dance shows created this type of viewer identification was through appeals, both verbal and nonverbal, to the specifics of gender, ethnicity, class, and especially to family. Part of this had to do with the medium of television itself, its newness, and its ability to relay images of "reality" that translated into viewer empathy. "Television," as John Fiske notes, "tries to construct an ideal subject position which it invites us to occupy."[66] The spectator is then "rewarded" with "the pleasure of recognition" of her or his own worldview. In the 1950s, this worldview prioritized, and gave concrete representation to, the social values of family, togetherness, order, attractiveness, and heterosexual romance.

For Black teenage viewers, as explained in Chapter 1, the sense of identification was far different since in this televisually segregated terrain Black teenagers were not the primary viewers being appealed to except on the euphemistically called "special guest days," or "Blacks-only days," when they danced separately from their white counterparts.[67] As mentioned earlier, Black performers were permitted and even encouraged to perform on the shows and to interact with the (white) teenagers, but the real problem—or source of consternation and fear—lay with dancing between Black and white couples, which the Frankie Lymon imbroglio revealed so well. The decision to appear on the Black-only days was a complex one. A former dancer on *The Milt Grant Show*, Mickey Teague, recalls how he got the chance to dance on Grant's show:

> I can't remember just how it came about; all I know is that they said we—
> you know, the Blacks—could start to come on once a week, which was—
> either it was a Tuesday or a Wednesday—and so we called it Black Tuesday
> or Black Wednesday. And it was funny because when we danced the white
> kids stayed and watched us. . . . And then we weren't able to watch the white
> kids, but we watched them on TV. I think Milt, kind of, he started leaning
> a little toward us being on longer, and a couple of more days because of the
> way we danced.

Teague continues about his relationship with his white peers and explains how and under what circumstances Black and white teenagers might engage with one another:

> You danced all the time, even in school, at lunchtime we could dance. Then
> in junior high school, junior high school they called it when I was in school,
> we had corner stores that had jukeboxes; the white kids would go to one
> store, we would go to another. Then there was a third store we would go to

that was Blacks and whites, usually the white kids, they wanted to learn how to dance, how we would dance.

Teague recalled, too, that on the Blacks-only days, many of the white kids would "hang around" so they could learn their dances and then bring them back to the show:

> Yeah, they'd bring 'em back to the show and then you could kind see some of the stuff they had seen with us. Some of them wouldn't ask. . . . But the ones that asked, we showed 'em.[68]

Teague notes that Grant, for instance, tried but failed to get Teague and other Black kids on the show to compete in a dance contest. But these entreaties fell on the network's deaf ears. Nonetheless, of course, televisually Black and white teenagers, as Teague alludes to, were watching and copying each other's dances and dance moves despite cultural and institutional barriers.

Another teenager (or young adolescent) who danced on Buddy Deane's "Blacks-only day" was Donald Thoms, who was only twelve years old when he appeared on the show in 1957. Thoms noted that every kid in his neighborhood watched the Blacks-only day on *The Buddy Deane Show*. "Every kid [that he knew] considered themselves good dancers. They had practiced at house parties, and to be on these shows was their chance to 'show everyone they could dance.'" He emphasized how there "no Black people anywhere on TV, so in a sense this was 'a big deal.'" For many home viewers, it was an opportunity to revel in the talents and abilities of young, Black teens. In a very candid and revealing interview, Thoms expresses the psychological conflicts that he had with this setup and notes how at twelve years old he was still coming to consciousness about segregation and racial politics. As the civil rights movement took on steam, by the early 1960s, and as he got a bit older, he saw "the tension mounting," and ultimately came to see this practice as deeply offensive.[69] Teague, too, describes a similar experience, which, for both young men, was a kind of gradual political radicalization:

> You kind of like were feeling around in the dark, finding out stuff on our own, and then when it hit you in the face all you got was, "well that's the way it is." Never an explanation. But then you start to get the feel of what was going on and why.

Teague was aware of where the primary animosity emanated from, though. "As kids," he said, "we just heard the music." He continued, "We got along as far as kids; it was the adults that didn't want to see this."[70]

It is not insignificant that the close of *The Buddy Deane Show* coincided with the 1964 Civil Rights Act legislation prohibiting discrimination in public accommodations and employment. As the civil rights movement had gained momentum, and as TV itself covered civil rights uprisings and protests, it became increasingly difficult for the networks to enforce this type of "televisual segregation." By the mid-1960s, so-called Blacks-only days— which the Black teens either resisted or were resigned to—would become a thing of the past. Deane himself wanted to add more "special guests" days, for Black teens only, but, as protesters made clear, that was not the point. As Bob McKenzie, a former teen dancer and teen assistant on the show, noted years later, "There was fear that a Black boy would ask a white girl to dance in front of the camera and if she said no, what would happen"?[71]

Two major protests occurred at the studio that forced the producers' hand and spelled the demise of the show. On June 28, 1962, twenty white and Black students of the Civic Interest Group (CIG), an integrationist group formed at Morgan State University, picketed WJZ on one "special guests" day, when Ray Charles was to make an appearance. The teens were hoping to intercept Charles and prevent him from entering the studio, but unbeknownst to them, Charles's performance had been taped days earlier.[72] *The Afro American* newspaper reported on the protest and noted an inscription on one of the picket signs: "Buddy Dean [sic], Do You Have Georgia on Your Mind"? The picketers, who insisted that they were committed to nonviolent protest, were turned away—although their aim was never to get on the show, but to demonstrate against it.[73]

It wasn't until the protest in August 1963 that another group of protesters were actually successful in getting on the show: the Baltimore Youth Opportunities Unlimited (BAYOU), an integrated group, a branch of the civil rights organization Northern Student Movement. It was another "special guests" day, but this time the protesters caught the station off guard as a busload of Black and white students entered the studio and then danced together. Wexler quotes a viewer of the show, Mary Curtis (a former columnist at *The Charlotte Observer*): "A white guy would grab a Black girl and the screen would dissolve into squiggles and squares—like the producers were trying to hide what was really happening. I've never forgotten it." Another former audience member, Bill Henry, remarked, "I remember that the lights on the show got so dim the kids were silhouettes. But you could still tell it was white and Black kids dancing together."[74] The show stayed on the air for another four and a half months, but as a result of mounting protests, hate mail, and death threats to station personnel (from both white and Black audience members), *The Buddy Deane Show* went off the air on January 4, 1964.

As TV increasingly covered the events of the civil rights movement, it became far more difficult to ignore the racial discrimination occurring on the shows. Each of the shows established during the 1950s handled segregation differently, but most of them died out by the mid-1960s (if not earlier) for this and other reasons, as I will discuss in the final chapter. By this time, styles of music were also changing—the Beatles arrived in 1964 and "rock 'n' roll" music gave way to "rock" music—as were styles of dance. And, too, the nature of the programs changed; some, such as *The Lloyd Thaxton Show* and *Shindig!*, were much more performance-oriented and featured professional dancers instead of amateurs, which radically changed the tenor of the programs.

As this chapter has shown, the shows did their best to domesticate the teen dance and the rock 'n' roll phenomenon within a televised simulacrum of the white, suburban family that prized togetherness and conformity at the same time that they proved to be testing ground for rebellious youth. Despite the attempts by network producers and advertisers to mold the programs into a narrative about middle-class solidarity, the Black and working-class origins of the dances could not be wholly contained. Ruptures continually shot through the façade, as in the instance of Frankie Lymon forgetting not to touch a white girl on Alan Freed's *Big Beat*. While the United States appeared to present a face of consensus in the aftermath of World War II, latent racial as well as class divisions lay submerged, and the teen programs brought some of these anxieties to the surface. In the following chapter, we see how several all-Black local teen TV shows negotiated these divides.

3

"Movin' and Groovin' "

Black Teen Dance Shows of the 1950s and Early 1960s

Many of the local televised teen dance shows, because they were not nationally syndicated, could override TV's unwritten racial "codes" and discriminatory practices, particularly if they had a cooperative advertiser or sympathetic network. In these cases, some Black youth might be allowed to appear on the shows. The four all-Black shows described in this chapter—*The Mitch Thomas Show*, *Teenage Frolics*, *Teenarama*, and *Richard's Open Door*—aired out of Delaware, North Carolina, Washington, DC, and Illinois. That three of these shows appeared in Southern states speaks both to the economics of the media markets in these cities (Wilmington, Raleigh, and Washington) and the stations' desire to appeal to a growing Black population. The longevity of two of the programs in particular (*Teenarama* broadcast until 1970, *Teenage Frolics* until 1983) suggests that these shows dug deep roots into their communities and became places for expressive communication, camaraderie, and embodied pleasure. Social dance, beyond mere recreation, can become a space for rejuvenation, testing of behaviors, and assertions of identity outside the confines of the ordered, everyday world. Dance theorist Thomas DeFrantz calls social dance "a primary site of improvised selfhood."[1] In this respatialization, now, of the (white) TV dance studio, the Black teen dance shows, like other sites of social dance, whether house parties, social clubs, YMCAs, church basements, or school dances, were not only places for Black teenagers to "show off" what they knew, and the skills they had honed, but to test their own capacities, innovate, and in the process ·create group cohesion.[2]

The Mitch Thomas Show

Hosted by radio deejay Mitch Thomas, *The Mitch Thomas Show* debuted on the unaffiliated TV station WPFH, Wilmington, Delaware, on August 13,

Dancing Black, Dancing White. Julie Malnig, Oxford University Press. © Oxford University Press 2023.
DOI: 10.1093/oso/9780197536254.003.0004

1955, every Saturday, from 2 to 4 P.M., and drew area teenagers from cities in New Jersey, Pennsylvania, and Delaware.[3] The show, then, would have been accessible on television to teens in the Philadelphia area who were avid *American Bandstand* viewers. For some, though, attending *The Mitch Thomas Show* was not possible. Alonzo Kittrels, a former fan and chronicler of the show, explained that "Few had train or bus fare for such a trip and access to automobiles were limited. Also, there was no interstate 95, back then, so an automobile ride involved a long drive through the heart of Chester, Pennsylvania, to reach the show."[4] But the show had a devoted TV viewership. He recalls gathering around a thirteen-inch black-and-white Zenith television, watching his peers dance to the music of Black performers including Chubby Checker, Fats Domino, Chuck Berry, Mary Wells, and more.[5]

Mitch Thomas himself began his career, like many other teen TV hosts, as a radio deejay; in fact, he was the first Black deejay in Wilmington working at WILM and then at WDAS radio.[6] Born in Palm Beach, Florida, Thomas moved to New Brunswick, New Jersey, and then received a bachelor's degree in business administration from what is now Delaware State University. Both he and the well-known Black deejays Jocko Henderson and Georgie Woods, partners at WDAS radio, often collaborated on teen events and rock 'n' roll dance shows, such as the 1956 "Rock and Roll Number Five" concert at Camden, New Jersey's convention hall that drew a biracial crowd of 4,500 teenagers; in fact, many of the performers featured there, such as The Five Satins, The Moonglows, Ella Johnson, and Screaming Jay Hawkins, were then brought to his TV show. Thomas was the first of his peer group to appear on TV on his own show.[7]

Both Black and white kids watched *The Mitch Thomas Show*, and while the studio audience was primarily Black, white teenagers were also known to attend.[8] Following a model similar to *American Bandstand*, *The Mitch Thomas Show* had the same type of "committee" that oversaw the dancers, attended to the proper dress code, and welcomed the show's guests. These dancers became local celebrities featured in several "teen columns" published in the *Philadelphia Tribune*, including "Teen Talk," "Teen Events," "Philly Date Line," and "Current Hops," that kept abreast of the latest local musicians, dancers, and dances. As "Philly Date Line" noted, "The Bee-Bee-Bop [a local dance] seems to be picking up in South Philly. Watch the *Mitch Thomas Show* on television each Saturday for a good demonstration of this dance."[9] Just as the white teen dance shows galvanized a white teen culture, so too did *The*

Mitch Thomas Show create a vibrant Black teen culture that reveled in a show dedicated to them and their community.

That WPFH would have chosen to air an all-Black teen dance show was more a matter of economics than of enlightened egalitarianism (Figure 3.1). As Matthew Delmont explains, "Eager to complete with *Bandstand* and the afternoon offerings on the other network-affiliated stations, WPFH hoped that Thomas's show would appeal to both Black and white youth in the same way as Black-oriented radio" did.[10] Clearly, the show came to have significant influence in the Philadelphia area and became as important as *American Bandstand* in supporting the market for rock 'n' roll music. In the documentary *Black Philadelphia Memories*, Thomas himself notes that "The show was so strong, I could play a record one time and break it wide open. Wide open, believe me. They'd [the kids] be jumping in the record stores buying it." And, too, the show's visibility made it somewhat of a local philanthropic hub and an aid to Black community projects. Like many Black radio deejays of the time, the televised teen show hosts became important civic leaders in their respective communities; many of them advanced civil rights causes. Thomas used the show to find homes for orphaned children. He also advertised other events and organizations such as for the NAACP, or local fraternities. Said

Figure 3.1 Mitch Thomas, the popular host of the locally aired Black teen dance program *The Mitch Thomas Show* (Wilmington, DE), ca. 1957. From *Black Philadelphia Memories*, Trudy Brown, dir., WHYY-TV, 1999.

Thomas of his largess, "They wanted something to be known, I'd do it. Free of charge."[11]

Mitch Thomas and the other Black teen dance show hosts discussed here were extremely influential actors in molding their shows in the spirit of Black institution building—that is, autonomous Black spaces that affirmed and upheld Black existence apart from or in resistance to segregated spaces delegated by white business owners, politicians, and educators, among others. What sociologist Maxine Leeds Craig calls "sites of cultural production" were the many Black newspapers, churches, women's clubs, and political organizations whose leaders promoted "varied ways of interpreting race."[12] These acts of institution building were similar to what the Black radio deejays did some years earlier for their listening public and the Black teen dance show hosts accomplished for Black social dancers (and TV viewers) in the late 1950s and early 1960s. The hosts were instrumental in fostering such an expressive culture and providing a safe, supportive environment for the teenagers. All of them saw themselves, and their programs, as contributing to the civic life of the community and in so doing created a community and culture *around dance*. While the programs needed advertising to secure sponsorship, the hosts made special efforts to specifically support local Black stores, businesses, YMCAs and WYCAs, and cultural enterprises. It is significant that each of the four teen TV hosts discussed here attended local Black colleges—what are known today as Historically Black Colleges and Universities—that no doubt instilled in them what cultural critic Jelani Favors calls "race consciousness"—a sense of their mission as leaders and activists.[13] It can be argued, in fact, that television in these early years, with the guidance of the hosts, helped make Black dance an institution in and of itself.

With the nurturing and supportiveness of the teen dance show hosts, the shows became important cultural spaces where Black youth might identify and compete with one another while creating and innovating news steps and styles. One particularly talented dancer was Otis Givens, a student at Ben Franklin High School, who with his partner Vera Boyer, became one of the "stars" of *The Mitch Thomas Show* (Figure 3.2). Givens was an avid watcher of the show for over a year before he was able to make the trip from South Philadelphia to Wilmington to dance on the show urged by his friend (and another acclaimed dancer) George Gray—or George the Walk as he was known.[14] Givens explains how the process worked; just as on *American*

Figure 3.2 Popular dance team of Otis and Vera (Otis Givens and Vera Boyer), on *The Mitch Thomas Show* (Wilmington, DE), ca. 1957. From *Black Philadelphia Memories*, Trudy Brown, dir., WHYY-TV 12, 1999.

Bandstand (as Joan Buck described), the host would "spotlight" a dancer or dancers who were particularly outstanding:

> So, it was a while before I could get on the camera because every time I asked them if me and Vera could dance—he [Thomas] never saw us dance before—so, he, you know, he was reluctant to just put the camera on us. But anyway, one day we were there and this record called "Talk to Me" by Little Willie John. It came on, and when we started dancing everybody was amazed at the type of dancing that we were doing, and, so, they really stopped dancing and watched us, and then they had to put the camera on us.[15]

Givens and Boyer were childhood friends who had started dancing together at an early age. Givens says that "we learned from the street," and then as they improved they took themselves nightly to different dances and dance clubs in the neighborhood, among them St. Simon's in South Philly at 22nd and Reed, St. Charles on 20th and Christian, the Girls' Y on 16th, and the Boys' Y on 17th and Christian. As they got more proficient, they went to some of the major city clubs such the OV Catto, Quaker City, and then to North Philly at Town Hall and Reynolds Hall. "We used to steal the show wherever we went," said Givens.[16] From photographs, and from a *Mitch Thomas Show* reunion in which Givens and Boyer reprised their dancing, it seems that their specialty was indeed a variation on the Strand, a version of the Lindy done to slow music (and copied by Buck and Peatross). Givens, today, recalls that he and Boyer also brought to the show their own distinct brand of free-style dances along with variations on the Bop and the Cha-cha.

Like many of his peers, Givens knew of *American Bandstand*, of course, but didn't watch it as a rule; he remarked that he and his friends might tune in "if it happened to be on." But, as he pointed out, "The music wasn't the same music that we liked, you know? I'm not saying all the music wasn't; they played some music we liked. But if we wanted to dance, I mean, you would have to pick and choose the records that you would want to dance to on his show." He recalls actually trying to get onto *American Bandstand* when it was hosted by Bob Horn. "We got in, but we really, you know, didn't like the atmosphere, and no, we just never went back." He continues, "I think more or less we were tolerated."[17]

It is apparent from interviews with those who performed on and watched *The Mitch Thomas Show*, as well as from Thomas himself, that it was marked by a spirit of inventiveness and camaraderie and was the birthplace of many new dance steps. According to the *Philadelphia Tribune*, when recording artist Hal Singer appeared on the show,

> His number "Movin' and Groovin'" was such a hit with the jockey's teenager guests that some of them were inspired to invent new and tricky dance steps to accompany the musician's clever recording. Mitch Thomas, emcee . . . was as surprised as Hal and the televiewers when he noticed that some of his young guests were cutting some unfamiliar steps which looked like a cross between "The Itch" and "The Chicken."[18]

We can assume that many dances performed on the show were presented for the first time, only then to be copied and brought to the white teen dance shows where they of course reached a wider circulation and became part of the popular dance culture. Mitch Thomas recollected on his surprise at the dancers' talent and initiative and his admiration for them:

> We had kids who could *dance*. I used to stand up there and watch it [their dancing], and I said, "Man, I can't believe this." They created a dance called the Stroll, where they were dancing in a line, this was before the Madison

and all that. I said, "Hey, what are y'all doing out there?" "Man, it's the Stroll." And I said "Oh." And the Stroll became a big thing. Mercury Records had the Diamonds to record it, and these kids, I don't know, I think they waited for a Saturday, just to have a good time.[19]

The Stroll was like so many Black social dances that have been "layered, copied, recreated, and regenerated" (Figure 3.3).[20] The musical composition was, in fact, initially inspired by the R&B number "C. C. Ryder" by Chuck Willis, which told the story of an unfaithful lover (originally sung and recorded by the blues great Ma Rainey in 1924).[21] In 1957, the white rock 'n' roll group The Diamonds, at Dick Clark's urging, created their cover version and named it "The Stroll," which then became a song describing the actual dance steps. Contrary to Clark's claims that the Stroll originated on *American Bandstand*, the dance was in fact created by Black teens and first seen on *The Mitch Thomas Show*. Apparently, Thomas had complained to

Figure 3.3 Teenage dancers performing the Stroll with the musical group The Diamonds at the head of the line on *The Mitch Thomas Show* (Wilmington, DE), ca. 1957. From *Black Philadelphia Memories*, Trudy Brown, dir., WHYY-TV 12, 1999.

Clark for taking credit for a dance that originated on his show, and, to his credit, Clark issued an apology on his show. But this is a classic instance of when borrowing becomes appropriation—even though credit was given to the Black teens, a major inequity remained since the dance continued to be performed on Clark's show, an affiliated station with ABC, that broadcast across the country. As Delmont notes astutely, Black teens could never be properly credited since "they were not depicted as part of a national youth culture *American Bandstand* broadcast to viewers."[22]

The Mitch Thomas Show was unfortunately short-lived. It ended in the summer of 1958 due presumably to the financial vicissitudes of the parent company, Storer Broadcasting, which had purchased WPFH in 1956. Storer changed the call number to WVUE and moved the station headquarters in Wilmington closer to Philadelphia. The station suffered in the move, however, and Thomas's show was one of the first to be let go. The station's unaffiliated status—the fact that it was not attached to the major networks, ABC, CBS, or NBC (Dumont was gone by now)—also contributed to its financial difficulties. Despite the popularity of the show, the primary reason cited for dissolution of the program was lack of sponsorship. This was still a problem for the handful of Black TV programs that existed in the 1950s; while many sponsors were keen to jump on the bandwagon for the Black media market, just as many were fickle, particularly in the South, and fearful of association with a Black show during a time of civil rights turmoil. Mitch Thomas himself continued to work in the radio industry but eventually retired in 1969 when he became a counselor to gang members in the city of Wilmington as well as a staff member at the South Price Run Community Center and the Martin Luther King Jr. Center. In the 1970s, he became a social worker for the Delaware Department of Health and Social Services.[23]

Teenage Frolics

Teenage Frolics vies with *The Mitch Thomas Show* as the "first" regularly scheduled television show hosted by a Black deejay and featuring Black teenage dancers and studio participants. It was also the longest-lasting. *Teenage Frolics* aired from 1958 to 1982, every Saturday at noon, on Raleigh, North Carolina's WRAL-TV (Channel 5), which was part of the Capitol Broadcasting Company, and an affiliate of NBC. The show was so popular across the state that some teenagers and teen groups would travel 100 miles to take part.[24] While tickets were not required for admittance to the show (most simply turned up hoping to get in), most teenagers, student groups, and others wishing to participate on the show wrote to the station to reserve a place for a specific date. *Teenage Frolics* featured its own house band, Irving Fuller and the Corvettes, as well as noted local and national performers. As a measure of the intense racism and fears of broadcasting a Blacks-only show, at its inception *Teenage Frolics* alternated Saturday with a wholly white teen show. As with Black radio of the early 1950s, white teenagers gravitated to the Black show. According to Yvonne Lewis Holley, "We're talking about segregation. When it started, one week it was a white show, the next Saturday it would be a Black show. The white show was so bad. And the white kids in the community wanted more of the Black show that they just stopped the show and he [Lewis] got every Saturday."[25]

A part of the reason for the longevity of the show, and, indeed, for the strength of the station, was J. D. Lewis himself, who was instrumental in securing the station's TV FCC license in 1957 (WRAL had begun as a radio station) (Figure 3.4). According to Paul Pope, former vice president at Capitol Broadcasting, Lewis "was the pioneer African American in that company." He started out as a radio announcer, became host of *Teenage Frolics*, and also worked in Public Affairs for the station (where he hosted a community affairs show called *Harambee*) and was the station's first personnel director. But it was also Lewis's deep ties to the Black community in Raleigh that endeared him to the city's populous and made him a valuable player at the station. As Pope recalled, "Fred Fletcher [the white owner of the TV station] had a relationship with the African American community, and he was smart enough to use J. D. Lewis.[26]

Lewis himself had a very distinguished career; after attending Morehouse College, he enlisted and was one of the first 200 Black men accepted into the Montford Point Marines (who trained at Montford Point). As a result of his training during service, which left him skilled in radio technology, when he returned home, he began announcing the local Negro League baseball games from a mobile sound truck at the historic John Chavis Memorial Park.[27] Fletcher spotted him at the games and was so impressed with his voice and demeanor that he hired him as a morning radio deejay at WRAL-AM radio where he hosted *JD's Jukebox*. He played a cross section of music from jazz to R&B that reached a wide listenership.[28] Soon after he became host of *Teenage Frolics* and remained host for nearly thirty years (Figure 3.5).

Figure 3.4 J. D. Lewis, the celebrated radio deejay and host of *Teenage Frolics* (Raleigh, NC), ca. 1958. Courtesy of Yvonne Lewis Holley.

Figure 3.5 Host J. D. Lewis on the set of *Teenage Frolics* (Raleigh, NC), WRAL-TV, ca. 1958. Courtesy of Yvonne Lewis Holley.

Like that of *The Mitch Thomas Show*, the significance of *Teenage Frolics* can best be understood within the context of Black institution building, but perhaps even more so because its longevity enabled it to establish deep roots in Raleigh and surrounding areas during the Jim Crow years. Chavis Park, for instance, so named for the nineteenth-century free Black preacher John Chavis and built in 1937 under the Works Progress Administration, became a place to address the community's social needs created by racial discrimination and oppression. It became a coveted center of community activity offering educational and cultural programming of many kinds. Lewis often broadcast episodes of *Teenage Frolics* from Chavis Park. Yvonne Lewis Holley, J. D. Lewis's daughter, explains that "Chavis was an African American park, which also contained a very large swimming pool. . . . Visitors would go to *Teenage Frolics* that morning and then they'd go to the park, to the pool and cook out and all that stuff."[29] Former social dancer Virginia Talley, a friend of the Lewis family through her church, remembers taking dance lessons at the community center at Chavis Park in tap, jazz, and ballet. She attributes those dance lessons with providing her with physical fitness and self-discipline, "which gave me an incentive to really want to dance before groups of people, namely the Chavis Park Outdoor Dance Station, to show off my rock 'n' roll dance steps."[30]

Several former dancers on *Teenage Frolics* reveal how different dances and dance steps were learned and transmitted; often it was intergenerational (Figure 3.6). Talley remembers learning dances up North from an aunt in New Rochelle, New York, whom she visited during the summers. She recalls bringing some of these regional variations to the showcase at John Chavis Park: "Different ones [teenagers] would show off their steps, and then we would copy their steps. We would learn from the others."[31] The Reverend Gwen Horton, another former *Teenage Frolics* dancer, said that she learned rock 'n' roll dancing "at home from different cousins and relatives. I had a large extended family of different relatives that would come down from New York and Philadelphia. I think they were a year ahead of us as far as dancing is concerned. And when they would come home every summer, we would put on music, and they showed us different dance moves. I could usually pick up on it."[32]

Among the dances that both Horton and Talley remember were the Hand Jive, the Stroll, the Madison, and the Twist. Said Horton of the Twist: "Yeah; it was very popular. You stand up and twist, and then we would go all the way down to the floor and twist to the floor, and then jumped back up to do it

Figure 3.6 Teenage dancers on the set *Teenage Frolics* (Raleigh, NC), ca. 1960. Courtesy of Yvonne Lewis Holley.

all over again." And of the Stroll: "We used to have something that we called stroll down the line. You have a line on either side and each person takes a chance, has an opportunity to go down the line and do your best dance moves."[33] *American Bandstand* actually aired on WRAL just before *Teenage Frolics*, so the teenage dancers were privy to the styles introduced there. Remarked Horton:

> Yeah. We watched that [*American Bandstand*] sometimes to try to figure out something that we could do on J. D. Lewis's show. Could they dance better than we could, or could we dance better than they could? We didn't know one another, but it became a rivalry. When it came time to dance on the show, then, we made certain that we would outdance them.[34]

Teenage Frolic's remarkable longevity speaks, in part, to the symbolism of having one of the first Black hosts on TV in North Carolina. Yvonne Lewis Holley recalls countless people, including strangers, who would come up to her expressing their gratitude for her father's contributions. She remembers one individual, in particular, who told her that "J. D. Lewis was the first Black man I saw on TV who wasn't pushing a broom and was allowed to be himself."[35] A former TV producer and director and colleague of J. D. Lewis, Clarence Williams, remarks that the popularity of the show was immense all over the state. Said Williams, "It offered Black teenagers a chance to get out there and have others see them on TV locally or regionally. It also captured viewers from outside the immediate viewing area [that ran to South Virginia]. They would sometimes bring busloads of kids to appear on the show."[36] Williams also noted how the show, in its later years, drew people of all races to "watch these unique dances." J. D. Lewis had built up a reputation and following and was a major a "conduit," as Williams called it, to the Black community because of all his civic and community work. As Virginia Talley remarked, "He was actually instrumental in helping teens to express their gifts, or their talents, through music. And this was also a means of displaying one's self esteem, and other traits, such as integrity and kindness. . . . He was a bit ahead of his time, I thought. Mr. Lewis's criteria spoke to helping to improve the quality of life for all citizens."[37] And from Paul Pope: "If you were a teenager, and you could get on *Teenage Frolics*, you were somebody."[38] Lewis himself continued to host *Teenage Frolics* until it ended its run in 1985.

Teenarama Dance Party

Another groundbreaking Black teen dance show was *Teenarama Dance Party* that aired on WOOK, Channel 14, out of Washington, DC. *Teenarama* debuted on March 7, 1963, and ran through November 20, 1970. The show emerged from the Black radio station WOOK, which was owned by United Broadcasting and by white businessman Richard Eaton, who also owned television and radio stations across the country; many Black-oriented networks were run by white owners during this time, eager as they were capitalize on the "Negro market."[39] Commercial radio was facing drastic competition from the rise of television, so in order to avoid going out of business, many white owners quickly moved to acquire TV stations. Eaton had pioneered a Black format as early as 1948 when he hired Hal Jackson as his first Black announcer and deejay.[40] Specializing in R&B music, WOOK radio eventually gave birth to its television spinoff, *Teenarama Dance Party*.[41] Although a series of hosts rotated throughout *Teenarama*'s seven-year run, the most

Figure 3.7 The popular host Bob King with teenage dancers on the set of
WOOK's *Teenarama Dance Party* (Washington, DC), ca. 1963. The Bob King
Collection, courtesy of Beverly Lindsay-Johnson, *The Teenarama Dance Party*
Photo Collection.

celebrated host of that show was R&B deejay Bob King, who hailed from
WRAP radio in Norfolk, Virginia. He handily made the transition to
Teenarama, the TV show, which was broadcast live six days a week from 5 to
6 P.M. from the WOOK studio in Northeast, Washington, DC, at First Place
NE near Riggs Road[42] (Figure 3.7).

Teenarama was "resurrected" as such in 2006 with the groundbreaking
documentary *Dance Party: The Teenarama Story*, produced by filmmaker
Beverly Lindsay-Johnson and directed by Herb Grimes and Curt Simmons.
Like so many other teen dance shows of the period, tragically no footage
exists—only still photographs of the dancers remain (Figure 3.8). To remedy
this, the documentary recreated dances and dance styles of the early 1960s
by using contemporary teenagers dressed in vintage clothing from the era
and made up in hairdos from the era. The *Teenarama* documentary project
auditioned and taught teen dancers from the area dances including the Bop,

Figure 3.8 Promotional photo spread for *Teenarama Dance Party* (Washington, DC,) ca. 1965. The Bob King Collection, courtesy of Beverly Lindsay-Johnson, *The Teenarama Dance Party* Photo Collection.

Jerk, Hand Dance, Cha-cha, and Boogaloo. Herb Grimes, the co-producer of the documentary, wrote that "These hip hop teenagers mastered the old dances and when we turned on the cameras, it was *Teenarama* again."[43] One of the most popular dances on *Teenarama* was the Hand Dance, a form of Swing dance, in which dancers moved smoothly and seamlessly on a four-count beat. (For more on this dance, see Chapter 4.)

Like other Black teen-dance shows, *Teenarama* served as a community hub for Black youth. According to papers filed with the FCC in 1961, part of *Teenarama*'s role was to serve as a "community outreach program geared towards teenagers in Washington, DC's Black communities." Of course, it became a major stopping-ground for Black R&B and rock 'n' roll musicians, as well as a showcase for dance styles of Black youth who, according to Beverly Lindsay-Johnson, "In a time plagued with social injustice and civil upheaval . . . managed to express themselves through a creative outlet to spare them from reality."[44] Similar to *American Bandstand*, *Teenarama* enlisted teenagers from local high schools, such as McKinley and Coolidge, to dance on camera. Generally, the kids wrote in for tickets, although that could take a long time; other times one could become a dancer by being invited by a *Teenarama* regular.[45] Many, instead, simply appeared at the station, hoping for the chance to get admitted. Only if the station had not met its daily quota of forty teens, though, would those waiting in line be considered.

As with *Bandstand*, local, district high schools got "showcased periodically."[46] The "regulars" were responsible for appearing on the show at least three days of the week and enforcing dress and dance codes. And, too, they selected dancers from the lines of teenagers waiting outside the studio and selected the daily set of recordings. The dress code was de rigueur: Boys were required to wear sports jackets and ties, girls neat dresses and what were called "19s"—$19 shoes "that came in a variety of colors and fabrics."[47] *Teenarama* dancer Laverne Parks recalls wearing the leather shoe, which actually sold for $21. "Don't ask me how we got started wearing them, but it was the thing to do."[48] Regulars sometimes distributed suits and ties since, according to former dancer Barnett Williams, "some guys in the Black community didn't own them."[49] Parks noted, too, that for those who couldn't afford the "19s."[50] there was a $9.99 version of the shoe "and if you couldn't afford either of those then you would buy the $4.99 pair and those are called 'slingshots.'"[51]

The thrill for the Black teenagers, similar to white teenagers, was to see their idols perform; many, in fact, got the opportunity to meet them

(Figure 3.9). During this era, DC's Howard Theatre—the historic show-case for Black music and performance—featured the major Black R&B and chitlin' circuit artists (among them James Brown, Smokey Robinson and the Miracles, Lou Rawls, Billy Stewart, and Martha & the Vandellas). In an arrangement with the theater, the show regulars served as chauffeurs and hosts who ushered the stars over to the *Teenarama* studio, at 5321 First Place NE, before or after their concerts.[52] The excitement, too, was that of being seen on TV by their peers, becoming a local celebrity, getting noticed. Said James Preston Jr., a former *Teenarama* dancer, "Being on the show had a lot to do with your self-esteem. You had to have a certain amount of etiquette, camera presence and personality.... Being in that environment, you picked up certain traits from other people and all of these variables helped people become who they are today."[53] Various former *Teenarama* dancers had similar reactions to the effects of being on the show. Said Yvonne Mills,

Figure 3.9 R&B singer/songwriter/showman James Brown with teenagers on the set of *Teenarama Dance Party* (Washington, DC), ca. 1966. The Bob King Collection, courtesy of Beverly Lindsay- Johnson, *The Teenarama Dance Party* Photo Collection.

"*The Milt Grant Show* was a show you watched, but you weren't a part of." For her, *Teenarama* "provided an opportunity for Black youth to have fun, meet entertainers, and have our own identity."[54]

On the surface, there are certain obvious similarities between the white and Black teen dance shows—the concerned host, the specific dress codes, and the general sense of camaraderie and friendly competition that developed among the teenagers. But these surface details belie the underlying meaning of the shows for both sets of teenagers. The clean-cut dress code for white teenagers, for instance, was meant to bolster criticism of rock 'n' roll dance itself and specifically its association with Black culture. Although referring specifically to the situation in the South, Brian Ward's observation held for the North, as well, that "the campaign against rock 'n' roll became inextricably linked to the rise of organized white resistance to desegregation and Black insurgency."[55]

For Black teenagers, though, the dress codes and other "regulations" also assumed other connotations particularly those connected to "respectability politics"—the idea and discourse that can be traced back to the nineteenth century, which suggested that, as historian Kevin Gaines notes, "African Americans' material and moral conditions through self-help would diminish white racism."[56] (This is a theme that will be taken up again in Chapter 5 in relation to teenage girls.) Born of the emancipation era, racial uplift ideology was rooted in a middle-class ideology of individual improvement and social advancement and aspiration. Continued racial stereotyping, which was pernicious during the Jim Crow era, fueled many Black Americans' desire to counter racist attitudes and white supremacy with overwhelmingly positive images and behavior. The dress code for Black teenagers, however, at the height of the civil rights movement, was in part a way for Black parents to signal the white community that their children were not to be feared; some Black parents had objected to *Teenarama*, at first, fearing that images of Black children dancing would reinforce negative attitudes about the Black race.[57] While clothing and dress styles for both white teenagers and Black youth could serve as markers of "in-crowd" status, for Black teens the "dressing up" that so many of the former dancers spoke of may also have been a way to form solidarity, or a collective identity apart from their white counterparts. As historian Robin Kelley notes, "dressing up" challenged "stereotypes of the black body" and "reinforcing a sense of dignity that was perpetually being assaulted."[58] It's important to point out, though, too, that in this recreational and leisure space of the teen dance TV studio, not least of the emphasis on dress styles was a desire to experience bodily pleasure and freedom *through* dance and unencumbered by the "white gaze."

The first host of *Teenarama*, Bob King, was already a well-known WOOK-radio deejay. While hosting *Teenarama* daily from 5 to 6:30 P.M. and 4 to 6 P.M. on Saturdays, he also spent more than thirty hours a week on the radio. King, a graduate of Morgan State College in Baltimore, was a budding thespian, but after a stint in a radio drama on Baltimore's WBAL, he took a job at WCBM, also in Baltimore, as a deejay on a late-night R&B radio show. His philosophy of radio carried over into television and no doubt accounted, in part, for his success: he didn't try to "improve" on the taste of his audience, but rather chose to expose them to various R&B and rock 'n' roll tastes. Many Black teenagers felt a particular kinship with King; it was not only his knowledge of music and easygoing manner but his love of teenagers and desire to see them succeed. *Teenarama* dancer Mike Goodwin said of King that "He was like a father to all of us. When times were lean, he said, well, come on over to dinner."[59] As King told Beverly Lindsay-Johnson, "I know we have saved some kids, sometimes without even knowing it. Maybe for the first time these kids feel they belong to something. Maybe for the first time they have a sense of importance."[60]

The collective sensibility that inhered in the Black teen dance programs in part echoes Beverly Lindsay-Johnson's observation of the DC Black community, that it was not unlike many other Black enclaves during the Jim Crow era in developing its own businesses and establishments to maintain a sense of self-sufficiency in the face of outright racism. *Teenarama* dancer James Preston Jr., a retired management consultant for the Treasury Department, reflects a sensibility often felt by others: "My parents sheltered me. Until I saw Martin Luther King [Jr.] get arrested on TV, I didn't really know I was segregated."[61] Although a leisure space, and not on overtly political space, the Black teen dance shows were nonetheless important "alternative" spaces and institutions that fostered community, identity, and a sense of self. Robin Kelley quotes the historian Earl Lewis who, writing of Southern Black people during the Jim Crow era, noted that they "turned segregation into congregation," which "symbolized an act of free will, whereas segregation represented the imposition of another's will. . . . They used this space to gather their cultural bearings, to mold the urban setting."[62] But for most of the Black dancers—whether dancing at house parties, dance halls, or teen dance shows and whether on the all-Black shows or on the "special guest" days—the attraction was to be with others with whom one had a shared knowledge; with the teen shows, it was the dancing.[63] The Black teen dance shows, in fact, can be seen as a continuum of the Black "jook joint," an arena that dance historian Katrina Hazzard-Gordon explains "has demonstrated a cultural resilience and recuperative creativity."[64] For *Teenarama* dancer and regular James Sator, *Teenarama* was "an opportunity" and "a responsibility."[65] Because of this, he felt that the show had a "revolutionary" psychological and cultural effect on those teens who performed there. Former *Teenarama* dancer Donald Thoms, and his peers, were carving out a territory of their own, even on the "special guest days," and thus were able to "use" this televised space to display to a mixed-race audience of TV viewers their dance prowess and stylistic sophistication.

Regarding class issues, both white and Black teen dance shows attracted middle- and working-class teenagers. While, as discussed, *American Bandstand* was typically described as appealing to middle-class kids from the [white] suburbs, this was not always the case; *American Bandstand*, broadcast originally out of Philadelphia, for instance, featured many Italian American working-class teenagers. Historian Thomas Hine notes that "They didn't look like juvenile delinquents, though they looked urban and ethnic and thus faintly exotic to those watching from suburbia."[66] *The Milt Grant Show* featured urban working-class as well upper-middle-class "daughters and sons of generals."[67] Of course, everyone was required to dress alike, in a "uniform" designed to connote middle-class sartorial and cultural values, but that only masked the actual demographics of the teen dancers. *Teenarama* for the most part reflected a cross-section of the Black population of Washington, DC. As Beverly Lindsay Johnson has remarked, the teenagers were primarily from middle-class Black families to those of lower economic classes: "During that time, in the early 1960s, many Black families were working their way up the economic ladder with government jobs that were stable. Those with lower income worked to see that their children had a good education regardless of their economic status."[68]

Richard's Open Door

Although short-lived, and not *solely* a teen dance show, *Richard's Open Door*, a variety program that aired out of Chicago on WBKB-TV, Channel 7, in 1956, is important to mention as it demonstrates how TV stations during the 1950s were willing to gamble on Black shows due to both the burgeoning white market for R&B and the increasing Black audience spurred during the postwar migration from Southern states such as Alabama, Mississippi, and Georgia to the North and Midwest. It also reveals how white broadcasters, most of them well-intentioned, were eager to capitalize on this new and booming demographic. And, not least, it reveals the desire to attract a teen audience that was increasingly captive to R&B music.

The host of *Richard's Open Door* was Richard E. Stamz, one of Chicago's first Black deejays and a major radio personality of the day, who along with Al Benson, Ric Riccardo, and Sam Evans were featured on WGES-Radio, one of the most powerful Black radio stations in Chicago owned by white Missouri doctor John ("Doc") A. Dyer.[69] According to Patrick Roberts, Stamz's biographer, these deejays were known for their "unpolished and spontaneous" on-air delivery as much as the "gut-bucket, rock-bottom blues music" that they played and that fans adored. As we've seen earlier, radio deejaying was often a stepping-stone to TV hosting, and Stamz's story was no different. Stamz himself was a charismatic and enterprising figure whose peripatetic career spanned business, politics, and entertainment. The TV show was directed at a primarily Black audience, and over the course of thirteen episodes at thirty minutes each, it featured interviews with Black guests, a dance sequence with Black teenagers, and news read from the Black-owned *Chicago Defender*.

Stamz himself was from Memphis, and before even stepping inside a television studio, he was part of Ma Rainey's traveling minstrel show (where he was known for his buck dance) and traveled with various big bands before settling back in Chicago, where he attended Memphis's all-Black LeMoyne-Owen College (according to his résumé he also spent some time at Fisk University in Nashville). Throughout his career, he was heavily involved in community organizations; he was, for instance, director of the Englewood Prevent Project, in Chicago's South Side, and organized several pickets to protest racist hiring practices at a local Woolworth's as well for the city's streetcar lines, and served as a volunteer at numerous city agencies. In Chicago, Stamz steeped himself in the music business and became known for his "sound truck"—a vehicle with speakers to broadcast the latest hit records and signboard for advertising local community events, including dances. As Stamz recalled:

By 1955 I had met most of the people who were involved in Chicago's independent record business, and I was not even on radio yet. I bought a new sound truck, a large package van, and brought in a business partner by the name of Harry Rudsky. Like so many others during that period, I met Rudsky while driving Miss America [the name for his car]. He and I called ourselves the "Sound Merchandisers."[70]

Stamz also used his sound truck to advertise music and dance events such as a Thanksgiving weekend concert of The Five Chances, an early Chicago doowop group, at Drexel Hall, which also featured a mambo concert, a talent show, and "Holiday Teen-Age Dances."[71]

White business owners and advertisers clearly saw the potential in the market for Black programming. While at WGES-Radio, Stamz's primary advertiser was the soft-drink company 7-Up, which, unfortunately, did not carry over its sponsorship to his TV show. It was actually a local clothier—the Martin Clothing Company—that sponsored *Richard's Open Door*. Apparently, the owner, Irving Weisberg, spotted him doing promotional work for businesses along Roosevelt Avenue while Stamz was acting as pitchman; he then teamed up Stamz with Sander Rodkin, of the Sander Rodkin Advertising Agency, who said he would back him on TV and bought thirteen weeks of airtime. Deejays during this time were primarily paid through a portion of the commercial time that they themselves sold; a good deal of the airtime, thus, was devoted to ads for Martin Clothing Company, which, of course, determined Stamz's salary. In fact, at least one segment of each show contained a "Fashion Counter" featuring at least four models advertising the company's latest styles of women's coats, suits, and dresses.

Richard's Open Door, as the TV show was called, reflected Stamz's freewheeling entrepreneurial style, his community connections and political interests, and his showmanship. The show premiered on January 21, 1956, from 11:30 P.M. to midnight. The dance sequence—called Smokey Joe's Café—was named after a hit song of the period by the doowop group The Robins that Stamz wanted to promote.[72] For this section, the studio resembled a nightclub, with small tables, and the teenage dancers Hoyt Torrey and Judy Davis claimed the spotlight. Phyllis Stamz, Richard Stamz's daughter (and the first Black woman hired at the prominent Garmisa Record Distributors in Chicago), recalls that she was the one who recruited Torrey and Davis from Parker High School, which all of them attended. The show also regularly featured Black performers Jimmy Payne and his Calypso Dancers. (This Calypso dance, which was popular with teenagers, seemed to have eclipsed the other Calypso dance that become popular on *American Bandstand* around 1957.) Like other Black deejays and hosts of the day,

Stamz understood the significance of connecting his teen dance to civic and community causes. For the opening show, for instance, Stamz featured an interview with Edith Spurlock Sampson, the first Black woman judge to be elected in Chicago and the first Black woman alternate delegate to the UN. Phyllis Stamz, in fact, recalled that interview with Sampson and "how great it was talking to her" and learning about her work in civil rights.[73] Featuring prominent members of the Chicago community on the show was also, of course, a way for Stamz to showcase successful Black Americans to potential white viewers.[74]

Revealing among Stamz's archival records are reports detailing the Black population's spending and consumption patterns; these reports, "Chicago's Huge Negro Market" and "Population Trends of the Negro Market in Chicago," were prepared by the radio station and culled from various studies published by the Chicago Urban League, the University of Pennsylvania Study on Consumer Expenditures, and noted Black sociologist Dr. E. Franklin Frazer (author of *The Negro Family in the United States* and *The Black Bourgeoisie*). All the statistics and information contained in the reports served to bolster the network's desire to create programming designed to appeal to Black audiences and create faith in Black deejays to cultivate this "market." The numbers given illustrate how the Black population was becoming increasingly urban (as opposed to rural), and that spending in the areas of furniture, food, personal care, and, in particular, entertainment had increased across "all income classes."[75] The report stated that "The figures clearly indicate that any product manufactured for a mass consumption will have to count this market in as part of its customers."[76] To be sure, Stamz played to his advertisers, but, like Mitch Thomas, he was also very interested in having his show serve as a kind of community bulwark and to assume the role of civic leader.

Richard's Open Door lasted only until December 1957; according to Stamz, the station refused to sell him any more airtime. While ratings may have dropped, it's clear that racism play a major role. In his autobiography, he laments that "The newspaper critics had been writing some horrible things about me, even before I went on TV. One critic even said, 'He moves too much.'"[77] Stamz does note, however—referring to the teen dance portion of the show—that "I did get a lot of complimentary mail from white people who had never seen Black kids dancing before."[78] Clearly, white adults, as well as white youth, were watching Black youth dance. As *Teenarama* producer Beverly Lindsay-Johnson has noted, perhaps somewhat optimistically but also truthfully, given the separation of the races during this time, television "prepared whites for the future of integrated dancing by allowing them to practice and incorporate African American dance skills in the privacy of their own homes."[79] The following chapter will explore those dances and skills in greater depth and discuss the Black roots of rock 'n' roll dance and their adaptation by white youth.

4

Rock 'n' Roll Dance and
the Africanist Aesthetic

This chapter will explore the makeup of some of the most popular and notable dances of the period and discuss the process in which the dances
were popularized or "mediated"—that is, disseminated, filtered, and
reconstituted—through the apparatus of television to a mass, and largely
white, audience. The basis for the rock 'n' roll dances and dance forms of the
1950s and 1960s is the Black vernacular social dance tradition. In part, this is
a story about the popularization and commercialization of social dance and
the attempts at the erasure of race, even though, as previous chapters have
illustrated, racial consciousness seeped through the shows—and the dances.
The dances became products of this new mass-media technology. Essentially,
the televised teen dance programs "sold" dance to the public through the
machinery of commercial culture and thus became emblematic of a host
of social and cultural ideologies concerning race, of course, but also class
distinctions and attitudes about the role of women and girls. In addition to
describing what kinds of dances audiences would have seen on their television screens, this chapter illustrates how the dances were adapted for the televisual space, and made palatable and accessible to a broad and largely white
audience. When there is available evidence, the chapter indicates how Black
and white versions of the same dances differed from one another.

Before going further, it is important to note those dance historians and
theorists, anthropologists, and art historians whose groundbreaking research and writing inform this study. Scholars such as Lynne Emery, Katrina
Hazzard-Gordon, Brenda Dixon Gottschild, Robert Farris Thompson, Sally
Sommer, Jacqui Malone, and Thomas DeFrantz have mapped out what can be
termed the African or African-diasporic aesthetic as it applies to social and
vernacular dance forms. Certain stylistic traits and tropes, which are known
to social dance scholars, have been identified as belonging to this tradition.
These styles, as Malone explains, were perfected in "the coming together, on
American soil, of central and western African dance with European dance."[1]

Dancing Black, Dancing White. Julie Malnig, Oxford University Press. © Oxford University Press 2023.
DOI: 10.1093/oso/9780197536254.003.0005

A brief summary of this constellation of traits follows, and I will also refer to these characteristics throughout the chapter in describing the central social dances of the 1950s and 1960s.

These stylistics include the following:

Polycentric rhythm. This descriptor, as Gottschild explains, refers to movements that emanate from different parts of the body simultaneously, and which Malone describes as contributing to that propulsive sense of forward movement, asymmetry, as well as a lowered or crouched body stance.[2] The bodily crouch loosened the waist, enabling the dancer to emphasize those different parts of the body.[3] This weight of gravity in the hips and pelvis sets off the Africanist-related movement from European-derived movements, which tend to be centered higher in the abdomen and solar plexus.[4]

Improvisation. Characteristic of dances such as Charleston, the Lindy, and the swing dance performed by teenagers of the 1950s, the term denotes the improvisational "breaks" in which couples momentarily separate to enable maximum movement.[5]

Aesthetic of the cool. This is the term coined by art historian Robert Farris Thompson, in his essay of the same name, to refer to the West African–based sense of composure, clarity of movement, and almost effortlessness sense to the dance.[6]

Call-and-response. This is the antiphonic structure in which the dance functions as a response to either a musical or danced "call." In turn, there may be a call-and-response pattern between spectators and performers who spur on the dancers while experiencing their own kinesthetic reaction.

Apart dancing. Originally referring to drummers playing different, overlapping rhythms while contributing to the whole of the musical piece, in dance this is the practice of paired partners moving apart at points, without touching, "as they relate playfully to each other and to the same rhythmic impulses."[7]

Dances of derision. This manner or trait refers to African and African American forms of social dance in which "pride and pretention are targeted by dancers."[8] This might take the form of dancers satirizing other dancers showing off their moves. This showing-off of one's stuff, though, on the 1950s dance floor (or TV studio dance floor) was often an attempt to outdo one's fellow dancers or best them in a spirit of competitive camaraderie. It was also a form of improvising moves on the spot.[9]

These techniques, or strategies, are not just steps, though; they are all part of an aesthetic tradition, or as Malone describes it, a "movement system" that has grown out of specific cultural imperatives rooted in Western and Central African traditional society and culture and carried through slavery and onto the shores of North America. Aesthetic traditions are rooted in cultural traditions. This brings to mind sociologist Marcel Mauss's path-breaking essay "Techniques of the Body," which claims that such traditions, and aesthetics, are ones that are taught and learned and belong to a set of conventions developed by the exigencies of a particular society and its cultural needs.[10] Cultural historian Gena Dagel-Caponi makes the case for an aesthetic as "a set of factors that are not incidental, occasional, or ornamental but which serve as the foundation of an art form."[11] The use of the term "aesthetic" suggests artistic abilities that are acquired and perfected over time and not some sort of essentialist, or biological predisposition to dance prowess.[12] Thomas DeFrantz argues that these are not just "particular movements" but "propositional strategies." Writes DeFrantz, "they are recurrent aesthetic imperatives that may be employed both by African diaspora artists and, significantly, by others following this tradition."[13]

And, of course, we are not talking about a static style, one overarching set of unwavering movements. As dance scholar Yvonne Daniels writes, "This is the course of popular dance. It is always borrowing, returning, imitating, shifting, reversing, inventing, improvising, and in the process shaping and polishing yet another named creation of the current day."[14] This is, in part, what makes social dances so difficult to pin down and to document. Their structure and form "has evolved over time in relation to their social function."[15] And as they evolve, they take on new meanings. Dance historian Marya McQuirter has considered how dances are learned in Black communities, in particular; if social dances are connected to the creation of individual and group identity, then, McQuirter asks us to consider "the performative dimensions of Blackness and community": how, in other words, individuals use dance performatively, and how it is an invented, deliberate, action to create one's identity on the dance floor.[16] This idea coincides with that of historian Robin Kelley, who contends that social dances, like other leisure activities, may become an "alternative" space in which to express one's individuality and identity through sonic and physical pleasure.[17]

Swing Couple Dance

The social dances of the 1950s that one would see in ballrooms, nightclubs, and in a variety of social gatherings (weddings, proms, and the like) were a mix of couple dances including Lindys, Fox Trots, and Rumbas, mostly derived from the African American tradition, as well as a variety of Latin-inspired dances such as the Mambo, Cha-cha, Samba, Merengue, and Bossa Nova. The dances born of rock 'n' roll music, however, and those seen mostly on television, included couple, group, and then eventually solo-oriented social dances. Whether in concert halls, theaters, social clubs, or on television, both Black and white social dancers demonstrated an immediate response to the beat of the music. They also responded to the movements and gestures of their peers, thus uniting them in a shared social and communal experience. The couple dance most frequently exhibited on the televised teen dance program was actually an old dance—the Lindy—but a newer version, of course, set to the rhythms of rock 'n' roll music. Dance historian Sally Sommer explains how the dance changed and morphed to accommodate to the "tempos and accents" of rock 'n' roll music.[18] Sometimes it was referred to as the Boogie-woogie, or Bop; whatever name or variation, though, the dance was essentially a simplified Lindy couple dance characterized by weighted hips, small rotations in the hips as partners held hands punctuated by short breaks in which the couples turned out and away from one another and might improvise steps or hand movements.[19] Here, instead of performing one move after another, couples danced together in place while holding hands.[20] The televised teen dance shows were responsible, in part, for creating this kind of variety and competition; dances seen on the shows were picked up by teen viewers, and new variations were then created and taken to local high schools or neighborhoods.

Another variation on the Lindy, or Swing, was the Bop (not to be confused with a solo bop, described below). Former *Buddy Deane Show* dancer Bobbie Burns recalls how her version of the dance differed from that on *American Bandstand*. As she notes, "They called it the Bop and it was more of a back-and-forth motion than the Baltimore jitterbug, where the guy more or less took you around and it was like a swivel step and then around again."[21] In Black communities, dances also varied from neighborhood to neighborhood and school to school, but unlike in white communities, these dances were most notably passed on from generation to generation. According to dance historian Benita Brown, who has written about social dances in Black communities in 1960s Philadelphia, the Bop as performed by Philadelphia social dancers can be traced to the Bebop era of jazz music from the mid-1940s. In fact, a young person first learning to Bop was named a "teeny-bopper."[22] Different styles abounded: the North Philly Bop, the South Philly

Bop, the Chester Bop, and so forth denoting different regions of the city. According to Brown:

> During the 1960s in Philadelphia, this dance was the staple genre, done as a finale or standard, that invoked full participation from everyone present, transforming an empty dance floor into a soulful space filled with dancers who were showing off their stuff and lifting their spirit.[23]

The Bop, though, could also be performed as more of a solo-oriented dance; here dancers still formed as couples, lightly touching each other's hands, but as demonstrated in various of the recorded films, they are seen moving apart from their partner in a kind of crouched position and executing fast, Charleston-like steps, with slightly turned-in toes and sometimes a hopping motion. In one version, a young white dancer, on *American Bandstand*, jumps up and down, and when he lands, grinds his feet into the floor. The 1956 dance manual *How to Dance the Bop!*, by white dance teacher Art Silva, announces on his opening page that "The Bop is a brand new distinctively American dance, but one that has its origins in the dances of the past."[24] Of course, it was not brand-new; one could reach deep down into the Black dance lexicon to find its roots.

Another couple dance known as the Slow Drag, was essentially a slow Two-Step or reconstructed Fox Trot, also of Black derivation. It has been described as a couple dance with shuffle steps, "plenty of grinds," and breakaway steps reminiscent of the Lindy.[25] As performed by in the Black dance community in Philadelphia, Benita Brown explains that it was more of a stationary dance (as opposed to moving across the floor) and contained dips and hip grinds. As Brown notes, the dance "mimicked sexual overtures."[26] One clearly, though, would not see this kind of suggestiveness on a TV dance-floor set; it was enough, in fact, that mostly white couples were now dancing together without the requisite six inches apart and added hip sways. (A slightly more up-tempo version of the Slow Drag was a variation of the dance called the Strand, discussed in Chapters 2 and 3.)[27]

A particularly popular variant of Swing dance that took hold in Washington, DC, and favored especially by teenage dancers on the Black televised dance show *Teenarama*, was the Hand Dance, also known then as Fast Dance. The dance can be traced to the Savoy Ballroom in Harlem of the late 1920s and the Swing dancing that originated there; when it landed in DC, it took on qualities unique to that area.[28] Performed to a six-, eight-, or twelve-count rhythm, Hand Dance is an urban partner-dance involving fancy footwork with smooth, upper-body control, in which couples generally freely sweep the dance floor. Historically, the music has fueled variations in the basic dance style; while in the 1950s Hand Dance was performed to upbeat tempos, by the 1960s it was danced easily to the music of Motown. Hand-dancer Maxine Grant recalls Fast-Dancing at house parties, church dances on the weekends, and, of course on television on *Teenarama*: "Anytime we found an opportunity to go someplace to dance, we were there."[29]

All of these variations on Lindy and Swing dance are characteristic of the stylistics that developed according to the specific places, environments, and cultural settings in which the dances themselves took root. Regional styles flourished in the 1950s and 1960s, thus producing a cascade of named social dances around the country. At the same time, too, in the Lindy and the Bop (both its couple and solo-oriented versions), one could actually see the coming changes that would distinguish rock 'n' roll dances of the mid-to-late 1960s in which couples faced one another yet performed individual movements while in rapport with the crowd around them.[30] Rock 'n' roll music encouraged and permitted greater improvisation, more moments of breaking away from the couple, and an overall looser movement style, which would become a hallmark of 1960s dances. Here they were facing each other but both turning outward to face their fellow dancers during the "breaks."

Group Dances

The other category of dances one would see on the TV screen in the mid-to-late 1950s, also derived from the Africanist tradition, were group dances: the Hand Jive, the Madison, and the Stroll, most notably. That the group dances were compatible with and popular on the teen dance shows is not surprising; these dances were a kinesthetic match, in a way, to the overarching production aims of the shows, which were to promote group solidarity and community. In the group dances, teenagers essentially used the music to liberate themselves from the constraints of their parents' values, yet at the same time, conforming and comparing themselves to the "group."[31]

One of the most popular of the group dances was the Madison, in which we see a rich history of Africanist antecedents. The notion of dancing as a group in and of itself can be traced to the 1920s Big Apple, for instance—a dance performed in circle formation which, in turn, can be traced back to the plantation ring shout "with its counterclockwise circling and high arm gestures."[32] The use of the line, too, has great significance in Black culture and can be traced back to parade formations that marked nineteenth-century Black, Southern festivities. As dance historian Katrina Hazzard-Gordon has observed, nineteenth-century May Emancipation Day festivities in Alabama featured celebrants in "line walks," as they danced to the beat of drums.[33] The aesthetic and cultural glue that provided the impetus for the dances was the dialogue created between the group/community and spectators. Benita Brown discusses how this participatory activity *among* dancers and *between* dancers and spectators created community bonds, spirit and "soul" that, as she notes, "affirm[ed] our status as an African American urban community, as a family."[34]

The Madison and the Stroll, both group dances, are useful examples of how Black-derived forms of music and dance get picked up by white producers and dancers and then brought to mainstream attention. The emergence of the Madison is widely credited as having emerged nationally on Baltimore's *Buddy Deane Show*. Two musical compositions were recorded to accompany the dance, "The Madison" by noted Black Baltimore songwriter Al Brown and his band Al Brown's Tunetoppers, and "The Madison Time" (written a bit later) by prominent Black jazz pianist and composer Ray Bryant and his band, the Ray Bryant Combo, the house band for Philadelphia's Blue Note jazz club.[35] Both versions were of the call-and-response variety of music. Cookie Brown (Al's brother, also a musician) made the calls on the Brown version, while famed Black Baltimore deejay Eddie Morrison, the host of an R&B radio program on WEBB-AM, made them for Bryant's rendition. While there is some dispute about the dance's origins, existing sources lay claim to its popularity in Baltimore, Chicago, and Columbus in Black social clubs and communities; clearly the dance predated the songs that were eventually created to accompany it.[36] According to a reporter for the *Baltimore Sun*, in 1960, the dance had a wide following among Black youth: "First teenagers and younger children began dancing the Madison in the aisles of a record store [General Radio] in the 500 block North Gay Street. Then they danced it on the sidewalk in front of the stores, inventing new steps by the score."[37] That it was popular in Baltimore probably had much to do with the influence of Eddie Morrison's radio show in that city. Musicologist Tim Wall surmises that Morrison, as a deejay, would have hosted numerous record hops where he could have picked up on what the teenagers were dancing and thus gotten cues as to determine appropriate narration.[38] At the same time, the Madison was also very popular among Black youth in Chicago, where Al Brown's version of the song reigned. Other sources contend that the actual "birthplace" of the Madison was in Columbus where William (Bubbles) Holloway supposedly introduced the dance in 1957 at the LVA Club near the Cameo Theatre on Mt. Vernon Avenue.[39]

In a video clip from 1960, Buddy Deane promotes the number on his show in a rather aggrandizing manner (typical of the teen dance hosts) and notes how the dance had become "probably as successful as the revival of the Charleston or as successful as the Shag. Perhaps even more successful, the biggest dance we've seen in a long, long time."[40] Although Ray Bryant's version of the Madison was most often featured on the show (as it originated in Baltimore), that wasn't uniformly true; sometimes the Al Brown number vied for accessibility. According to former Buddy Deane dancer Joe Cash (Deane's first "teen assistant"), one number was easier than the other: "I'd mostly be demonstrating the steps of Ray Bryant's version to both the studio audience and to those at home, but I'd occasionally perform to Al Brown's as well. But I found it [the latter] more difficult to follow because of the rhythm."[41]

What made the Madison challenging, according to some former dancers, was its count and number and variety of steps.[42] It was performed to six counts, instead of the typical eight that the teenagers were used to and demanded that the different "calls" be executed on the beat.[43] An apt description of the Madison seen on the shows is that it was a kind of "stylized movement imbued with the insolence and understated swagger of youth," consisting of a combination of shifting weight from left to right and back and forth with a short sweeping action of the feet.[44] In viewing short clips from *The Buddy Deane Show* and photographs from an issue of *Ebony* magazine, clear differences are evident in presentation style between Black and white dancers. The basic dance featured several long, parallel lines of dancers facing in one direction; it could actually be performed within a narrow area as the trunk and torso remained relatively stable and controlled while leaving free room for the arms and shoulders. On the whole, white teenagers kept a very erect torso at all times and tended to step with the balls of the feet. Black social dancers were much more prone to use the flat of the feet, and they are generally seen in a slight but distinctive hunched or crouched position at the torso, which left more room to maneuver the legs. In one variation displayed in *Ebony* magazine, two Black dancers perform what was referred to as the "Ernie Banks Swing" (gracefully mimicking the baseball player's swing of the bat) in which they bend at the knees and twist the torso to one side while their outstretched aims move in the opposite direction. The kind of "cool" that Robert Farris Thompson refers to can be seen in an image of one dancer in the "Pennsylvania Stroll" step with both hands tucked in his pants pockets in a leisurely strut.[45]

Mass Mediatization of Dances

The power of the teen dance shows to break open a new dance was great, and, as was so often the case, that success and visibility came about in large measure as a result of the popularizing and promoting of Black-invented dance forms. In a sign of how racial politics operated, and how a Black dance got "popularized" for white audiences, after the Madison broke open on *The Buddy Deane Show*, white dancers Joe Cash and Joan Darby were recruited by Columbia Records to tour the East Coast and Midwest visiting other televised teen dance shows, including *The Milt Grant Show*, to teach the dance. Apparently, Columbia's Baltimore-based promotion manager, Victor Gregory, assisted in making a short film of the two dancers that was sent to the TV stations for broadcasting in advance of their arrival. The promotional efforts also included a full, feature-length insert in the album jacket for Bryant's "The Madison Time" featuring foot-patterns for the dance so TV viewers could ostensibly practice at home.[46]

This type of promotion of the dance by record companies was typical of the time; for instance, a briefly popular dance known as the Swivel was marketed by United Artists Records to help promote its latest song release of the same name. Again, as with the Madison, two white teenagers—the young actors Diane Skylar and Hunt Stevens—toured the country appearing on the teen dance shows (such as *The Buddy Deane Show*, *Detroit Bandstand*, and *The Ted Steele Show*) as featured guests demonstrating the dances there and, too, at local record and dance hops. In addition, United Artists printed over 250,000 "dance cards" in a promotional tie-in with Arthur Murray (of the Arthur Murray Dance Studio chain) containing instructions for the dance that could be distributed at the shows and hops[47] (Figure 4.1).

A major mass-mediated means of spreading social dances, as Sally Banes and John Szwed point out in "From 'Messin' Around' to 'Funky Western Civilization,'" was the dance-instruction song, which became ubiquitous in the 1960s.[48] These sheet-music covers, album inserts, and newspaper and magazine articles with step directions all functioned like dance manuals that

Figure 4.1 Cover of *Teen* magazine, May 1962, containing an article and photo spread, "Dancetime U.S.A.," by Charles Laufer, illustrating the variety of regional variations of dances occurring across the country. Magazine publications, such as this, were other vehicles for helping promote and popularize dance crazes. Courtesy of the Glenn Pitts Collection.

helped "democratize" social dance and spread Black dance forms and style. Clearly, though, because these records and instructions were also intended to reach a white audience, it is questionable as to whether the instructions featured dances as performed in Black settings. If the sheet music cover for The Tunetoppers' recorded version of the Madison is any indication, they probably did not: it was titled "The Madison Dance Party" (a nod it seems to the teen TV shows) and featured four generations of a white family—a young woman and boy, a middle-aged couple, and a grandmother.[49] Banes and Szwed are correct, of course, in asserting that the dance instruction songs nonetheless allowed for "repeated infusions of Black style into white mass culture."[50]

The Stroll exemplifies how a Black social dance form got mediated and "sold" to the public through the machinery of commercial culture. The Stroll step itself was a simple walking/shuffling step to a six-count measure characterized by low slides into the beat. The "solo stroll" of each couple is a major characteristic of the dance; as the couples meet at the top of the line, they dance down the center aisle, as such, in either a traveling version of the basic Stroll step (or an improvised step or movement).[51] A relatively slow rock 'n' roll dance generally performed in two parallel lines, it is sometimes compared to what we know as the Virginia Reel, in which dancers on either side (girls on one side, boys on the other) advance to the top of the line and then proceed down the line as the couple meets and improvises or performs a "shine" demonstrating their dance prowess.[52] The Stroll is actually a dance that represents the kind of creolization of African American and Euro-American American dance forms that anthropologists John Szwed and Morton Marks describe in "The Afro-American Transformation of European Set Dances and Suites."[53] As they explain, at the turn of the nineteenth century, formation dances involving lines were prominent in quadrilles, cotillions, and reels, at which enslaved and freedmen would have participated. In the quadrille, two lines face one another as in the Virginia Reel.[54] This cross-cultural formation suggests an interpenetration of Black and white dance forms; in the Stroll, the African American aesthetic can be detected in the improvisatory inventions the dancers insert as opposed to mere traveling steps of a Euro-American reel.[55]

The Stroll, though, quickly became synonymous with a white rock 'n' roll tradition. The 1950s song "The Stroll," recorded by The Diamonds, was designed to fit a dance craze, and although not a dance instruction song as such, the opening bars refer to the dance as the teenagers should perform it. As Banes and Szwed point out of the dance instruction song, there is usually an *exhortation* at the beginning to participate in the dance. In the Stroll, it was this:

> Come, let's stro-oh-oh-oll
> Stroll across the floor
> Now turn around, baby
> Let's stroll once more.[56]

The difference between Black and white renditions of the Stroll is striking; in a photographic image from the film *Philadelphia Memories*, for instance, *Mitch Thomas Show* social dancers can be seen dancing in a line with a low center of gravity with shoulders slightly hunched, as they step and slide in a forward motion. Even though the dance calls for a "lean-in" of the body as weight is transferred from one side to the other, this move is much more accentuated by the Black dancers who actually jut their hips. In what seems to be a variation of the dance, boys and girls, lined up sequentially, lightly hold the waist of the dancer in front of them, as the line peels off into a circular motion. Interestingly, in this image from the film, at the top of the line is the white lead singer of the vocal quartet The Diamonds, Dave Somerville (in a striking upright position, by contrast), revealing that Black dancers also performed The Stroll to The Diamonds' cover version. But, in another sign of the racially discriminatory practices of the shows, the Diamonds' song "The Stroll" outsold the other version as it became synonymous with *American Bandstand* dancers' rendition of it. Not only did the continuous airplay of the cover version on *Bandstand* help popularize the dance with white audiences, it associated it with *Bandstand* instead of *The Mitch Thomas Show*. *American Bandstand* episodes regularly employed extended close-ups of the dancers, which often spotlighted their feet. In his careful reading of *American Bandstand*, sociologist Matthew Delmont describes how this kind of close-up, which revealed a level of detail not otherwise seen, could have the effect of creating an intimacy between white spectators and viewers, further reinforcing the idea that this dance "belonged" to *American Bandstand*.[57] And, too, the continuous advertisements for instructions of the Stroll as danced on *Bandstand* that appeared in popular magazines, newspapers, and teen magazines all helped promote the idea that *American Bandstand* was the birthplace of the Stroll.

More Group Dancing

The Hand Jive, one of the most popular communal dances of the late 1950s, took flight on the TV screen in the summer of 1958. Again, we see the phenomenon of a song helping popularize a dance and containing instructions for the dance, in this case "Willie and the Hand Jive," by iconoclastic R&B singer, songwriter, deejay, bandleader, and civil rights activist Johnny Otis. Born Johnny Veliotis to Greek immigrant parents, Otis lived his life as an African American; in an interview in 1994, Otis said, "Genetically, I'm pure Greek. Psychologically, environmentally, culturally, by choice, I'm a member of the Black community."[58] Many have claimed that more than Alan Freed, it was Johnny Otis who deserves the moniker "the godfather of rhythm and blues."[59] A guiding preoccupation of Otis's was to support, promote, and credit the music of Black singers, songwriters, and musicians, among them R&B singers Etta James and Esther Phillips ("Little Esther"), soul singer Jackie Wilson, and Hank Ballard (original writer of "The Twist").

One of the first televised versions of the Hand Jive was on Johnny Otis's own TV variety show, *The Johnny Otis Show*, which aired from 1954 to 1961 on Los Angeles's KTLA.[60] "The song became a hit for the show and reached #5 on the *Billboard* R&B charts and #9 on the top 100 list."[61] From a segment of the show featuring the gospel-based singer Marie Adams and her two sisters, Sadie and Francine McKinley (and known professionally as the musical trio Marie Adams and Three Tons of Joy), we get a glimpse of the percussive use of the body working in sync with the music. As Otis sings and plays the piano, the three women perform a sequence of hand gestures (hitting the right and left wrists with a clenched fist, rolling the wrists around one another in a circular motion, and clapping their thighs). A dance such as the Hand Jive illustrates the strong connection between music and movement—another cornerstone of Black aesthetic characteristics; in addition to its emphasis on the percussive nature of performance, the dance draws on other characteristics such as multiple meter, apart playing, and a type of call-and-response. As Jacqui Malone has pointed out, writing about the Africanist aesthetic, "A good dancer is one who converses with music, clearly hears and feels the beat, and is capable of using different parts of the body to create visualizations of the rhythms."[62] This was the challenge of the dance—dancers needed to not only remember the sequences but keep to the number's quick tempo. We see this exquisite movement-off-the beat in the

Marie Adams and Three Tons of Joy sequence where the singers respond to the instrumentalists.[63]

   That the Hand Jive could also be performed while sitting was demonstrated at many of Otis's concerts; apparently his guest performers would demonstrate the gestures and teen audiences would perform them in their seats. In the Hand Jive as performed on the teen dance shows, dancers typically faced each other in two rows (boys on one side, girls on the other) and enacted the dance's series of percussive gestures (Figure 4.2). In an extant filmed segment, white teenagers can be seen dancing the Hand Jive on New York City's *Studio Party* (hosted by Herb Sheldon). As Otis begins singing, the teenagers move through and repeat the sequence of percussive gestures. In typical dance-instruction song format, the song alludes to other names dances of the time that teenagers would have been familiar with including the Stroll, the Susie Q, and the Walk.[64]

Figure 4.2 Teenage dancers in typical line formation for the Hand Jive on *Detroit Bandstand*, hosted by Dale Young, ca. 1957. Courtesy of Dale and Deborah Young.

Latin and Afro-Caribbean Styles

Afro-Cuban and Afro-Caribbean styles of music also fueled a variety of dances during this time. Spurred by the Cuban migration of the late 1940s, the Mambo had become a sensation at New York City's Palladium club by the early-to-mid-1950s. As historian David Garcia explains, before the Mambo's wide commercialization in popular culture, "it involved new ways of playing and dancing."[65] A combination of Cuban son rhythm and swing, Mambo stood out with its sensuous hip rolls and isolations and syncopated rhythms done in *contratiempo* (an "offbeat accentuation" with the musicians). Out of the Mambo developed the slower-paced Cha-cha considered simpler for most social dancers. While the Mambo's downbeat in the first musical measure could be difficult to coordinate with the music, the Cha-cha's opening triple step with a slight hop was easier to grasp for American dancers.[66]

The dance seen on most of the televised teen dance programs, though, was what was called the "Chalypso," so named for the dance's combination of Cha-cha steps and Calypso dance, the latter a descendant of the West Indian dance that became a craze of the late 1950s and early 1960s fueled, in part, by appearances by singer Harry Belafonte and his 1957 album "Calypso." Rock 'n' roll historian John A. Jackson suggests that it was Dick Clark and his *American Bandstand* producer Tony Mammarella who christened the Chalypso, which may be the case, although what was referred to as a chalypso beat—that combined Cha-cha steps and calypso rhythms—was already a musical form already attributed to Black performers in the early-to-mid-1950s. In 1956, Dee Clark, the Black R&B singer, recorded "Gloria" and "The Kangaroo Hop," which utilized a chalypso beat.[67] According to former deejay and teen-dance show host Clay Cole (of *The Clay Cole Show*), the popular Bo Diddley song "Love Is Strange," recorded by Black R&B duo Mickey & Sylvia, in 1956, also helped propel the Chalypso dance craze.[68]

The Chalypso was clearly a dance invented by teen dancers for the purposes of television. And *American Bandstand* dancers didn't have the monopoly on it. The Chalypso appeared on teen shows around the country; in fact, on the popular *Detroit Bandstand*, hosted by Dale Young, teenagers added a feature that caught on called the "Chalypso Train," essentially a Conga line characteristic of the Cuban carnival dance that became popular in the United States in the 1930s.[69] It's fair to say that the Chalypso was only the palest of imitations of a Trinidadian-based music and dance form. Indeed, looking at *American Bandstand* teenagers dancing to Billy & Lillie's "La De Dah," dancers seem to be doing a variety of steps, not all of them certainly from the Cha-cha (as performed in its club and ballroom version).[70] The dancers, in male-female pairs, primarily dance in apart fashion, inserting solo twirls and turns, with just the slightest rotation of the hips. The significance of the Chalypso, though, is that it heralded the more solo-oriented dances that would emerge in the early 1960s; the teenagers here do a kind of free-styling, non-contact dancing, in which teenagers of the same sex can be seen dancing with one another.

The Twist

The signature dance of the early 1960s was, of course, the Twist. Dancers, particularly Black teen dancers, were experimenting with the dance well before it caught on with white teenagers, not to mention New York's café society. The rather tangled history of the Twist, and its evolution as a musical composition, has been well documented, but a few salient facts are relevant here that point to the way a dance number got popularized in the commercial sphere. "The Twist," written and composed by R&B performers Hank Ballard and the Midnighters, who based the song on Clyde McPhatter's "What You Gonna Do?," was recorded in 1958 by Federal Records but then released in 1959 by King Records (the parent label to Federal). It was the dance "B" side of the "A" side love ballad "Teardrops on Your Letter." Even though Ballard was convinced that it was the B side that would become the hit, his producers thought otherwise and heavily promoted "Teardrops." According to Ballard:

> We were doing the Twist for approximately two years before it caught on. We were in Baltimore on a ten-day engagement at the Royal Theater. And the kids saw us doing the Twist there. There was a show in Baltimore, *The Buddy Deane Show*, which was similar to *American Bandstand*. Deane saw those kids out there doing the Twist because they had seen us doing it at the Royal. So he called Dick Clark and said the kids over here are going crazy over a record by Hank Ballard and the Midnighters called "The Twist," and they're not even touching![71]

Not to be overlooked in the development of social dance styles are those movements and gestures initiated by professional R&B vocalists, like the Midnighters, who developed the twisting motion of the hips from side to side that caught on, first, in Black communities. In Ron Mann's documentary *Twist*, Ballard demonstrates how the step involved lifting a leg, bent at the knee, and then turning it out while rotating at the hips while the body moved in a kind of corkscrew motion.[72] Ballard states that he was not sure how the Midnighters came by their movements,[73] but this type of vocal choreography was very typical of R&B performers of the time and an essential vehicle for the transmission of Black vernacular styles of dance. Ballard's "The Twist" also demonstrates one of the core aesthetics of Black expressive culture— the strong relationship between musical rhythm and dance and call-and-response in which, in this case, audiences picked up, and then transformed the steps into a dance that would take root in the culture at large.[74]

The twisting of the pelvis and shaking of torso and hips demonstrated in the Twist had long been characteristic of Black vernacular dance styles; Katrina Hazzard-Gordon, in fact, has traced the Twist to the "wringin'" and "twistin'" vernacular dances of the North American enslaved in the seventeenth century, and, too, to dances in the nineteenth-century jook described earlier.[75] Some of the earliest dance-instruction songs such as Perry Bradford's 1912 "Messin' Around" exhorted dancers to:

> Put your hands on your hips and bend your back,
> Stand in one spot, nice and light
> Twist around with all your might
> Messin' round, they call that messin' round.[76]

While Stearns suggests that the dance was interpreted as "protruding the pelvis in a circle" while the body bounces on the toes with each beat, its unmistakable twisting of the hips and pelvis in a circulate motion mark it as an early precursor of the Twist of the early 1960s.[77] In the Twist, which could be performed solo, with a partner, or as part of a group, dancers, while rotating their hips to the upbeat tempo, transferred weight from one leg to the other while pivoting slightly on the balls of the feet. The arms moved in counter direction to the hips. Teen dancers might improvise by alternately raising either leg from the knee (although, perhaps, not as suggestively as Ballard's) or executing partner twirls or turns.[78]

Even though dancers on *The Buddy Deane Show* were dancing to Ballard's "The Twist," the version that ultimately caught on with the public was Chubby Checker's cover version issued in 1960 by Cameo-Parkway Records.[79] As the story goes, Dick Clark was instrumental in making stars of previously unknown artists on record labels that he either had part interest in or controlled, Chubby Checker (nee Ernest Evans) among them.[80] According to Ballard, Dick Clark wouldn't think of showcasing the Midnighters' "Twist." Mimicking Clark, he said (as he laughed), "I don't want to hear. I don't even want to hear, 'cause I know it's another one of those dirty records, you know."[81] For Clark, Checker, who was younger and seemingly more clean-cut, was the surer bet, and he got Cameo-Parkway to issue more of a pop-sounding version of the song. "The Twist" went on to become number one on the *Billboard* charts—not once, but twice. The song was re-released in 1962 when it reached number one again and got picked up by New York Society, most notably at The Peppermint Lounge.

A veritable cottage industry of "Twist" songs followed into the early 1960s by both white and Black recording artists, among them Chubby Checker's own "Slow Twistin'" (1962), Sam Cooke's "Twistin' the Night Away," Gary Bonds's "Dear Lady Twist," Joey Dee and the Starliters' (the Peppermint Lounge house band) "Peppermint Twist," and Danny and the Juniors' "Twistin' USA."[82] By this time, though, the dance had moved out of the Black dance community and gotten picked up by white and Black dance teachers, dance studios, and Hollywood choreographers (in which many theatrical variations were created), then went on for yet a couple of more years as a national and international phenomenon cutting across class and generational lines.

The significance of the Twist, what made it and many of the social dances that followed it so revolutionary was, in part, the dissolution of the dance couple once and for all; for decades, many prior social dances had hinted at this development, as in the improvisational breaks of the Lindy, or the Bop, but with the Twist it became complete. Individuals now performed in loose associations of couples attuned to the surrounding group. Yet at the same time, there was an increasing sense of improvisatory display—a kind of freestyling—that allowed for individual expression to the rhythms of the music.[83] The effect of this was to provoke the dancer's inward focus rather than strict attention to one's partner.[84] The Twist essentially set the stage for the expressiveness and permissiveness that would come to characterize "the 1960s."

By the early 1960s, there was a parade of dance innovations (close to a hundred), including the Jerk, the Slop, the Frug, the Horse, the Pony, the Monkey, the Watusi, the Continental, the Skate, the Swim, the Freddie, the Twine, the Locomotion, and the Mashed Potato, among others. In the popular Jerk, for instance, the signature move is the back-and-forth or up-and-down whipping motion of the arms as the pelvis tilts outward and back. The Watusi (which like the Twist caught on famously with white, middle-class society) employed a quivering-like motion of the hips as the arms, stretched up over the heads, propelled themselves forward and back. The majority of the dances came out of song numbers by Black musical artists (e.g., Dee Dee Sharp's "Mashed Potato Time" and Little Eva's "Locomotion," in 1962, and Alvin Williams's "Twine Time," in 1964).[85] And, too, they were greatly influenced by the dance routines of Black musical performers such as the Motown vocal groups coached by choreographer Cholly Atkins.[86] The famed 1964 T.A.M.I., or Teenage Awards Music International, concert in Santa Monica, California (discussed in Chapter 6), featured the major R&B and rock 'n' roll musicians and singers of the time, among them James Brown whose memorable performance there combined bits of various Black vernacular dance steps.

The fact that some of these dances were short-lived does not, though, devalue their significance. Without a doubt, some of these dance creations were the work of record executives and advertisers who rushed songs into publication in order to take advantage of—or spark—a new dance craze.[87] And, too, cover versions and spin-offs of the Twist proliferated. This "popularization" process was as much about selling records and promoting dances as it was about commodifying and mediatizing them (on shows such as *American Bandstand*) as white dances.[88]

Whether the dance manuals were even read or practiced by teenagers is anybody's guess—more likely that they were aimed at teens' parents to diffuse consternation about the sexual overtones of rock 'n' roll dances. Some critics have contended that Chubby Checker, for instance, created a more palatable Twist, that he "downplayed the hip movement and ramped up the lateral waist movement while gently rocking back and forth."[89] While it is true that Checker was cultivated by Dick Clark, who favored his rendition of the Twist over Hank Ballard's, and promoted it on the heavily white *American Bandstand*, as Reebee Garofalo points out of the Twist: "[i]ts leading exponent was a Black man, however unthreatening, and it released middle-class white bodies from their repressed stiffness while anticipating more openly sexual dances like the 'Monkey,' the 'Jerk,' and the 'Philly Dog.'"[90]

The fact is, while on the one hand white teenagers, unlike their Black counterparts, may have been dancing modified versions of the Twist (and other dances), the era still witnessed white bodies taking Black styles into

their own. As Banes and Szwed so aptly remarked, "emerging generations of white youth eagerly learned the bodily and cultural codes of Black
Americans by practicing its dances."[91] Steps and rhythms from the Black
dance tradition—twisting, tilting, or shaking hips; swiveling on the balls of
the feet; quick transfers and shifting of weight from one foot to the other; and
slightly bent knees with lightning-quick marching or pedaling steps—were
at play in their dances. The bodily codes learned on the dance floor mirrored
and instantiated cultural changes occurring in society. By the mid-1960s, in
light of major civil rights legislation, dance floors (including that of *American
Bandstand*) were becoming integrated, Motown had created an audience of
both Black and white teenagers (and adults), and social change was in the air.
That story will be taken up in the final chapter on the fall and then the rise,
again, of the televised teen dance shows of the mid-1960s.

5

Girl Power

Youth Culture and Female Fandom

Because it's almost time. Whatever our race, color, or creed, my
peers and I are getting ready to:
Sidle
Slump
Pout
Pose
Sashay and foot-drag
Into adolescence.
Devious and careless
Feverish and slothful
Living in the moment that's so often the wrong moment,
                                        —Margo Jefferson, from *Negroland*

Two images dominate the pages of mass-consumption magazines of the mid-
to-late 1950s. One is of the screaming, seemingly half-crazed female fan at a
large, rollicking rock 'n' roll concert in thrall to the live presence of one of her
male recording idols. Her fandom here is seen only as a kind of blind devotion to male rock 'n' rollers (or male movie stars) who seemed to create in girls
a post-pubescent mass hysteria. Although we associate the seeming frenzy
at rock 'n' roll concerts with white girls, because those were the images most
widely projected (then and now), Black girls at these events *were* as equally enthusiastic and excited. In an article from the *Pittsburgh Courier*, in December
1957, famed Black deejay "Professor" Nat D. Williams recounted the reaction
of young Black girls at a Memphis Elvis Presley concert—the same kind of reaction that was troubling white middle-class parents and commentators: "A thousand Black, brown and beige teen-age girls in the audience blended their alto

Dancing Black, Dancing White. Julie Malnig, Oxford University Press. © Oxford University Press 2023.
DOI: 10.1093/oso/9780197536254.003.0006

and soprano voices in one wild crescendo of sound that rent the rafters . . . and took off like scalded cats in the direction of Elvis."[1]

The other image is of a white, adolescent girl, alone, sometimes with a friend or two, sitting on her bedroom floor, feet curled under her, and sifting through her record collection, about to place an album of (perhaps) Little Richard or Elvis Presley on the spindle of her record player. Sometimes outfitted in a buttoned-down sweater and saddle shoes, she appears to the viewer as if involved in a surreptitious activity that she must keep from her parents, or else involved in some type of private ritual in which she expresses her devotion to the gods of R&B. She has been called by some scholars as "the bedroom girl," a designation that sees the girl fan as inextricably linked to the home and domestic sphere and the culture's construction of girlhood as one tied to cultural consumption.[2] Media theorist Simon Frith, in particular, has suggested that girls' involvement in rock 'n' roll music (and youth culture generally) was limited by cultural constraints on her behavior. She was, he argues, excluded from boy's "street culture" where, unlike girls, they were "learning the rules of loyalty, bravado, and public leisure."[3] (Of course, they were learning about sex, too.) Girls, on the other hand, were understood to be using the bedroom as a place to primp and prepare themselves to meet those boys.

But might there not be more to these images than meets the eye?

Like all media-constructed images, these were only partially true. While social and sexual mores indeed limited girls' behavior, and their passion for rock 'n' roll music and dance more often than not did play out in the sanctity of their bedrooms (listening to music or dancing with their friends), neither were they agency-less. As youth culture historian Mary Celeste Kearney has written, opposing Frith's argument, it "ultimately reproduced the dominant notion that girls are capable only of cultural consumption."[4] Girls' obsession with rock 'n' roll most often got translated as her being a "passive consumer" of the music. Youth historian Jon Savage cites a 1956 headline from *The Musical Express Annual* that asks, "Are Bobbysoxers Musically Ignorant?," suggesting that girl fans were more interested in their male idols than the music.[5] While it is clear that young girls were as transfixed by rock 'n' roll music and dance as were boys, the idea has persisted that girls of the era were somehow the more conformist, listening to rock 'n' roll music in the privacy of the home, tethered to consumerist notions of beauty and dating, and more hesitant to break gender norms. Of course, because of constricting gender admonitions (and "rules"), girls often had to engage in what youth scholar Wini Breines (writing primarily of white girls) refers to as "covert dissidence," quiet, less dramatic acts of passive resistance (such as identifying with Beat culture, which was primarily male).[6]

While Breines, and others, contend that young girls' "mute rebellion" actually presaged and paved the way for the more outwardly rebellious protestors of the late 1960s, I want to explore the ways in which both rebellion and conformity were in constant dialogue with one another, and where and when young girls might gravitate toward one pole or the other to assist them in negotiating the sexual and racial boundaries of adolescence. How both Black and primarily middle- and working-class white women accomplished this, and to what ends, forms the basis of my argument. Black and white girls were *affected* differently, but all of them were embedded in "teen culture" of the 1950s, and R&B and rock 'n' roll music and dance were an influential part of their coming of age. Because there were so few all–African American teen dance shows, in this chapter I discuss more broadly all of those locations where rock 'n' roll dance took place—not only on the televised shows, but in the concert halls, auditoriums, and teen clubs, in order to best capture the experience of both Black and white girls alike. Ultimately, I hope in this chapter to take up historian Rachel Devlin's charge to view this era neither nostalgically, on one hand, or as a gateway to the 1960s, on the other, and to see it in its own right. We will see what went on from the voices of those who lived it, with all its conflict, contradictions, and partial resolutions to young girls' quest for sexual autonomy and self-identity.

A word about sources: part of my discussion concerns the way that young girls found immense *pleasure* in rock 'n' roll dance, both physically and emotionally, that helped propel their fandom. Documenting what constitutes girls' pleasures, though, particularly in the 1950s when so much of their behavior was monitored and proscribed, often remains elusive in the historical record and all the more so for young Black girls, who because of segregation and racial animosity had to guard and often conceal their actions and demeanor. As gender historian LaKisha Simmons writes, in her groundbreaking work on Black girls' coming of age in mid-twentieth-century New Orleans, "The various silences that seem to constitute and consume Black women's sexuality are reflected in the archive. Newspaper articles, 'expert' discourses on Black sexuality, court documents, reform home records, and even oral histories are filled with silence."[7] Not content to accept these silences, Simmons looked at various under-researched sources, such as public spaces, YWCA dances, and writings in high school yearbooks, to determine how young girls created their own pleasure cultures. Looking at life "behind the masks" that both Black and white girls were forced to wear has been a challenge of this inquiry, but interviews with former social dancers, and recollections of their experiences, have been an important part of gleaning how young girls' found pleasure within constraints. The chapter revolves around the interlocking issues of coming of age, sexual desire, and identity formation and how rock 'n' roll figured into these developments. And, too, the chapter showcases some of the roles young girls and women played in teen dance culture, since so much of it has been credited to male deejays, performers, and fans.

Setting the Stage

Historically, girls' experience within popular culture has been viewed as ancillary to boys'. In matters of concern about youth of the time—whether juvenile delinquency, the high school experience, rebellions against one's parents, sex and sexuality, or the effects of rock 'n' roll music—the default model was always male. Even though girls were seen as consumer engines for the purchase of rock 'n' roll music and paraphernalia (one critic reported that "Persons under the age of 18 and predominantly female, buy 80 percent of all 45 revolutions-per-minute recordings"),[8] rock 'n' roll *culture* was the purview of boys. Recall that the 1954 US Senate Subcommittee Hearings on juvenile delinquency and the deleterious effects of comic books were all focused on boys' experience. It was in 1956 that sociologist Paul Goodman, in *Growing Up Absurd: The Problems of Youth in the Organized Society*, stated that "our 'youth troubles' are 'boys' troubles." As Rachel Devlin notes, even though the end of the Second World War through the 1950s saw a spike in female juvenile delinquency, the media "alternately sensationalized and ignored the problem."[9]

In 1994, media theorist Susan J. Douglas wrote that "Elvis Presley and rock 'n' roll made rebelliousness acceptable for boys. But what about the girls?"[10] Since then, several youth historians, gender theorists, and feminist sociologists have addressed this question. Scholars such as Angela McRobbie, Wini Breines, Norma Coates, Susan J. Douglas, Mary Celeste Kearney, Kelly Schrum, Susan Cahn, and LaKisha Simmons have attempted to correct the record and revise our understanding of the plight of both Black and white girls during this era.[11] A focus on young girls, of course, helps us to fill a gap in the historical record, but it also enables us see the contradictory nature of the 1950s as a whole that much more clearly—the push and pull between complacency and conservatism on the one hand and deviation from those norms on the other. How the culture responded and reacted to rock 'n' roll music and dance, and teenage girls' involvement in it, serves as a kind of template for how "adult society" grappled with gender and racial divides in the country during this time.

Part of shifting our focus onto young girls necessitates changing the lens through which we view rock 'n' roll culture to see how young girls incorporated rock 'n' roll into their lives. When we do, other possibilities emerge. Musicologist Leah Branstetter, for instance, writing about both Black and white female singers, suggests of rock 'n' roll that

> When we begin to examine the huge variety of performances that occurred and records that were sold under that banner, an equally wide array of women's performances becomes visible. We might set out looking for a female rock star who resembled Elvis Presley—and some did—but she might just as well have been founding her own vocal group, recording a witty retort to a song by a male contemporary, or bringing rock and roll to Japan.[12]

To that list I would add creating or popularizing a rock 'n' roll dance, as many young girls did on the teen dance programs; for many, the shows served as a launching pad for pre-professional rock 'n' roll singers and dancers. Branstetter contends that hundreds of girls either performed or recorded rock 'n' roll in its early years, but not all of them were necessarily pursuing fame—some were also behind the scenes writing songs, working for record companies, or managing talent. And even for the hundreds (and thousands) of amateur rock 'n' rollers there were many who became as proficient as pre-professionals. By embracing the music and dance wholeheartedly, they were forever changed by it.[13]

The Double Standard and the Double Bind

How young African American and white girls achieved "girl power" through the rock 'n' roll ethos is not clear-cut, nor was it uniform. There was no one "universal" girlhood; rather, there were essentially multiple girlhoods based on race, class, nationality, regionality, and even among different high schools. Certainly, too, the experiences of working- and middle-class Black and white girls' experiences differed from one another. But at the same time, there were overlapping beliefs and practices. As historian Susan Cahn writes about the experience of coming of age, it generally refers to the years between twelve and eighteen, and involves "physical, emotional, sexual, and psychological changes shaped by the idea of adolescence itself, by processes of identity formation and change."[14] Childhood and adulthood, as she notes, have come to be seen as "stable bookends," around a time of life that is known for its instability, unpredictability, if not tumult and confusion.[15]

Although young boys were the focus of much of the study of adolescents in the 1950s, young girls were taken hold of by the mass media and their experience commodified and popularized at the hands of journalists, advertisers, and the fashion industry. The teenage girl, as Devlin points out, with her expenditures on records, clothing, and a host of teen paraphernalia, became the poster child of sorts for the country's economic boom.[16] *Seventeen* magazine, and its star promotional director, Estelle Ellis, created the prototypical "teena" figure to refer specifically to young girls in order to lure potential advertisers to this new demographic group.[17] Although teena (girls between thirteen and eighteen who represented a $2 billion market) was also a civic-minded person who was concerned about her home and community and not afraid to buck her parents, there's no question her "power" was seen in her ability to be an avid and wise consumer. The widely popular Black magazine *Ebony*, too, with its essays and articles about the achievements of middle-class, female youth, their coming of age at debutante balls, and the like, represented a distinct market for girls and girls' products.

There's no question, though, that by the early 1950s there was, as Cahn adeptly notes, "a 'coming out' of teenage girls' sexuality with rock music at the conspicuous center."[18] Rock 'n' roll music and dance, it was clear, was a breakthrough in terms of young girls' acknowledgment that they could *express* sexual desire.

Unlike the immediate postwar years, in which discussion of girls' sexuality tended to focus on the promiscuity of the so-called Victory Girls who frequented soldiers' camps, by the 1950s there was a belief by the experts that sexual feelings formed a part of all adolescent girls' development—both working and middle class. Although active pursuit of sexual experience still signaled female delinquency, as it had in the mid-to-late 1940s, the difference now was that it was understood that girls could demonstrate that desire through "dating, dances, and teen romance" spurred on by heterosexual high school culture.[19] Throughout the 1930s and 1940s, high school enrollment had grown, accommodating rural, immigrant, as well as Black students, as it moved from a more elite status to a universal one.[20] The acceptance of girls' sexual natures intensified as high school culture developed in tandem with consumer market culture; high school girls' purchasing power grew alongside all of the activities associated with dating and dancing that were sanctioned by the schools. As Sherrie Inness, in *Delinquents and Debutantes*, has noted, teen culture has in the past been created and shaped both by adults (as in the editors of *Seventeen* magazine) seeking to link girls to consumerism, yet it has also sprung from the girls themselves attempting to carve out a space for themselves in a culture that was limiting, and even at times debilitating, regarding choices offered to them.[21]

This was a paradoxical time for women and young girls. On one hand, sexual activity, while acknowledged, was also highly sanctioned. As Cahn points out, although adult society might disapprove of young girls' "public displays of 'hysteria'" and "lack of inhibition," "they did not assume that female eroticism, in and of itself, signaled victimization, pathology, or poor and immoral family background."[22] Young girls were surrounded by a highly sexualized popular culture in the form of pin-ups, movie magazines, and lingerie advertisements, yet it all "unfolded amid prudish families and narrow, even cruel sexual norms."[23] The power of the sexual double standard—which professed, for example, that young girls, unlike boys, could date but not go "all the way"—was such that young girls' innate desires were often silenced or repressed. (Early matrimony, espoused by experts, was a way to control sexuality and to contain it within marriage.)[24] As historian Amanda Littauer notes, in most aspects of life around her, young girls learned that "it was men's right to sexual self-determination and self-expression that was on the table."[25]

Paradoxes were everywhere. Although the era actually saw a rise in women's employment (the "working girl" was replaced by the "working mother," according to Devlin),[26] women's ties to domesticity were hailed and reified. Much of teenage girls' rebellion was aimed at the heart of what various scholars have referred to as the "domestic containment ideology."[27] The idea is that just as Cold War fears led to the political containment of the country's perceived enemies, forcing the country inward, so too, on the cultural front, were supposed internal "threats" that upset the traditional order, such as racial integration, teenage rebellion, working women, and the encroaching loss of women's "separate sphere" (the ideology that maintained strict boundaries between male and female domains). Writes Wini Breines,

"Working mothers, homosexuals, and single women were categories of the excluded. So were Black people."[28]

The sexual fears surrounding women and rock 'n' roll music and dance were also racialized ones. If the culture was about upholding masculinity, it was also about maintaining whiteness; the so-called consensus mentality of the era cohered around the notion of "belonging" to a group with shared values and attitudes. It conceived of "outsiders" as threats to middle-class norms and aspirations. The consensus, though, was in large part an illusion— the celebration of whiteness and white femininity reflected anxiety about integration of the races and meant precisely to stave off "the claims of those who had been excluded."[29] In the conservative climate of the 1950s, one that still upheld sexual puritanism, the fact that young white girls might experiment with morally suspect music and dance uninhibitedly to raucous guitar riffs by Black and working-class men was met with suspicious and outright condemnation. Sexual possibility continually floated through the often erotically charged lyrics and the pulsating rhythms that coursed through bodies on the gym or TV studio dance floor. But, of course, what lay underneath the opprobrium was the deeper fear of the possibility of interracial dancing and the ultimate threat of interracial dating and sex. Cahn explains that "High schools and dance floors had two things in common. Each constituted a shared physical space that teenagers—Black and white—had claimed as their own, forging a heterosexual youth culture beyond the control of adults."[30] Although many schools, of course, particularly in the South, were not yet integrated, the rise of Black-derived R&B and rock 'n' roll music and dance raised the specter of what *might* occur were schools to become desegregated. Here, white teenage girls were still expected to uphold the deeply entrenched belief that "vulnerable white women" needed protection from "Black male sexual aggression."[31] This fear of interracial dancing was occurring just at the time, of course, that the South was preparing massive resistance to the desegregation of schools (in the aftermath of the *Brown v. Board of Education* decision, in 1954) and of public transportation.

Black girls were equally subject to the cultural messages surrounding sexuality, sexual permissiveness (and its dangers), as well as ideas about beauty and romance. Then, as now, white measures of beauty were applied in estimating Black women's attractiveness and the popular culture of the time— whether in the pages of *Seventeen* or *Ebony* magazine—emphasized the importance of romance.[32] (The pulp magazines *True Confessions* and *Love Story* were equally popular among white and Black girls.[33]) The double standard was alive and thriving; Beverly Lindsay-Johnson, the producer and director of *Dance Party: The Teenarama Story*, recalls how there were penalties for not adhering to what were deemed appropriate feminine norms, which were also created by and normalized by the public schools, that attempted to elide ethnic and racial differences to create a uniform teen culture. Said Lindsay-Johnson, "You had to look a certain way, you had to present yourself a certain way, in order to be accepted. But that's also what the schools required."[34]

But Black girls had a double burden, that of maintaining "purity" as well as fending off and protecting themselves from racist attacks. In the segregated society of the 1950s, Black girls, as Devlin states, "were afforded none of the public protections that extended to middle-class white girls such as the assumption of dependence, the notion that children ought to be free of economic exploitation, or security from public violence and sexual harassment."[35] Black girls' adolescence was marked by fears of being struck by white men for not giving up a seat on a bus or targeted by white gangs on the way to school.[36] As a result of this reality, Black parents, teachers, writers, and social activists preached the discourse of "respectability," as discussed in Chapter 3, that young Black girls needed to maintain as a means of active self-preservation. LaKisha Simmons refers to the "double bind" that Black girls and women faced, the burden of having to negotiate "the violence of white supremacy" with the discourse of "respectability."[37] As historian Darlene Clark Hine has written, "chaste modes of self-presentation were institutionalized into racial projects," and young Black girls, then, grew up living with the expectation that it was their responsibility to uphold a set of mores and behavior that might prevent unwarranted attacks—physical or verbal—or mitigate negative stereotypes.[38]

The issue of "respectability politics," and the idea of advancing oneself for the public perception of the Black race, was clearly gendered. During this time, Black women actually bore the burden of comporting themselves with dignity. As Maxine Leeds Craig writes in *Ain't I a Beauty Queen: Black Women, Beauty, and the Politics of Race*, "Incorporating prevailing sentiments that women were the caretakers of morality, black writers of the day stressed the importance of the position of women in the progress of the race."[39] The attraction to R&B and rock 'n' roll, then, was all the more fraught for Black girls. If indeed the advent of rock 'n' roll coincided with the "coming out" of teen girls' sexuality, then there's no question that Black parents might have particular concerns about their daughters exhibiting that sexuality, especially in a climate where, as Devlin explains, judges and lawyers in court cases involving school desegregation routinely castigated young Black girls for their innate promiscuity.[40] Writer and memoirist Margo Jefferson describes this balancing act, particularly for middle-class Black women and girls:

> Between the 1940s and the early 1960s, Good Negro Girls mastered the rigorous vocabulary of femininity. Gloves, handkerchiefs, pocketbooks for each occasion. Good diction for all occasions; skin care (no ashy knees or elbows); hair cultivation (a ceaseless round of treatments to eradicate the bushy and nappy). Manners to please grandparents and quell the doubts of any white strangers loitering to observe your behavior in schools, stores, and restaurants. We were busy being pert, chic, cool—but not fast.[41]

Recalling her adolescent foray into rock 'n' roll, Jefferson writes that

> I had a few years to go, but I started to get involved—half conscript, half worshipper—when Denise [her older sister] starts listening to Jam with Sam on WGES weekend nights; when she persuades our mother to drive us both to a weekend showing of *The Girl Can't Help It* ("Little Richard is excellent and Jayne Mansfield is a very good actress," we assure her when she picks us up).[42]

That Black girls' excitement could reach unexpected crescendos over their favorite rock 'n' rollers is revealed by an *Ebony* journalist writing about a Fats Domino concert in Albany, New York, in 1957: "When Elvis Presley sings, teen-agers swoon and drop for dead. Pat Boone hits them in the limbs and they flop around like headless chickens. But when Fats Domino sings, mass hysteria sets in."[43] This critic continues that

> as Fats builds up to a climax, riding along on the locomotive-like beat of his seven-man combo, pandemonium erupts. Teen-agers shriek and contort their bodies, their limbs jerks in spastic rhythm, their eyes roll. Gradually, the "big beat," as Fats calls it, takes hold of the initiates and shakes them like leaves. Three times in the past year, the beat shook them too much and riot squads were summoned to restore order.[44]

Elvis Presley, too, won devoted acolytes. Although the response to Presley in the Black community was mixed—some feeling that he was appropriating Black musical forms, others that he seemed to pay homage to them—he had the power to attract audiences of both Black and white youth, and Black and white girls, in particular. According to Arnold Shaw, the music writer and publisher, Colonel Tom Parker, Presley's manager, had said of the singer that "Presley had not really made his mark on wax, that he was dynamite in personal appearance, affecting Southern girls, white and Black—as Sinatra once had."[45] In December 1956, WDIA—the Memphis radio station whose programming was aimed at a Black listenership—hosted its annual revue to help the Goodwill Fund charity whose goals was to help "needy Negro children." The revue, held at the Ellis Auditorium featured Ray Charles, B. B. King (a former deejay for WDIA), the Moonglows, and others, and a surprise appearance by Elvis Presley. At the revue was Carla Thomas, daughter of heralded Black R&B singer-songwriter Rufus Thomas and a member of the Teen Town Singers, who sang backup for singers on the show. (Thomas would go on to become known as the "Queen of Memphis Soul.") She remembers the thrill of seeing and meeting Elvis Presley, who made a surprise appearance at the end of the event. Music writer Peter Guralnick quotes her reaction:

> He [Elvis] stayed around for a long time after the show.... My sister Vaneese and I had our pictures taken with him, and there was an old piano backstage and he played some little runs on it. The audience was gone, and there were just the people getting dressed, and finally the stage manager said, "All right now, y'all got to go." He stayed that long, and we were just having a lot of fun. I remember *that* Elvis.[46]

In a *Pittsburgh Courier* article quoted earlier, Nat D. Williams seems to wonder how the Memphis community might feel about its Black girls reacting so wildly to Presley: "Beale Streeters are wondering if these teen-age girls' demonstration over Presley doesn't reflect a basic integration in attitude and aspiration which has been festering in the minds of most of your folks' women folk all along. Huhhh?"[47]

While Black and white girls reportedly displayed similar modes of behavior in response to rock 'n' roll celebrities, the Black press was apparently not as derogatory toward the girls' reactions and didn't treat the phenomenon as a "moral panic" as did the white press. This absence of Black girls from the popular press, which bears out Simmons's findings regarding the archive's "silences," suggests that either the press didn't *focus* on these images or that the young Black girls, bound by the conventions of middle-class "respectability," were simply not as *overt* in "acting out." As Shayla Thiel-Stern points out in *From the Dance Hall to Facebook*, given the "racialized codes of public conduct" of the time, young white girls were afforded the license to rebel in a way that young Black girls simply were not. "Black teens," Thiel-Stern notes, "regardless of social class, were hardly afforded the same tolerance."[48]

Consumerism, Advertising, and Girls Culture

The teen dance shows, both Black and white, as discussed, were fueled by advertising; it was what literally kept them in business. Product endorsement was rampant on the shows, and the advertisers courted by the producers of the shows were for those products of special worth to a teen audience—radios, record players, Good Humor ice cream, Clearasil, Coca-Cola. Of course, the mass media of the day, including popular magazines, teen magazines, teen advice columns, and movies, also participated in the formation of a teen culture that prized heterosexual dating and thus emphasized physical attractiveness, grooming practices, as well as athletic prowess (particularly for the boys). For the girls, the emphasis on popularity and peer culture, also fostered in high schools, translated into anxieties around beauty and acceptable beauty standards, all of which got mirrored and reproduced on the teen shows. This national teen culture cut across racial, ethnic, and class lines to affect all young girls who were encouraged, as Wini Breines notes, toward "similar feminine patterns."[49] Although *Ebony* magazine, for instance, always highlighted Black women's achievements and engagements in the workforce in its feature stories (it was careful to counter the racist perception of Black women, as historian Jacqueline Jones notes, "as domestic drudges"), its advertising nonetheless was similar, on the surface, to white publications in its emphasis on clothing, beauty treatments, and a young woman's manner of self-presentation.[50]

Youth-studies scholars have wrestled with the question of whether and where young girls exerted any type of self-agency or independent-mindedness within teen culture, fixated as it was on the teen-culture market. Consumer culture, dependent on sales and profit, traded on traditional notions of femininity and beauty; gender stereotypes were built into promotion and advertising. Many of the types of activities sponsored by the teen dance shows directly fed into this emerging reality of teenagers as budding consumers. Girls of the era were deemed to have a special relationship to consumer culture; they were viewed as especially "skilled consumers," according to cultural critic Dwight Macdonald, who were well versed in consumer trends and the fashions marketed to them.[51] Dick Hebdige, pioneering author of *Subculture: The Meaning of Style*, has ably demonstrated that subcultural practices are never completely divorced from the parent culture of which they are a part (in this case consumer capitalism). This is why he terms subcultural practice a "*symbolic* form of resistance." Clearly, the girls were participating in and promoting the values of the consumer culture. Yet, within those restrictive frameworks, young female rock 'n' rollers often managed to create a kind of group solidarity in how they manipulated and used those products and promotional strategies to create a distinct subculture setting them apart from their parents and from their male counterparts. Again, there was pleasure to be found physical adornment, pleasure in physical expression through rock 'n' roll music and dance. The accouterments of this culture—the hair, the dresses, the shoes, the makeup—were all a part of creating or developing their own worlds. The young girls were indeed "actors" in a complex economic system, as Kelly Schrum points out, at once responding to teenage consumer culture yet also driving the niche markets that markets then capitalized on.[52]

A feature found on many of the shows were beauty contests or fashion shows whose female participants were eligible to win all sorts of products ranging from televisions to luggage sets. While these events were an obvious way of showcasing the sponsor's products, they at the same time replicated what was an essential part of the actual high school experience of the time.[53] Beauty contests (along with homecoming queen celebrations) became ubiquitous in high schools, with their emphasis on a heterosexual peer culture and the intensified focus on dating. Black schools, too, were caught up with this more sexualized culture, particularly in the South. Susan Cahn points out how after the Supreme Court's 1954 *Brown v. Board of Education* decision, Southern schools, in order to avoid integration, built newer and improved Black high schools, whose activities began to resemble those of the white schools.[54] A national cosmetics and bath products brand—April Showers—became a major sponsor of several teen dance shows. On a 1957 episode of Alan Freed's *Big Beat*, substitute host singer Bobby Darin opens a segment devoted to claiming the winner of the Miss April Showers Contest. The winning contestant gets singled out by Darin, who declares her the winner of a month's supply of April Showers products. Similarly, *Oklahoma Dance Party*, broadcast out of Tulsa, featured its own Miss April Showers contest; at the so-called coronation (and it was that—the young woman dressed as a debutante was handed her crown by host Lee Woodward) the prize was actually a Nash "Metropolitan" automobile, a "little bitty coupe they produced from 1954 until 1962."[55]

Some of the few Black teen shows, too, were apt to feature beauty contests or beauty or fashion-related offerings. *Richard's Open Door*, for instance, the all-Black teen show that aired out of Chicago, regularly featured a segment on every show called "the fashion counter," in which young women from the Crest Modeling Agency and Charm School modeled the latest day and evening wear fashions to the background music of "I Only Have Eyes for You."[56] The dresses and suits they modeled were from Martin's Clothier, on Roosevelt Avenue in Chicago, owned by Irving Weisberg (who had spotted host Richard Stamz doing promotional work near his store and thought he would be great on television).[57] Like the white teen dance programs, similar Black shows were beholden to advertisers. But unlike the white shows, the emphasis on beauty, attractiveness, and glamour needs to be seen in the context of the standards of beauty that emerged within Black life. The emphasis on beauty was in one respect a protest against those racist and degrading conceptions of Black women and girls that abounded in white, mainstream culture. As Maxine Leeds Craig points out, many images of white femininity were born out of and created "in specific opposition to real and mythical Black women. The position of lady was distinguished by those it excluded—men, prostitutes, and Black women."[58] This was particularly true in the South where white racism was upheld in the name of protecting vulnerable white women. Writes Craig, "An African American woman who was simply showcased as pretty made an effective counterclaim to caricatures of Black women as humorously or monstrously ugly."[59] To offset these claims, the Black middle-class-oriented publications, among them *Ebony, Jet, Tan,* and *Sepia,* as well as schools, social clubs, the YWCA, and social protest organizations of the mid-century were actively invested in countering these images as a matter of Black pride (or in accord with the politics of respectability).[60] All of these were attempts to revise definitions of beauty as presented in the white mainstream. The Black pageants, homecomings, and other beauty and popularity-related events, for instance, most often had a social function not seen in the white community; the organizers often donated the proceeds to charities and fundraising projects.[61] Richard Stamz, in *Richard's Open Door,* had as one of his motives for using the Crest Modeling Agency a show of support for local Black businesses. While these events still traded on gender biases of the era, and most often played into white, mainstream conceptions of beauty, nonetheless, as Craig points out, they did so as "nonconfrontational ways of expressing racial pride"[62] and might serve the larger community.

The Politics of "Being Seen"

The beauty pageants and contests, the homecoming celebrations, and all other manner of shows of popularity, as well as the televised dancing, were all essentially sources of pleasure for adolescent youth, and for girls, in particular. Part of that pleasure was the reality of "being seen." In her seminal 1979 essay "Visual Pleasure and Narrative Cinema," Laura Mulvey coined the phrase "to-be-looked-at-ness" to refer to the way in which women in Hollywood films were positioned and objectified within the framing of the so-called male gaze. This type of viewing, or gazing, bespeaks an asymmetry in how women and men are "seen" by audiences; the women in the audience relate to the women on screen who are being objectified and sexualized. Although Mulvey revised her theory in a later essay (to provide more agency to the female spectator), the issue her essay raises about how women see themselves in a media context is relevant to the teen dance shows.[63] Of course, for *both* young boys and girls, the televised teen dance shows were vehicles in which to become seen, known, and revered, particularly among one's friends and peers; that was part of the allure. Garnering popularity was a matter of how one was seen—how one looked and dressed—and with whom. Because the shows were so tied to high school mores and manners, it's worth considering the nature of adolescent dates, which, as historian Beth Bailey points out, functioned "as tools for acquiring popularity."[64] But for the date to matter, it has to be *public*; the young girl had to be seen as someone who *could* date. The date also had to be displayed and shown off (like a consumer good). Dating was performative in this sense, then, a kind of accomplishment that one could exhibit, especially on TV. Interestingly, even when dance couples were not dating (but were simply dance partners), teen audience members projected onto the dancers an aura of romance. Citing the popular romantic movies, teenage love ballads, and movie magazines that permeated the time, Wini Breines emphasized that females were in a constant stay of display and "were to be chosen by males on the basis of their media-defined sexual allure."[65] But the notion of watching and "being seen" might have had other less injurious connotations. It might not have always been associated with "judgments about desirability,"[66] about sexualization and objectification. For many young female teenagers, the opportunity to dance and participate on the teen dance shows was also a means of being seen in the sense of taking up space—of *claiming* a space as their own. Many adolescents, preoccupied with how they appeared to others and the outside world, saw themselves as "stars" of their own dramas; according to one developmental psychologist, they played to an "imaginary audience," "believing themselves to be watched by an eager if sometimes judgmental public."[67] Girls, too, particularly on the teen TV shows, were watching each other for cues on how to look and behave. Just as fashion and beauty magazines were means of identifying with other (young) women, the shows were places where they could actually enact these behaviors, on the studio dance floor. In a culture that proscribed so much of their behavior, the teen dance studio could become a place where girls might "try out" identities, if you will; it was a way of flouting those rules, of showing off, of inhabiting space before the camera as so many young girls often did. For some young girls, this claiming of space went hand-in-hand with the ability to imagine themselves differently and dream of a better future. As Bunny Gipson, a former "regular" on *American Bandstand*, recalled:

> I knew when I was a little girl—no matter what went on in my house—and I would go to sleep and dream that there was more out there. I dreamed that there was more. Whatever that was—the dream, the hopes, the vision— pulled me to that show to go find it. I'd open those doors and there was a wonderful world of fun and happiness and dance and joy.[68]

Even though the teen dance shows themselves had a prescribed dress code, like the public schools, and forbade certain types of behaviors, the studio dance floor was a still a place to experiment with dress style, demeanor, and new styles of bodily expression. To resist traditional modes of conduct, of course, might risk being labeled a juvenile delinquent, but part of teen rebelliousness was about exploring one's own identity and in a public fashion. Beverly Lindsay-Johnson (the producer of the documentary film on *Teenarama*) recalled her own behavior in school in the Bronx in the early 1960s, and her attempts to buck the dress code:

> There was this really big discussion about pants, okay; we still could not wear pants to school, and we couldn't wear the go-go boots, right, and my mother had bought me some culottes, and I felt that because the culottes were wide legged if I put my legs together it could look like a skirt, you

know, and I went to school and I had my culottes on, and the hall mon-
itor pulled me over to the side, sent me to the principal's office, called my
mother, and told my mother to come and get me.[69]

Former *Teenarama* dancer Yvonne Mills, known to her then-peers as
"little bits" because of her petite size, recalls an experience that illustrates
how experimenting with fashion styles was a means of rebellious exhibi-
tionism, and, too, how teen girls watched each other for signals of appro-
priateness. Mills (a speech pathologist with a PhD in communications and
speech disorders) mentions wearing "the very nice clean blouse, a little belt,
and the skirt with all the crinoline under it. I looked like that; I've even got a
picture." But she did notice that some other girls, presumably from another
school, "wore dresses that were a bit more provocative . . . their dresses were
a little tight. The guys would love for them to walk up the steps first, so they
could watch. They didn't look at me. I was like a little pencil." Mills concluded,
"I was shy, but I was observant." For Mills, what mattered most, though, were
the accolades from her peers who watched her dance:

> The recognition, oh, it was exciting. It was exciting because people would
> say, "I saw you yesterday. I really like that dance." Or you know, "I didn't
> know you could dance like that." As I was walking through the hallways of
> the school the next day, someone was always telling you that they saw the
> show and "Oh, you did a great job." And "Oh, you guys look like you were
> having so much fun."[70]

Wini Breines, writing about the standard dating system foisted onto young
teens of the 1950s, has written that "Complex rules and conventions were
the underside of media glamour. . . . Teenage sexual etiquette, dating and
going steady, channeled female sexuality into a routinized sexual system that
controlled and punished female spontaneity."[71] But the televised teen dance
shows, despite their rules and regulations, were in many respects a way out of
that routinized trap for many young girls. For Bunny Gipson, it represented
a world beyond the confines of her home that let her imagine a new self. For
Yvonne Mills, it was both the freedom to express herself and her competence
on the dance floor and at the same time get recognized for it.

It's important to consider that the girls felt free to exhibit themselves in
an unfettered way, usually in the company of their female friends. Much of
girls' behavior occurred for each other as they tested bounds of propriety

and custom. At the same time that girls used the music to feed their adolescent rebellion, and break from their parents' culture, they looked to each other for what 1950s adolescent psychologist James Coleman called "social rewards."[72] Although all teenagers looked to their peers for social approval and confirmation, for girls a special kind of camaraderie developed, in part as a result of their discovery that they shared a common passion: the love of music—particularly R&B. It was understood that girls "bought the records in millions" and made a huge contribution to the success of stars such as Elvis Presley and others.[73] But it wasn't only the stirrings of sexual feelings that spurred their desire for the music or, even, the momentary release from proscribed gender constraints; I believe it was also the music itself that sparked their devotion. Judging from high school yearbooks, and other memorabilia, Kelly Schrum concludes that girls "identified music they liked and sought avenues for expressing their enthusiasm through singing, dancing, and fads while searching for acceptable public places to enjoy music with peers." She also notes that, along with the purchase of records and radios and attendance at dances and concerts, girls were taking music lessons in droves and learning instruments.[74] Apart from the lyrics and content of the songs, mostly about dating and seduction, and the vicissitudes of teenage love, it was the music itself, and the dancing it inspired, that linked female adolescents in a kind of affective force—a *communitas*, if you will, as they heard and felt the music in unison. It is difficult to listen to soul singer Shirley Ellis's 1963 hit "The Nitty Gritty," for instance, with her sweeping vocal registers from soprano to alto and her sassy vibrato capped by a searing saxophone, and not imagine young girls swiveling their hips in a Watusi or lifting and swinging their arms for the Pony in an orgiastic rite of the self.

"It's Got a Good Beat, and You Can Dance to It"

Although the conventional wisdom is that rock 'n' roll performance was a world unto boys and young men, there were, in fact, many young women who were not only great appreciators and lovers of the music and dance but who wanted to be a part of the scene itself. One of the arguments about female fandom typically espoused among feminist popular culture scholars is that, deprived of a sense of their own agency as a result of 1950s sexual double standard, young women found in male rock 'n' rollers the object of their own fantasies and desires; that is, the swooning and screaming was

"to imagine being the idol as well as being with the idol." With their infat-
uation with the "girl groups" of the 1950s and 1960s, female adolescents
could indeed project themselves onto the life of the performer and fan-
tasize themselves as "exceptional" instead of someone's girlfriend.[75] Susan
Douglas, in a quasi-autobiographical chapter in *Where the Girls Are*, points
out that

> Some of us wanted to be good girls, and some of us wanted to be bad. But
> most of us wanted to get away with being both, and girl group music let us
> try on and act out a host of identities from traditional, obedient girlfriend
> to brassy, independent rebel, and lots in between.[76]

Young Black girls, alike, found inspiration in the girl groups. Said Lindsay-
Johnson, "Every girl wanted to be a Chantel or a Shirelle. And then when
Motown came, every one wanted to be the Supremes, you know."[77] As author
Sheryl Garratt, writing about female fandom, concludes: "The girl-group era
told women they could be stars, that they could dress up and look strong and
sexy, get up there with the boys."[78]

Some of these same girls, with the same aspirations, could be found among
the dancers on the televised teen dance shows. Antoinette Matlins, for instance, a "regular" on *The Milt Grant Show*, got a chance to record her own
rock 'n' roll 45 rpm as a result of a chance meeting with Vernon Wray, the
brother of the pioneering R&B singer Link Wray whose gritty, 1958 "Rumble"
was banned from radio stations in New York and Boston.[79] Matlins came to
The Milt Grant Show having trained seriously in ballet—she had been invited
to join the Royal Ballet—and ballroom dance (in part because her father's
gemology business was located in the same building as an Arthur Murray
Dance Studio). But she also loved rock 'n' roll music and dance. For her, it
was the sensuousness of dancing together that had "a romantic kind of exciting quality to it as teenagers coming into our own awareness of so many
things. . . . I had a couple of guys who were like, wild, but it was fun, and it was
a healthy way to explore your changing hormones and the influence they had
on you."[80] In her role as a regular, Matlins also assumed a certain authority.
One of her responsibilities was to help novices learn to dance:

> You had these groups that would come from schools and different clubs and
> whatever, and you could always spot the shy boy who didn't know how to
> move his foot. He didn't even know his right foot from his left foot, and I'd

always pick out of those guys, and they'd say, "Oh, I can't really dance." And I said, "sure you can. Everybody can dance." "Well, I can't dance." I said, "Can you count?" He said, "Well of course I can count." "I said can you count to four?" And they'd laugh. I'd say if you can count to four, you can dance.[81]

Matlins had no real desire to become "an actress or an actor or anything like that," but she had a voice, and she remembers coming early to the studio and learning about being in a sound room, using microphones, and how to deliver lines from a script.[82] She particularly loved writing lyrics:

> I could remember melodies. So, I'd make the song in my head, and I'd start to sing it to myself, and I'd write down the words, and I'd keep thinking it over until I got the sounds and the words just right. Then my brother would record it on our Wollensak tape recorder.[83]

Matlins, like other middle-class white girls, was very influenced by the African American girl groups who appeared on the show: "I liked them a lot, and I think that's one of the reasons I wrote music; because the girls were successful at it."[84] Although teen dancers were forbidden to dance with the guests on the show, they were free to talk and socialize with them, and many teenagers made professional contacts in this way. It was during a commercial break that she got to meet Vernon Wray (who went by Ray Vernon), who urged her to record.[85] Matlins's brush with a recording career unfolded in a way that may have been true for many young and naïve recording artists—particularly young women. Under the name "Toni Lens," Matlins, who was nineteen at this point, recorded three songs for Wray's then fledgling record company, Vector Records. Matlins got a distributor and traveled to Vector's recording facilities in Nashville and recorded two numbers—a remake of Teresa Brewer's popular "Don't Sweetheart Me!" and Matlins's original composition "Sophisticated Kate" on the A side. As she has said of the numbers:

> "Someone" was a slow-dance kind of melody describing that perfect someone, and "Sophisticated Kate" was a youth rebellion [song] against parents: "I don't want to be a Sophisticated Kate. No, I want to have fun, be a blast on a date, I don't give a darn about my hat or gloves. All I want is someone to love" . . . that kind of thing.[86]

"Sophisticated Kate" apparently got excellent airplay on radio stations in the Virginia area, and the Teresa Brewer number hit the local top-ten charts. Matlins also appeared on *The Milt Grant Show* and other TV shows lip-syncing to the Brewer number. According to Matlins, just as "Someone" was starting to reach the charts, Vector Records absconded with her master tapes—never to be recovered. Said Matlins, "The whole recording experience, all of my optimism about actually becoming a part of this scene that I so loved, went up in smoke. He [Wray] just vanished."[87] Like so many of the former women social dancers interviewed for this project, Matlins—despite her misfortune as a budding recording artist—has remarked that as an adolescent, "finding the group and finding a way to feel included or part of something greater than yourself is really of paramount importance" and that she found that on *The Milt Grant Show*. And she found dancing: "*The Milt Grant Show* probably did as much for me, maybe more for me, than anything I ever did in terms of finding self-confidence, feeling that I had something to offer to somebody, whether it was dance or whether it was singing or whether it was helping that other couple on the dance floor learn how to dance."[88]

In Detroit, in 1963, the teen dance program *Swingin' Time*, hosted by former deejay Robin Seymour, was just getting on the air at CKLW-TV. Although not the first teen dance program to air in the Detroit area, it was the first to feature the performers who would go on to become some of the biggest names at Motown.[89] The show ran daily from 4 to 5 P.M.; on Saturdays the *Swingin' Time Review* featured performers and musicians only in variety-show format that was broadcast and taped from the Fox Theater (home to many Motown stars and Elvis Presley).[90] *Swingin' Time* appealed to teenage dancers on both sides of the Detroit River—CKLW-TV in 1954 had bought a license to air on the VHF channel in Windsor, Ontario, which drew mostly white teenagers. Leslie Tipton Russell recalls that the dancers on the show were mostly white kids, but she was not shunned as she might have been in an earlier decade. By 1965, according to Seymour, the show consisted of about 60 to 70 percent Black teenagers.[91]

Tipton Russell, with her twin brother Lester, became known as Lester and Leslie, a coveted dance team on *Swingin' Time*. Reminiscing about her time on the show, Tipton Russell remarked, "Yeah we'd get out of school—I got out at like 2:40, he [Lester] got out about 2:40 and we would get right on the Woodward bus and go to Canada."[92] Although they had no prior dance training or background, Lester and Leslie improvised and created many dances on the show, which the other teenagers would try to copy. Said

Seymour, "They'd make up their own routines, their own dances, and their own ideas." According to fellow *Swingin' Time* dancer Lana Drouillard, a regular on the show, Tipton Russell was particularly graceful and was always impeccably dressed (she and her brother would coordinate their outfits). "And you know, whatever was going to be in style, they would have it before anybody else. They were the best dancers you could ever watch. They sort of led the way."[93] Seymour, in fact, began to feature the team on his *Swingin' Time Review*. Their big "break" of sorts occurred in 1966 when Dick Clark apparently called Seymour to ask if he could recommend some dancers for a nationwide concert hosted by *American Bandstand*.[94] Seymour volunteered Lester and Leslie who won the contest; they got flown to California and received two Pontiac automobiles. While she loved the dancing, Tipton Russell also loved the camaraderie and the recognition. When she spoke of all the people and performers she met, who were so kind to her, she remarked: "Oh, Dennis Edwards of The Temptations, Smokey Robinson, Florence Ballard of the Supremes—she used to call me her baby sister. They would just come over to us." After *Swingin' Time*, she and Lester went their separate ways; she started getting acting works in movies and commercials and stand-in work for, among others, Diahann Carroll, Leslie Uggams, and Whitney Houston.[95]

Flirting with the Forbidden/White Girls and Navigating Black Culture

The gravitation of white teenagers to Black expressive culture was, in part, as I have discussed, a protest against the outmoded and repressive values of their parents and the hypocrisies of the era. In the Beat culture, most notably, that collective of white, mostly working-class male bohemians, Black culture served as an outlet for their own sense of alienation and frustration from mainstream culture and the American Dream. It was in many ways, though, a distorted, romanticized view of Black culture that, as Toni Morrison has explained in discussing white writers' used of Black characters, satisfied more their own unserved longings and desires, than was an authentic attempt to understand or inhabit Black culture.[96] Many young, white girls were attracted to the Beats, although their well-documented chauvinism kept the girls from fully embracing this world. As Wini Breines writes, citing cultural theorist Kobena Mercer, their "collective disaffiliation" with American culture, their estrangement from it, was "apparent in the countercultural influences such as R&B, rock 'n' roll, working-class styles and behavior, the Beats, and unacceptable boyfriends, all of which were employed to subvert dominant notions of white femininity."[97] While young girls, too, may have looked to Black expressive culture, as a "salve" for their own sense of alienation, their rebellion, in their gravitation to rock 'n' roll music and dance, was aimed precisely at those racial and sexual strictures that were so inextricably linked. For young girls there was always a particular type of danger involved in their rebellion—that because they were watching, enjoying, and expressing emotions for Black men (i.e., Black musicians or Black social dancers), they were "crossing the color line"[98] and that might spell their downfall were they to go one step further to date a Black man. In the girls' case, it could be argued that, in their attraction to Black music, their expressive dancing, and, in some cases, their Black boyfriends, they were recouping what was lost to them and/or rebelling against the nationwide backlash against minorities and empathizing with anyone deemed "other."[99] In such a refusal, they sought to affirm their own identity. The girls' rebellion wasn't solely about employing Black culture to accrue cultural capital, in sociologist Eric Lott's formulation, or to "try on the accents of Blackness" to become hip.[100] They were grappling for a language with which to self-identify.

An interesting case in point was "jitterbug" Peg Desonier, for whom the attraction to Black music and dance was not some "mystical" sense of Black culture, but a recognition of another way of life. A resident of the Old Greenpoint section of Washington, DC, for low-income whites, where houses were built especially for returning GIs, she was a frequent viewer of the all-Black teen dance program *Teenarama*. Desonier spoke passionately of her love for R&B music. She was especially drawn to singers such as Frankie Lymon, Etta James, the Platters, and the girl groups, especially the Shirelles. Although Desonier socialized primarily in white environments, in school and in her neighborhood (Greenpoint was segregated), she nonetheless experienced a strong affinity with Black culture spurred by her proficiency in hand dance—a smooth, synchronized style of dance with slides and intricate footwork known to various communities in DC.[101]

In part, Desonier's love of R&B was nurtured by her brother who used to listen to Ray Charles: "I went to parochial school; I would pretend I was sick, and I would stay home and dance—put his records on and dance for seven hours straight."[102] At that point, she was only about seven or eight years old. "You know what it shows me? That if . . . you know how people always try and make the distinction between people with rhythm and people without rhythm? If syncopated music is part of your upbringing, and I think I made it part of mine, you will have rhythm." Desonier also practiced her dancing in the aisles of the famed Howard Theatre in DC—a stop on the Chitlin Circuit for musicians from Lionel Hampton to Aretha Franklin and others:

> I loved The Shirelles. I loved Martha Reeves. I used to sneak in to the Howard Theatre with a girlfriend. We were the two only white people there with the gay guys in their gold lamé fishnet dresses. Oh it was wonderful. We used to throw tomatoes at Flip Wilson, because he was so bad. Oh yeah.[103]

Primarily as a result of her dancing skill and concentrated efforts to learn to dance from her Black counterparts, she came to the attention of some older Black dancers and became a sought-after partner. It was her association with the so-called block boys deemed cool and hip, mostly young Black male dancers (some were white as in Berwyn, Maryland, near Greenbelt) who wore Peter's jackets, knit shirts with suede strips, and wing-tipped shoes, that took her to dance in bars and beer gardens, and it was then that Desonier remarked, she "started living a double life." Her parents had no idea of her whereabouts. The dancing for Desonier was transformative. A self-described "stick figure," who says that she "did not look like Annette Funicello" (nor did she want to), she felt in some ways out of tune with the traditionally revered "fifties" woman. It was the dancing that for Desonier transported her; in the same sentence that she expressed her love for singers such as Clyde McPhatter, Jackie Wilson, and the Drifters, she remarked "What R&B did for me was give me the hope of love."

Desonier was an avid viewer of televised teen shows and drawn, in particular, to *Teenarama* and the "Blacks-only" day of *The Buddy Deane Show*—"I knew if I were to go on TV, that would be the day I should go, you know, because I just didn't dance like the white guys." She also knew that her parents most likely wouldn't let her and that the show's producers would have prevented any interracial dancing.[104] When asked if the dancing on the mostly white *Milt Grant Show* differed from *Teenarama*, she answered: "absolutely." According to Desonier, in dances such as the Mashed Potato, the Twist, and the Shake-a-Tail Feather, the white dancers were stiffer and flatter; as far as the hand dancing, "The turns weren't there, and the dancers had a rough hand." Her male Black partners constituted essential relationships that that led to her ultimate radicalization.[105] Like famed musician Johnny Otis, who decided to live as an African American and who saw himself as "Black by persuasion," Desonier also joined a Black community and had Black friends. Her first husband was also Black ("We got married when it was still a felony in 17 states").[106] In her case, her pleasure in "dancing Black," her "investiture in Black bodies," to borrow from Eric Lott, was more than a dabbling in the culture of the "other" in the name of resistance, rather than an attempt to live her life truthfully (and with agency) according to her values and inclinations.

Professional "rock 'n' roller," Kay Wheeler was another young woman whose coming of age was transformed by R&B. Although she wasn't a teen dancer on televised teen dance shows, she did appear on them, in Texas, as a performer. Today Wheeler is known for her work in two of the earliest "teen exploitation" movies of the fifties—*Rock Baby Rock It* (1957) and *Hot Rod Gangs* (1958).[107] She was actually "discovered" at the Majestic Theatre, in Dallas, in March 1956 while dancing in the aisles at a concert of the local rockabilly singer Johnny Carroll, which marked the movie screening of *Rock Around the Clock*. A producer, whom she described as a "beatnik type of guy in his thirties," explained that they were making a local teen dance movie in Dallas and asked if she would perform in it. Two to three weeks later, her mother saw an advertisement for the movie in a local newspaper and encouraged her daughter to contact them.[108]

Wheeler's other celebrity occurred as a result of becoming the founder of the first international Elvis Presley Fan Club; she met him several times in this capacity. Wheeler has described a childhood infused with the sounds of R&B. She has described being "obsessed" with the music: "When I heard the first R&B song by the Clovers or Hank Ballard and the Midnighters, I immediately loved them. Whoever's doing this—I loved it. They're my kind of people."[109] Growing up, Wheeler dared to transgress, although she wanted to be both the "good girl" and the "bad girl." Even though she was well aware of the "rules" for young girls and women at the time—of what she could and could not do—she was idealistic. As Wheeler remarked of her adolescence and young adulthood, "I wanted to have fun and still take the high road."[110] Born and raised in Dallas, she rejected the music of her parents (e.g., Perry Como, the Andrews Sisters) and found in Elvis Presley and rock 'n' roll generally "a departure from the squares."[111] Wheeler became part of what she called the "underground youth following of Black R&B and rock 'n' roll music. We would smuggle home the 78 records of the Black artists and dance like crazy."[112] Wheeler remembers hearing a "pulsating, magical voice belting out 'Mystery Train.' We shrieked and turned the volume up!"[113]

The boys, though, were initially jealous of Elvis; the resentment toward him, in fact, could get violent. "At school, I was forcibly grabbed and had my two treasured, autobiographical photos of Elvis ripped up!"[114]

Many reasons account for Presley's huge success, and reams have been written about his perceived transgressive status, his appropriation of Black R&B, and his traversing of gender binaries, arguments that I won't take on here. For many observers of the time, of course, Presley was the apotheosis of rock 'n' roll—the "working-class tough," the outsider, the boy who young girls would be afraid to take home to their mothers. For many in the adult world, Black and white, young girls' frenzied response to Presley—their sexual desire exposed—was enough to arouse their consternation. But it was also his closeness to Black culture, his representation of R&B, that suggested "a kind of racial mixing," as Susan Cahn writes, that terrified white, middle-class observers, particularly those in the South.[115] Girls' attraction to Presley was, in part, because he represented and embodied Black style, and in that sense could be considered appropriative—that they were exoticizing Black culture in part to lay claim to their sense of alienation. But it was also more than that, I think.

When asked about her own and her friends' attraction to Presley, though, Wheeler emphasized that it was less a matter of his sex appeal (although there *was* that, of course) than about rebellion. "We didn't want to live like our parents."[116] And part of not living like their parents was to reject the kinds of racist and sexist attacks leveled at Presley and his Black-derived music.[117] Many Southern white girls, in particular, roundly rejected the idea that they were responsible for upholding Southern womanhood and needed protection from the supposed avaricious sexuality represented by Elvis Presley and Black R&B performers; part of their rebellion, true for all teenagers, was to embrace the very things that their society condemned. But for young girls, like Peg Desonier and Kay Wheeler (who never traveled to her various engagements without her mother), there was a tug-of-war between being a "good girl" and protesting existing sexualized and racialized codes of morality. And intertwined within their rebellion was an authentic love for the music and the dance and a recognition of its roots. Although she believes that Presley was a singular talent, Wheeler has remarked that "I'm not sure that Elvis would ever be Elvis if it wasn't for Black R&B and Black rock 'n' roll. Let's talk about it. When rock 'n' roll hit, it didn't matter who was doing it. We just got on the mystery train and some of us never got off."[118]

Perhaps the greatest homage that Wheeler paid to Elvis Presley was in her own expressive movement style, which, curiously, strongly resembled his. In *Rock Baby Rock It*, Wheeler, cast as seventeen-year-old rock 'n' roll dancer "Kay Lee," says the producers "let her go wild" and perform her "Rock'n' Bop." The number, based on a rock 'n' roll dance local to Dallas in the mid-1950s, was, in her words, "a smooth, full-body, free-styled dance, 100 percent based on R&B music."[119] She remarked that the most important aspect of it was to "get the music, get the beat, and let yourself go."[120] In the film, dancing to John Carroll's "Sugar Baby,"[121] Wheeler is barefoot and clad in Black trousers and a Black off-the-shoulder top and moves in a sultry fashion. As she faces the camera, she moves her arms akimbo in time with synchronized leg movements and a jutting out at the hips similar to an oft-seen frontal image of Presley with hips thrust outward and legs bent.[122] Unbridled and abandoned, her bare feet pound and grind the floor as she circles around the small dance space. It's interesting, too, that her number was performed against band members ("The Cell Block Seven") decked out in convict suits, seemingly in anticipation of Presley's 1957 *Jailhouse Rock*.[123] Like many other girls of her era, Wheeler married young—at eighteen years-of age—but divorced soon thereafter. After leaving her life in Hollywood, she attended Southern Methodist University in Dallas where she majored in English and then studied for a while at law school. She now makes her living as a writer.

The contradictions of the era manifested in young girls' differing responses to rock 'n' roll music and dance. For some girls, R&B and rock 'n' roll changed them forever—it altered their outlook and worldview. Others, who were a part of teen culture, and who attended concerts or teen dance shows, were attracted more to the affects of rock 'n' roll and to its lighter, more frivolous sides (the more mainstream, less disruptive music that according to Nelson George "made the young white consumers of Cold War America feel more comfortable").[124] For many young people, as Wini Breines explains, rock 'n' roll "provided a version of rebellion without requiring one to be a rebel."[125]

Some were rebels, some were not. However, for most young girls, rebellious or not, their coming of age and their sexual identity occurred at the nexus point of rock 'n' roll music and dance. It was here that they had to negotiate the bounds of respectability with their sexual desires and face the contradictions for women of their era. Although young Black girls and young white girls were equally affected by teen culture, and the structures and strictures of acceptable femininity, the "proper performance of gender and femininity," as Shayla Thiel-Stern writes, "was all the more crucial for teen girls of color in segregated midcentury America."[126] Black girls were no less affected by R&B and rock 'n' roll, but there was simply more at stake for young Black girls who had to uphold both sexual as well as racial codes of propriety, and, as Thiel-Stern surmises, it may be because of this that "Black girls were so often left out of the conversation about the advent of rock and roll in the 1950s."[127] As Mary Wilson, of the Supremes, has remarked about her coming of age in the 1950s, "We dared to dream when it was not a very good time for Blacks to dream."[128]

Both Black and white girls of the era, though, unlike their male counterparts, had to battle a double standard, Despite the cultural sexual prohibitions maintaining that girls not "go too far," on the one hand, and the exhortations from the media and advertising to display one's sexuality, on the other, girls seemed to find in rock 'n' roll music and dance a means of navigating these adolescent hurdles through the nature of the dances themselves—the freedom to change partners, and the ability to devise dances and dance steps in an equality with their male peers. But what often goes unsaid as part of that enjoyment was the pure pleasure derived from the mastery of the dance and the recognition of that dance by such a mass audience. The dancing was in its own way an artistic process of invention, of discovery of one's own potential, and joy in the expressive use of the body. This is what social dance can accomplish, and for women of this era, that was powerful.

6

Storming the Sixties

From Teen Dances to *Shindig!*

The early to mid-1960s saw a multitude of events that galvanized the eventual enactment of the 1964 Civil Rights Act, banning discrimination based on race in jobs, education, and public accommodations, and the 1965 Voting Rights Act.[1] Beginning with civil disobedience protests at city lunch counters, as at the Woolworth's store lunch counter and segregated schools; the Freedom Summers; the March on Washington for Jobs and Freedom, led by Martin Luther King Jr.; and "Bloody Sunday," when civil rights workers in Selma, Alabama, marched from Selma to Montgomery in support of voting rights were attacked on the Edmund Pettus Bridge; the country seemed at a breaking point. Three assassinations, too, occurred within the span of three years—those of John F. Kennedy, Medgar Evers, and Malcolm X. And, too, with the civil rights movement came protests born of the counterculture movement, of primarily white, college-age students, who, inspired by civil rights activists, were reacting against the hypocrisy and in equities of social and political institutions (from schools to the military). Theirs was a call to new forms of participatory democracy that, as historian Eric Foner has written, "announced a new conception of politics, whose function would be to bring Americans 'out of isolation and into community.' "[2] By 1965, this activism would also take the form of major protests against the country's involvement in the Vietnam War.

While the primary emphasis in this book has been on those televised teen dance programs that originated and flourished in the 1950s, the early 1960s, too, formed a vital era for the shows even though many of them began to take shape differently; this was a result of changes in musical styles, advances in television, and a changed cultural and political climate. There is no question that the 1960s ushered in both political and cultural changes that would come to define that decade. As I have argued throughout this book, despite the easy façade of the 1950s as a decade of acquiescence, and the belief that it represented the calm before the storm of the 1960s, there was in fact serious

Dancing Black, Dancing White. Julie Malnig, Oxford University Press. © Oxford University Press 2023.
DOI: 10.1093/oso/9780197536254.003.0007

and significant unrest and disequilibrium. Rock 'n' roll music represented, for many youth, particularly white youth, a break from the monotony and tedium of suburban life and middle-class mores and a defiant staking out of a world of their own. For much of white youth it was, as historians Maurice Isserman and Michael Kazin write, "a more extravagant style of alienation" in which "they sought refuge among and enlightenment from America's most dispossessed and despised groups-tramps, migrant laborers, black criminals as well as jazz musicians"[3] epitomized by Mailer's "white negro." But that rebelliousness didn't coalesce into a movement. By the 1960s, though, with segregation still a firmly entrenched way of life, mass protests, nationwide sit-ins, the freedom rides, other direct-action challenges, and several well-organized civil rights organizations including SNCC, SNCC, and CORE, as Foner has said, "announced that young people were now the vanguard of social change."[4]

Like the country as a whole, television was painfully slow—even in light of these major national events—to incorporate Black individuals in significant ways, both behind and in front of the camera. The changes were gradual and incremental.[5] "Televisual segregation," though, was increasingly untenable in light of TV's broadcasting of unpalatable scenes of churches being bombed and protestors getting hosed down. If anything, television hastened sympathy toward integration and the aims of the civil rights movement. For a teen dance show to survive, now, it had to adapt to new musical tastes and styles, advanced television technology, and, most important, changes wrought by the civil rights movement. But in 1964 and 1965, most teen shows were not segregated. It's fair to say that many of the existing shows that were previously segregated, as well as newly created shows, now allowed Black teenagers as studio audience members and dancers. This hardly meant that there was equal representation among Black and white teenagers; Black teenagers, though, were not officially (or "unofficially") excluded. Of course, one reason that greater numbers of Black teenagers were not seen on the shows had to do with the matter of self-selection; shows known as being primarily "white" were simply not as appealing, particularly if they had a history of segregating the teen dancers. Some Black teenagers, of course, had their own reasons for participating on the shows, or watching them, even if outnumbered by white dancers, such as getting to listen or dance to their favorite bands or singers. They might "jettison" those aspects of the shows that were unacceptable in order to partake of a part of that experience that served their own needs. Former civil rights activist and politician Julian Bond recalls how he gravitated to *American Bandstand* as "a rural, small-town kid." The white teenagers were actually his role models until things changed when, through television and the Black press, he got to know "the nine brave young people of Little Rock's Central High School—the Little Rock Nine" who replaced his "former idols": "They possessed something the *Bandstand* dancers did not—grace and courage under great pressure."[6]

As is true for most historical periods, decades don't always follow a strict chronological timeline; much of what we think of as "the 1950s," particularly social values and mores, bled into the early 1960s. For the purposes of this study, on the vicissitudes of the televised teen dance program, the years 1964 and 1965 signify an important dividing point, after which the televised teen dance shows would not have their same cultural impact. Until that point, though, they continued, but with a slightly different look and style from their 1950s counterparts. These changes were marked by an influx of new musical styles including the Beatles, the Rolling Stones (and the many other British male groups that comprise the so-called British Invasion), Motown (Berry Gordy's hugely successful crossover Black pop sound), the protest songs of the American folk music scene, and the rise of soul and funk music, epitomized by James Brown, that carried the message of the growing Black Power movement. It was a time when rock 'n' roll begins to morph into "rock": the rock album as opposed to the single record takes precedence, and new forms of creative expression include greater amplification in the form of the electric guitar and bass and instrumentation. Musicians are now creating songs not only for dancing, but, for their political messages as well as their musicality and sonic experimentations (such as the Beach Boys).

The Beatles arrival on American shores February 9, 1964, by way of *The Ed Sullivan Show*, was particularly dramatic and influential, and while the story of their ascent to fame has been told many times over, a few points are worth mentioning when considering the fate of the teen dance programs and their accommodation to changing musical styles. Musicologist Elijah Wald explains the Beatles' sudden rise to stardom in part because of their ability to synthesize many of the musical trends of the previous years "wrapped in a particularly attractive package."[7] Specifically, he notes that " 'I Want to Hold Your Hand,' their first hit in the United States, had the hand-claps of the girl groups, melodic sophistication, a rhythm perfectly suited to the new dances, and the loose energy of the surf bands."[8] According to Reebee Garofalo, the group helped invigorate a lagging music industry; that while record sales decreased by about 5 percent in 1960, after 1964, "the industry had double-digit growth every year until the end of the decade."[9] No doubt these numbers soared, too, as a result, of the many other British bands that appeared on the scene and filled concert stages.

Another trend of the period was the growing split between music for dancing and music for listening, which would reach its peak by the late 1960s when, as Wald points out, "Psychedelic dance halls, begun in San Francisco two years ago, and now rolling in other cities, have developed into a new form of concert hall where . . . young people are not dancing, just digging."[10] In the *early* 1960s, though, one could still easily see couples dancing variations on the Lindy; swing-styled couple dances had not yet completely died out (particularly on the local shows). What was emerging were the new solo-oriented dances such as the Twist and others (described in Chapter 4) that ushered in a revised idea of the "dance couple." We see social dancers, now, dancing less in strict partner formations and more focused on themselves in relation to a large crowd of dancers.[11]

Teen Dance Programs of the Early to Mid-1960s

Essentially, the local teen dance programs the 1960s were of three types: those that began in the late 1950s, and for a variety of reasons, including loss of station support and revenue, and most often as a result of segregationist policies, ended in the early 1960s, such as *The Buddy Deane Show* (discussed in Chapter 2).The second group was other regional shows that began in the late 1950s but *did* integrate in the early 1960s and revised their formats to accommodate changes in popular music and new televisual techniques. A final group of shows were those that arose in the mid-1960s in part as a result of the influx of the British bands, the rise of Motown, and the incredible and fast-paced crop of new solo-oriented dances that swept the country. According to TV director and producer Bud Buschardt, "One of the reasons bandstands survived the early years [of the 1960s] was the creative dances that stormed through the studios. The Stroll, Twist, Monkey, Watusi, Hand Jive, Mashed Potatoes, Jerk, Shimmy, Freeze, and the Madison were just a few from the 'The Land of 1000 Dances.'"[12]

Two important and revelatory music and dance concerts and telecasts, in 1964 and 1965, brought together some of the best and most exciting of British and American R&B and rock 'n' roll performers, which had a tremendous influence on televised popular dance. These were the T.A.M.I (Teenage Awards

Music International) Concert and The Big T.N.T. Show, significant primarily because of the TV techniques introduced, the dancing (by professionals),
and the overall sense of inclusiveness of Black and white performers that the
shows attempted to foster. At the T.A.M.I. Concert, Berry Gordy's Motown
artists vied with music mogul David Epstein's British bands. The concert featured The Rolling Stones, Gary and the Pacemakers, Marvin Gaye (and his
backup group The Blossoms featuring Fanita James, Jean King, and Darlene
Love), the Supremes, and Smokey Robinson and the Miracles. Others included The Beach Boys, Chuck Berry, Lesley Gore, and James Brown and the
Flames. Brown's (and the Flames') spectacular dancing in many ways pushed
the bar for more highly polished versions of contemporary social dances that
would begin to make their way onto television.[13]

Directed by major music concert director Steve Binder and produced by
Bill Sargent, the T.A.M.I. concert was notable for several reasons. It was one of
the first experiments with telecasts of large, live music concerts and employed
techniques that expanded the possibilities of what television might do for
dance. The concert itself took place on October 28 and 29, 1964, at the Santa
Monica Civic Auditorium and was filmed with the intention of projecting it
onto large movie screens aided by what was called Electronovision, which
provided enhanced resolution to allow for big-screen enlargement. Binder,
in an interview for the Television Academy Foundation, explained how although the show was shot with only four cameras, the combination of the
master camera, two close-up cameras, along with a handheld reverse camera
had the ability to provide "some of the most dramatic shots ever." The reverse
camera enabled shots from the stage itself looking out, "so when Mick Jagger,
for instance, sang, or James Brown, I could literally have the cameraman walk
out on the stage with them." There was minimal editing, and as Binder said,
"What you saw on the screen is what I shot."[14] The drama of the T.A.M.I concert, too, was in the dancing, which took several forms—individual female
dancers (or go-go dancers), a troupe of trained "jazz" dancers,[15] and the
dancing and dance steps and gesture of the musicians and singers and their
backup groups. The effect of the close-up, "you are there" filming, along with
the steady rock 'n' roll and R&B beats, and continuous movement, was a tour
de force.

In multiple interviews, Steve Binder has laid claim to developing the idea
of the iconic go-go dancer and "stealing" the concept from famed Whisky
A Go-Go nightclub, the popular Sunset Strip club in West Hollywood that
originated the concept of featuring a single dancer, wearing a fringed dress

and white boots, in a cage (actually a glass-walled booth) mounted above the floor.[16] The T.A.M.I. concert was choreographed by one of the most sought-after choreographers of the time, David Winters, who had created dance roles in both the stage and film musical versions of *West Side Story*. The now legendary West Coast choreographer and former dancer Toni Basil was the assistant choreographer.[17] Basil explains that there were essentially three levels of dancing on the T.A.M.I. show. One was the chorus of trained jazz dancers who could cross over to "go-go party dance." The second were "legit-imately deadly funky go-go dancers" who were pulled from local LA dance clubs, the Whiskey A Go-Go among them, and possessed a certain "swing and street funk." These dancers performed steps from the popular social dances of the day such as the Pony, the Jerk, the Mashed Potato, the Monkey, and the Watusi. The third type of movement exhibited on the show was that of the singers, many from Detroit, who according to Basil "had that high-class sophisticated funk never-break-a-sweat" demeanor.[18] The effect was one of continuous motion and dynamism—the go-go dancers suspended in the air, the jazz dancers running up to and dancing on three different levels of an industrial-looking steel structure, and the motion and dancing of the musicians and performers.

Arguably, though, the highlight of the dancing was that of James Brown, the penultimate act, just before The Rolling Stones, singing "Please, Please, Please" and performing what would become his iconic "cape man" routine, the apotheosis of rock 'n' roll energy, grit, and sweat. At the core of Brown's and his Famous Flames' mesmerizing, highly theatrical performance were recognizable social dance steps and gestures popular in the early 1960s. The Flames performed what Basil said was "something they called 18th-note steps" in which they tried to dance every note in the bar. Basil con-tinued: "They rehearsed constantly. They were doing the Skate, the Monkey, and the Popcorn, and the Mashed Potatoes. They would quadruple the count and do it then in repetition. And they never, ever stopped looking at James who would start and stop the band at will." As for Brown, "He took half a Monkey, half a Mashed Potatoes, half a Popcorn, and wove it into one dance style that he made his own." Of course, Brown added his signature splits, spins, and slides. Of his performance on the T.A.M.I. show Basil has said: "It was the Baptist Church goes to classical theater all rolled all into one."[19]

While it was not the stated goal of the T.A.M.I show producers, by any means, the concert had about it a certain egalitarian feel characteristic of the 1960s. The T.A.M.I. show modeled the idealistic sense of community, an almost communal sphere on the stage to rival what many protesters hoped would become a more harmonious public sphere or civil society.

A major innovation of the show was to have the dancers perform in the same space as the singers and instrumentalists in a very nonhierarchical fashion, as if to suggest that the dancers (whom teenage audience members could project themselves onto) were a direct part of the event. And the space was shared by both Black and white dancers and performers—a sight one would have been hard-pressed to see on mid-1950s TV. The conclusion of the T.A.M.I. concert, where Black and white dancers, musicians, house band members, and stars moved to the music *en masse*, director Steve Binder called "the great final scene" that communicated to viewers that "everybody was there; everybody participated."[20] That moment did not last, though, it seemed. As well-intentioned as the directors and producers may have been, change was hard-won. Another Binder production, the TV special *Petula*, which was to air in 1967, had a less benign outcome. British pop singer Petula Clark, who had introduced the hit "Downtown" on *Hullabaloo*, in 1964 sang her antiwar song "Paths of Glory" with Harry Belafonte, whom Binder had recruited to perform with her. During the number, at one emotional point in the song, Clark reached out her arm to touch Belafonte's forearm. The act, as Binder later recollected, created "an international incident picked by *Newsweek*, *Time* magazine. It was the first time a Black and a white had openly touched in primetime television."[21] The show ultimately aired, but the repercussions rippled around the world.

Shindig! and *Hullabaloo*

This rebirth of teen dance shows in the mid-1960s also owed much to two highly popular national youth-oriented television shows—*Shindig!*, which aired from 1964 to 1966, and *Hullabaloo*, which lasted from 1965 to 1966. *Shindig!* and *Hullabaloo* were essentially rock 'n' roll music and dance variety shows, not teen dance shows as such. The shows featured professional dancers and theatricalized versions of social dancers, although *Shindig!*'s focus, in particular, on the crowd's excited responses "made TV viewers feel like they were part of the action."[22] A twice-weekly half-hour show, which aired on primetime ABC, *Shindig!* was the brainchild of British producer Jack Good, whose rock 'n' roll show *Oh, Boy!*, produced by England's commercial TV network ITV in the late 1950s, brought a new, accelerated feel to rock 'n' roll television. The British had not only influenced new musical styles in the United States but rock 'n' roll television, as well. As media theorist Simon Frith explains of *Shindig!*, "Editing was tight to the music (the rhythm of shots determined by the rhythm of the song)" and "The pace was fast (no breaks between numbers) and the message seemed to be that what you see is what there is."[23] It was a style in some ways similar to Steve Binder's T.A.M.I. show that ushered in the idea of "the live version of the TV version of a live show."[24]

Shindig!, which opened on the ABC network on September 16, 1964, simply exuded movement. The early pilots were directed by Rita Gillespie, one of the earliest women to direct live television, and who had worked with Good on *Oh, Boy!* She became known for her lightning-quick directorial approach, which included aerial shots, tight close-ups, and edits that occurred on the beat of the music.[25] Her editing, which cut from musicians to dancers to backup singers to excited youthful audience members, was an attempt to create a total stage picture—movement, lighting, stage design—that matched the effervescence of the music. The show, hosted by LA-based deejay Jimmy O'Neill, featured the choreography of David Winters who, with assistant choreographer Toni Basil, carried through on Good's kinetic, non-stop dance style.

The Shindig Dancers, consisting of ten professional white female dancers, performed routines of the latest popular social dances and accompanied songs developed especially for the continuous crop of new dances from the Shimmy to the Watusi to the Twine. According to original *Shindig!* dancer Anita Mann, who had danced under Winters's tutelage, "It was go-go dancing, but we also had to learn routines. We all had to be together whether it was the Wobble, the Pony, the Zonk, the Jerk, the Monkey, the Philly Dog. We knew every step of those dances."[26] The dancers often performed lead-ins or backup support for the starring acts and typically closed the show with the final act on the bill along with the house band.[27] The choreographic technique of having dancers perform on elevated platforms and dance up and down ramps while the main acts performed enhanced the show's sense of continuous movement. Often, the dancers improvised and originated some of their own dances and steps. According to another former *Shindig!* dancer, Maria Ghava Henley,

There was a constant new generation of movement all the time. Sometimes we'd have to run down the ramp and do the Pony endless endless times.

You'd just Pony yourself to death. And then you'd get up there and you'd go into a pirouette and you'd have to do a turn on the spot. And a couple of times we'd lose a girl. She'd just fall right off the back ramp there.[28]

In a similar vein was *Hullabaloo*, an hourlong variety-cum-youth dance show, which aired on NBC in 1965 and ran until 1966, also on primetime, and directed by T.A.M.I. filmmaker Steve Binder.[29] As Binder explains, he was approached by NBC to create an opposing show to *Shindig!* and brought in David Winters (who had left *Shindig!* after a few episodes). According to Binder, when he took over the show it featured a New York City high school marching band and stand-up comedy routines. Eager to shake things up, one of Binder's several innovations was to feature the iconic go-go dancers at the spirited conclusion of the show (the "Hullabaloo A Go-Go" segment) who danced variations on the popular social dances of the day. Unlike *Shindig!*, *Hullabaloo* alternated hosts with famous names like George Hamilton, Sammy Davis Jr., Liza Minnelli, and Dionne Warwick, which was no doubt an attempt to appeal to a slightly older demographic.[30] *Hullabaloo* was for the most part much more slickly produced, with a nod toward Broadway musical stars and shows.[31] Most of the *Hullabaloo* dancers were ballet and modern dance trained, and the choreography of David Winters was stylish and sophisticated. As Toni Basil explains of Winters's choreography, "His jazz dancing [on *Hullabaloo*], you know, came from *West Side Story*. There were some of the greatest dancers of that time period."[32]

The go-go dancers, which to our eyes today may seem like a curious relic of a pre-feminist era, were either trained, professional dancers or talented, polished social dancers who had burnished their skills via months, if not years, of club dancing. All of them underwent auditions.[33] And it is actually in their dancing and dance routines that studio and home audiences could watch and learn the major solo-oriented social dances of the early 1960s. Unusual for the time, and groundbreaking for primetime television, were the two Black go-go dancers on the T.A.M.I. show concert, Essie Randall and Debbie Butler. A testament to the relationship that Berry Gordy hoped to establish with the variety shows supporting Motown dancers were the national *Hullabaloo* tours. During the summer of 1965, Black dancer Karen Hubbard recalls performing as a *Hullabaloo* dancer on The Motown State Fair tour with the French-Canadian singer Tony Roman (Figure 6.1). The dancers performed backup routines to musical acts at state fairs in Detroit, Columbus, Minneapolis, and other cities. As Hubbard remarked, "They

Figure 6.1 The NBC *Hullabaloo* Dancers on The Motown State Fair Tour with Canadian singer Tony Roman, ca. 1965. The second dancer from the left is former dancer Karen Hubbard. Photograph by James J. Kriegsmann. Courtesy of Karen W. Hubbard.

were obviously looking for a Black girl to go on tour."[34] Hubbard remembers dancing, in a short skirt and short white boots, to Chris Kenner's hit "Land of a Thousand Dances" (popularized by Wilson Pickett) performing renditions of the Jerk, Mashed Potato, the Swim, and the Monkey.

Many observers as well as historians felt that *Shindig!*, *Hullabaloo*, and other shows of its kind that featured Black musicians, singers, and performers were breaking down racial barriers and were a sign of the times. Popular performance writer Norma Coates, writing about *Shindig!*, notes that "Good's emphasis on the overall look of the sound, and the sound of the look, mitigated all other potential hierarchies, especially those constructed by race, gender, and region."[35] Producer/director Steve Binder's comment that *Shindig!* was an "entourage or family" (of dancers and singers moving to continuous, non-stop music) might explain how the show tried to foster a sense of interracial community and camaraderie. Of course, though, these kinds of statements were also made about the teen dance shows of the 1950s where Black performers and entertainers were regularly featured, and as discussed earlier, this fact alone hardly meant that the shows were integrated. The difference was that Black performers, white musicians, and Black and white dancers were now actually shown sharing the same physical space, where bodies might touch and brush up against one another. The fact, too, that the shows were aired on primetime was significant, as it meant that many more white audience members were witness to these interactions. But, of course, it was the changing political climate and expanding civil rights actions across the country that eased some of the former intransigence and racism of television network executives and producers to enable this to occur at all.

The Influence of the Variety Shows on Local Teen Shows

Even though teenage dancers were not present as participants on the variety dance shows, they were watching, and the dancers, particularly the go-go dancers, *suggested* a relationship between what professional dancers were doing and what "ordinary" dancers might be able to do. They became stand-ins for the aspirations of the youth audience (and perhaps adults, too) who might look up to and emulate the dancers similar to the way filmgoers looked up to the ballroom dancing of Fred Astaire and Ginger Rogers in the 1940s and took from them vicarious kinesthetic pleasure. This was a very different experience from the home-grown look and feel of the teen dance shows of the 1950s, which gave us a view of teenagers being themselves. By the 1960s, television's increasingly sophisticated technology allowed for far more dynamic and fluid action shots than was possible in the 1950s, which, in turn, enabled greater theatricalization of 1960s social dance styles. In a nod toward the 1950s teen dance shows, and as a way to conjoin TV viewers with the on-stage dancing, the cameras on both *Shindig!* and *Hullabaloo* often focused on riled-up studio audience members who are often seen dancing in the aisles.[36]

The influence of the rock 'n' roll dance-variety shows on the local, TV dance programs, and bandstand shows was great. To the extent that these national shows had "Hollywood-ized" the concept of teen dance show, the local shows around the country, as influenced as they were by the variety shows, kept intact the concept of a community-based show that spotlighted local versions of some of the most popular, contemporary social dances. Several of these local shows were syndicated, which meant that local and regional styles reached television markets around the country. In Los Angeles, in the mold of *Shindig!* and *Hullabaloo*, was *Shivaree*, along with those more like a typical bandstand show including *Shebang* and *The Lloyd Thaxton Show* (also syndicated). In other parts of the country and Canada were *The Clay Cole Show* (New York City), *Swingin' Time* (Detroit), *Upbeat* (Cleveland), *Red, Hot, and Blues* (Chicago), *Kilgo's Canteen* (Charlotte, North Carolina), *The Larry Kane Show* (Houston), and *Uptight* (Kingston, Ontario). The few that I will focus on here, though, are interesting and important because they illustrate vividly how local bandstand shows adapted to TV's increasing technological capacities, dealt with the incursion of the popular youth-dance variety shows, or responded to the increasing popularity of Black pop and soul music and the greater exposure of Black styles of expressive culture that were becoming a part of mainstream TV. With the advent of nationally aired and syndicated shows, such as *Shindig! and Hullabaloo*, the local shows became even *more* important as they fulfilled a function that the national shows could *not*—they bound teenage communities together in their shared appreciation and creation of local dance styles.

American Bandstand, it should be pointed out, had by 1964 moved its operation to Southern California (specifically ABC's Television Center in Los Angeles, the new mecca for televised dance shows). The show now aired only once a week, on Saturday afternoons, and even though it featured local, amateur California dancers, it had lost its former "community" sensibility, and many of the young people on the show viewed it only as a steppingstone to a possible professional career, hoping to be spotted by an eager TV promoter or producer.[37] But feeling pressure from the youth-oriented dance-variety shows, Dick Clark came up with his own spin on the genre called *Where the Action Is*, which debuted in June 1965. The show was a curious mix of dancing, only by professionals, musical groups (Paul Revere and the Raiders were the "house" group), shot strictly in outdoor scenes including Monterey beaches and Northern California mountain ranges. The dancers, known as The Action Kids, coached by former *West Side Story* dancer Peter Menefee, performed alongside the musicians as they lip-synced their latest hits.[38] The singers and musicians were also surrounded by what TV dance-show chronicler Jake Austen calls "faux-swooning, faux-grooving, carefully positioned extras."[39] *Where the Action Is* continued for two years, while *American Bandstand*, even as it lost some its previous luster, continued (until 1989).

Although it only lasted for fifty-two weeks, *Hollywood A Go-Go*, a local LA-based show, demonstrated that despite the influx of the variety-styled rock 'n' roll TV shows, the concept of the teen and young adult–oriented show with amateur dancing was not dead. It attempted to bring together the best of the variety format, featuring professional dancers and inventive staging with the feel of a more traditional bandstand-type show. A former dancer on the show, Steve Vilarino, who was fifteen at the time, recalls how unlike LA's *Shivaree*, which riveted on the stars and the go-go dancers, *Hollywood A Go-Go's* nightclub atmosphere allowed a mix of professional dancers and amateurs. He recollected that once he and other participants got to the studio, often an informal rehearsal would take place—"they kind of rehearsed us all on the side first. And then they picked me and other people. And you notice I'm in the front a lot of the time"[40] (Figure 6.2). Originally called *Ninth Street West*, the show aired on Channel 9 (KHJ) beginning in 1964 and was then named *Hollywood A Go-Go* when it went into syndication in 1965.[41] Produced by famed music television producer Al Burton, *Hollywood A Go-Go* dispensed with the pretense and glitz of *Hullabaloo*, featuring instead musical acts and dancers in a speakeasy/nightclub-type atmosphere with low-level lighting (the result of movie lights instead of television floodlights.)[42] As in

Figure 6.2 A clip from an episode of *Hollywood A Go-Go* featuring Dee Dee Sharp singing "Mashed Potato Time," with fifteen-year-old social dancer Steve Vilarino dancing at the front. November 27, 1965. Courtesy of Collection Administrators and Retro Video, Inc.

a nightclub, there was a stage for the house band (The Sinners), the musical acts, and dancers, but just as often the dancers performed on solo platforms or on the dance floor. What differentiated *Hollywood A Go-Go*, though (and made it reminiscent of the spatial arrangement of the T.A.M.I. concert), was the proximity of social dancers to professional dancers and performers—at many points, all of them shared the dance floor. According to Jim Freyler, "The overall effect incorporating faux brick walls and dimmer lighting, was a stunner for teen television. The television viewer would have no idea that the broadcast was coming from anything other than a cool nightclub."[43]

By 1965, as is clear from the shows discussed thus far, the West Coast had become a major television mecca; the New York recording industry, as well, had begun to move westward.[44] The Southwest was no slouch, either, regarding both music and TV production. Two shows emanating from the Dallas–Fort Worth, Texas, area merit some discussion, one for its pioneering advances in TV technology and the way in which it adapted national televised teen dance trends to a local audience, the other for its presentation of Black musical styles that were becoming popular around the country and that continued to reinvigorate social dances and promote Black talent. The first was *The Sump'n Else Show*, broadcast five afternoons a week from the WFAA (Channel 8) studios at the upscale North Park Center shopping mall from 1965 to early 1968. Like many other successful teen dance shows, *The Sump'n Else Show* grew out of earlier incarnations of the show (known first as *The Group and Harrigan* then the *Group and Chapman*) and was rated outstanding regional production of the year by the industry magazine *Radio & TV Mirror*. The host of the show was the beloved local deejay of KLIF-radio Ron Chapman, a Radio Hall of Famer, who had become a popular entertainer at local teenage record hops.[45] WFAA had become known as an innovator in television and known for its state-of-the-art equipment; it was one of the first stations to broadcast in color, and early on it programmed music shows—big band, rock 'n' roll, country, and pop music—to suit multiple tastes.

Although *The Sump'n Else Show* was clearly a bandstand show, with requisite amateur teen dancers, featured bands, and dance contests, it pulled from the *Shindig!* and *Hullabaloo* playbook.[46] As was the practice now for many teen dance shows, auditions were de rigueur. The show was geared to a slightly older demographic—one had to be at least a high school sophomore and not older than a college senior. While the show started out with recorded music, it eventually featured live acts and added a house band that played before and after the show.[47] The show's producer, Bud Buschardt, noted that upbeat rock 'n' roll and R&B played throughout the show and during the commercial breaks maintained a high energy level. Perhaps the most innovative element, though, was the addition of the four featured female dancers, each performing on a six-by-six-foot platform, known as "The Little Group" (so named as to differentiate them from The Big Group, the quartet of dancers featured previously on The Group and Chapman). The Little Group consisted of go-go dancers, but perhaps in a nod to the older audience demographic (Ron Chapman, like Steve Binder, wanted to reach adults, too) or because of Southern conservatism, the young women were not called go-go dancers. According to former Little Group dancer Calleen Anderegg, "I'm sure there were many who referred to us as 'go-go dancers,' but we didn't use that term ourselves. We weren't in boots and mini-skirts; each day we had a different out that we had to model [from Andra's Alley clothing store nearby]. And we could dance in them"[48] Anderegg explained that there was no choreographer for the show and that the young women devised their own routines consisting of the Mashed Potato, Jerk, Pony, Frug, and others. "We were pretty much on our own."[49] Like featured dancers on the primetime shows, Anderegg had had training in ballet, tap, and modern dance. It was a professional job—the young women were paid $25 a week and had to be at every show, five days a week, from 4 to 5 P.M. (Figure 6.3).[50]

The talent that appeared on the show was a great source of pride for the producers and directors. In addition to featuring some of the major recording artists of the day, in rock 'n' roll, R&B, and country, *Sump'n Else* promoted many local, Texas-based musicians, several of whom went on to national prominence.[51] Again, like other shows of the mid 1960s, *Sump'n Else* had legions of Black performers come through its doors, among them Jackie Wilson, Wilson Pickett, John Lee Hooker, Fontella Bass (of "Rescue Me" fame), as well as many Motown performers. But, still, the composition of the social dancers was all-white. Of course, in some ways this wasn't surprising; as Buschardt said, "You know we weren't integrating yet back in '64." There were no longer any type of restrictions or prohibitions—either explicit or implicit—forbidding Black teenagers and young adults to appear on the show, but it was more a matter of Black youth understandably not wanting to be on a show that "was pure white."[52]

Another WFAA offering that innovated within the Black televised music and dance genre was the 1966 all-Black variety-show *The!!!! Beat*. According to Jim Rowley, the music director for the show (who also directed some early episodes), "It was the latest, greatest thing—color, television, and music."[53]

Figure 6.3 A dance couple on the set of KTRK-TV's *The Larry Kane Show*, another Texas-based show (Houston) with host Larry Kane. The show, like other teen dance programs of the 1960s, required that the teenagers take dance lessons from professional dance teachers. These social dancers were featured in the May 1962 issue of *Teen* magazine. Courtesy of the Glenn Pitts Collection.

A showcase for R&B and soul artists, the show was the brainchild of Hoss Allen, the pioneering white Nashville deejay (see Chapter 1) who early on championed R&B and soul artists on Nashville's progressive radio station WLAC. More of a variety-type show than a teen-dance show, and with no studio audience, *The!!!! Beat* had one of the most stellar rosters of R&B and soul/funk artists that one might have a chance to see on television in 1966,[54] all backed by three Black go-go dancers, on Plexiglas cubes, in both fast and slow blues numbers. Dressed in sequined dresses and short white boots, they danced and improvised versions of the Pony, Jerk, Swim, and other 1960s social dances. At the start of each show, just as the band appears on stage, three Black male dancers perform a Mashed Potato with quick slides, James

Brown–style, that matches the energy and up tempo of the music. The musical director for the house band, The Beat Boys, was the extraordinary blues musician and instrumentalist Clarence "Gatemouth" Brown. At the finale of each show, all singers, musicians, and dancers joined one another for an impromptu song and dance as the credits faded.

The show, which aired only for twenty-six episodes, was also syndicated on thirteen affiliate stations across the country.[55] According to Rowley, the singing was both live and lip-synced.[56] One reason proffered for the short-lived nature of the show was that as a white-run production, it didn't locate the most appropriate sponsors and thus failed to connect with a Black audience. Another is that unlike Motown, which had a broad crossover appeal to white audiences, Southern soul singers were still mostly popular with a Black fan base.[57] Whatever the reason, the network executives clearly missed an opportunity to promote Black expressive culture at a time when television was both expanding its capabilities and featuring many more Black performers during prime time. It would seem that national audiences might have been predisposed to embrace—or at least welcome—such an all-Black show.

Conclusion

Social dance is a barometer of changing styles of music and of cultural and political change. Dance anthropologist Cynthia Novack has remarked that social dance can "encode" ideas prevalent in social movements "in a flexible and multilayered text, its kinesthetic and structural characteristics laden with social implications and associations."[58] The televised teen dance shows, as this study has illustrated, were just one indicator of how social and popular dance styles of the 1950s and early 1960s took root and became disseminated within mass, popular culture. As explored here, the teen dance shows were at once incubators of dance styles, self-defining spaces for suburban and urban youth, as well as microcosms of a larger society experiencing major upheavals in its social fabric, namely around race.

Because these shows took place primarily during an era of racial segregation and often extreme racial violence, and mirrored the kinds of legal and de facto segregation around the country, it would seem that this is a history of two different stories—one Black, one white. In many respects, of course, it is. We might think of this as a "split image," to use the title of the book by Jannette L. Dates and William Barlow on African Americans in the mass media. But it is also one story about a racially segregated society and the ramifications of that segregation on both white and Black youth. Within a framework that reinstantiated the destructive and insidious racial politics of the time, the shows, by virtue of being televised, masked but also made visible the Black roots of the dances and brought Black-based styles of music to youth (and adults) across the country. As this book has revealed, the actual practices by white and Black youth—both on and off the shows—as well as their television viewing habits bespoke a certain amount of interracial association and crossing of racial demarcations. As historian Ann Douglas has noted, American entertainment and popular culture, "whatever the state of American society, has always been integrated, if only by theft and parody." [59] But this story is not solely about appropriation; it is also about interracial collaborations forged within the fissures of "official" culture.

The teen dance shows, as demonstrated, were for white youth, in particular, places they could stake out as their own without parental eyes watching over them. R&B and rock 'n' roll music and the dances they fueled were, for many of them, a rebellion against the stifling mores of the era. Historian George Lipsitz, quoted earlier in this book, has also observed that the adoption of styles from Black expressive culture was motivated, in part, by the eroding of city life and the rise of suburbia. As suburban enclaves increased racial and class segregation, white youth found inspiration and purpose "by celebrating the ethnic and class interactions of the urban street."[60] Black radio, as described in a previous chapter, was instrumental in exposing white youth to Black culture through R&B music, and the radio deejays-turned-television-hosts became pivotal figures in fashioning 1950s youth culture, for both white and Black teenagers.

For girls and young women, the era had its challenges. To the extent that the televised teen dance shows were vehicles for rock 'n' roll music and dance, they enabled female teenagers to enact a different vision of themselves. The teen dance show was a public space distinctly apart from home and school where girls might explore their personhood and identity. Despite the shows' rules and regulations, girls' experiences, particularly their love for R&B music and dance, were confirmed and validated. A distinct, and what we can surmise was a pleasurable, sororal bond formed between and among the girl dancers and participants on the shows. One recalls the visual image of the teenage girlfriends, Meg Pryor and Roxanne Bojarski, from Jonathan Prince's *American Dreams* television series that aired on NBC in the early 2000s. Meg and Roxanne defied their parents' wishes and became regulars on *American*

Bandstand; the girls, joined at the hip, share their hopes, expectations, and escapades before, during, and after dancing on the show, which serves as the centerpiece of their teenage lives.[61] Given the segregation and racial bigotry of the time, as the book has shown, Black girls and white girls had distinctly different means for negotiating the "double bind"—the pressure to maintain respectability on the one hand and express their sexuality and desirability on the other. Many Black female teenagers had to uphold their "purity" in the face of dangers that white female teenagers didn't and were subject to sexual stereotyping based on their race. This is not to say that R&B music and rock 'n' roll dance were not a central part of their growing-up years; they were, indeed. But that experience came with internalized proscriptions against behavior that might be misconstrued as sexually overt.

This book, of course, demonstrates the power of the television medium and the televisual domain—how images constructed and transmitted on screen not only reflect reality but also create cultural conversation and discourse. That early television projected a sense of intimacy and immediacy may help explain why the teen dance shows became so popular. On this new and exciting medium, in which events occurred in real time, dance and dance styles were brought directly into one's living room where one might experiment with the latest moves and compete with, or compare oneself to, the dancers on screen. In this early era of television, when televised dance, as Novack describes it, "constituted both performance and behavior,"[62] social dance styles became popularized around the country and eventually the world. While there existed many other venues where Black and white teenagers might learn to dance to rock 'n' roll music, surely television, on which those same teenagers might appear themselves, was particularly exciting.

Probably previously unknown to many readers are the all-Black televised teen dance shows, although they were extremely popular within the local communities and cities in which they appeared. The power of the all-Black shows, of course, was their ability to unite teenagers around the shared practice of dance. In many respects the Black teen dance shows were similar to other institutions in those communities that helped develop a rich, Black cultural tradition. Michael Omi and Howard Winant, in *Racial Formation in the United States*, have written of the civil rights movement that it "rearticulated black collective subjectivity. It reframed traditional black cultural and religious themes to forge a new black politics."[63] While the shows were not "political" in this sense, they can be seen, in many ways, as forms of grassroots activism, which bolstered individual and collective identity and at the same time served as a means of personal expression in the act of creation and innovation. As dance theorist Thomas DeFrantz has written, "social dance offers a site where black motion can be generated, accommodated, honed, and appreciated." It is a "a place of aesthetic possibility."[64] And, as the book explores, the Black teen shows also served as spaces of racial "crossover" in that they were viewed by white youth as well as Black youth. As Yvonne Lewis Holley, the daughter of J. D. Lewis (the host of Raleigh, North Carolina's *Teenage Frolics*) explained, "It was an introduction to Black culture." She noted, too, how to this day she meets former white viewers who tell her how much they enjoyed the show.[65]

One measure of the power of the televised teen dance show has to do with cultural memory. For most former participants on the shows, white or Black, the combination of listening and dancing to rock 'n' roll music, meeting and consorting with rock 'n' roll stars, and presenting themselves before the live camera was a heady experience indelibly imprinted on their psyches. The long-lasting friendships and bonds made, too, were part of the equation. Also indicative of the resilience of the shows in cultural memory are the great number of fan groups, nostalgia sites, and annual reunions held honoring the spirit of the shows that exist to this day. And, of course, it was the dancing. The teen dance shows certainly drew in young people by a shared social and aesthetic interest, yet at the same time a community got created *because of* the dancing. *Teenarama Dance Party* ended in 1970 in Washington, DC. In 2006, television producer Beverly Lindsay-Johnson, mentioned previously in these pages, created the award-winning documentary *Dance Party: The Teenarama Story*, which brought together many of the former participants and reinvigorated the *Teenarama* legacy. In December 2021, Lindsay-Johnson's musical version of the teen show, *Dancing on the Air*, created in conjunction with writer/librettist Jiiko Ozimba, streamed nationwide. The musical was inspired by 1960s social dances and draws on stories from actual participants on the show. In our interview, Ozimba remarked how the show still has a tremendous following:

> Anytime you do anything regarding *Teenarama* in this area [DC], people really show up. The original dancers, people who watched it on television, it just meant so much to people. Even when we were at the Kennedy Center [for the musical's preview], they were literally pulling in chairs and pulling in chairs until finally they had to lock the door and some people didn't get in, because people were that interested.[66]

The life of the teen bandstand show remains in memory, but also in practice. The resurgence of interest in the 1950s over the past twenty years sparked
a reimagining of the televised teen dance show in theater, film, and television. John Waters's cult-film *Hairspray* (from 1988) ignited the Broadway
musical *Hairspray* in 2002, followed by a film remake starring John Travolta
in 2007. The Broadway musical *Memphis*, in 2009, told the story of the somewhat madcap Memphis deejay Dewey Phillips and his radio show *Red, Hot,
and Blue*, one of the first shows to feature Elvis Presley, and his foray into television. And, in 2002, NBC's hit drama series *American Dreams* centered on
a suburban family in late 1950s–early 1960s Philadelphia in which *American
Bandstand* becomes the fulcrum around which the story revolves. There has
been a revival, too, of dances of the 1950s as in the New York City–based
organization Sock Hop Sundays, which features monthly social dancing to
1950s and 1960s music. And internet sites of many teen-bandstand shows
continue to attract former dancers and participants eager to share their
stories. All these efforts help to keep alive the memory of the teen dance show.
What I hope will continue, as well (as in the *Teenarama* musical), is an understanding and recognition that the televised teen dance story of the 1950s
and early 1960s was biracial; it was one that unfolded in Black and white.

Epilogue: *Soul Train*

As the Lindy of the 1950s faded, social dance of the 1960s saw an even greater increase, as dance historian Sally Sommer has written, in "an infusion of American interpretations of Africanisms."[1] Social dancing took place in many venues—in clubs, at concerts, and in the discothèque, which would flower in the 1970s. The changing political landscape of the early to mid-1960s, the rise in civil rights actions and legislation, the gains in television technology and production, and the way that social dance styles might now be presented on stage as a result of that technology all accounted for the significantly changed look and style of social dance on TV. There is, perhaps, some irony in the fact that even as civil rights activity gained traction, and the traditional teen-dance show became desegregated, there would emerge no truly integrated teen dance shows. That moment, it seems, had passed.

What did occur, however, was the emergence of the all-Black dance program *Soul Train*, in 1971, on national, primetime TV, which reinvigorated televised teenage and young-adult dance shows.[2] By the mid-1960s, along with accelerated civil rights demonstrations across the country, was a growing Black Power movement that, as historian Eric Foner notes, indicated a shift in the idea of Black freedom identified "less with integration into the American mainstream than with group self-determination."[3] The assertion of racial pride became even more pronounced after the assassination of Malcolm X, in 1965, who, as historians Maurice Isserman and Michael Kazin note, quickly became "a powerful symbol of racial redemption."[4] While the 1950s and early 1960s brought about political and legal advances, by the mid-1960s, as Isserman and Kazin continue, "it had become obvious to black activists and their white allies that the authorities, both North and South, rarely aided the process of liberation unless—as during the Freedom Rides—the movement made it politically uncomfortable for them to stall."[5] The musical landscape was shifting, too, as Southern soul music, a "grittier r&b" ascended to the pop charts.[6] Although it was a synthesis of different sounds, soul music came to represent what Peter Guralnick calls "a statement of possibilities."[7] It fit in with the ethos of Black self-determination and self-sufficiency characterized by James Brown, for instance, who fought for and

154 EPILOGUE: *SOUL TRAIN*

won greater artistic control at his label King Records, where he produced a multitude of single hits. Other musicians, such as Otis Redding, Wilson Pickett, Percy Sledge, and Etta James, were making music at the studios at Stax-Volt Records, in Memphis, and Fame Studios in Muscle Shoals, Alabama, which enabled them to claim their artistic voices and make names for themselves within the music industry.[8]

By the mid-1960s and into the 1970s, the philosophy of racial pride and the notion of Black self-sufficiency that took hold was reflected in Black life and music. As music critic Reebee Garofalo notes, Black pride "had created a cultural space in which unrefined r&b could find mainstream acceptance on its own terms."[9] James Brown was still as popular as ever, but his "stripped-down, rhythmically charged proto-funk" style spoke to the Black Power movement.[10] Brown's 1968 hit single "Say It Loud—I'm Black and I'm Proud" became an anthem of sorts for Black liberation. At the same time, in the late sixties, Don Cornelius was working as a radio deejay as an auxiliary member of the iconic Good Guys—the legendary voices on Leonard Chess's WVON radio station in Chicago. Cornelius, though, turned his sights to television, and in 1970 premiered the televised dance program that would go national in 1971 and become a music and cultural sensation for nearly thirty years.

Soul Train is the subject of several books and numerous essays, so my aim is not to traverse that territory here, but rather to underscore a couple of key points in relation to my own study.[11] *Soul Train* began as a local televised dance program in Chicago in 1970, and then moved a year later to Los Angeles when it went national. In its local version, *Soul Train* typified the best of the televised teen dance *and* variety-dance shows of the 1950s and 1960s. Like the professionalized variety-dance shows of the 1960s, *Soul Train* featured top musical talent from The Jackson Five to the Chi-Lites, along with teenage and young-adult social dancers (in the mold of the bandstand-type shows), several of whom went on to professional success. Like other local shows, when *Soul Train* moved to Los Angeles from Chicago in 1971, the show's choreographer Pamela Brown traveled to high schools in towns all over Los Angeles scouting for dance talent. As *Soul Train* chronicler Christopher Lehman recounts, at least twelve of the dancers on the first syndicated show attended Los Angeles High School. Like teenagers on the 1950s televised teen dance programs, the dancers received hundreds of bundles of fan mail, and, too, like the professional dancers on the variety-show dance programs, they became in high demand for professional engagements around the country.[12] The most popular dancers came to be known as the Soul Train

Gang—Damita Jo Freeman, Tyrone Proctor, and Don "Campbellock" Campbell among them[13]—whose local, regional versions of social dances often became national crazes.[14] Reports Nelson George, "What viewers saw on *Soul Train* wasn't just one style but a polyglot of approaches, some indigenous street dance, some just individual flamboyance, and often happy accidents discovered in the heat of competition."[15] *Soul Train* was a colorful swirl of moving bodies decked out in colorful regalia and fantastic hairdos dancing to R&B, soul, funk, or hip-hop. The famous Soul Train Line, the line dance that concluded every show—two lines of dancers opposite one another through which dancers would dance down the middle—was an opportunity to strut one's stuff and improvise dance moves on the spot. (Nelson George has called the Soul Train Line "the human alley.")[16]

The fact that *Soul Train* lasted as long as it did on national television, and through different eras and styles of music, attests to the crossover appeal of the show with both Black and white audiences. According to journalist Marc Weingarten, "*Soul Train* became one of the ten most-watched syndicated shows in the country."[17] Writer Nelson George: "It was a music show that not only generated hit records but also connected all of black (and a hip section of white, Latino, and Asian) America into a groovy community."[18] *Soul Train* emerged, though, on the wings of other local-based Black Chicago dance shows from the 1960s, including *Red, Hot and Blues* hosted by well-known Chicago deejay Big Bill Hill. Gayle Wald, author of *It's Been Beautiful: Soul! and Black Power Television*, makes a valid point that once *Soul Train* went national it necessarily lost some of that essence of the local teen TV show, which is a sense of community and camaraderie among friends and peers. What *Soul Train* did provide, though, was the massive exposure of Black styles of expressive culture that were now actually becoming accepted by mainstream TV. Whether Cornelius knew of the earlier Black televised teen TV shows that emerged in the 1950s, such as *The Mitch Thomas Show*, *Teenage Frolics*, or *Teenarama*, is unclear. But these shows were definitely precursors.

Even though *Soul Train* lost some of its community appeal when it went national, it nonetheless became a cultural touchstone for Black youth across the country. In that sense, *Soul Train* continued the role of the Black teen dance show in representing more than a "dance show," but also a social institution, a professional training ground, a home away from home, and a place to test out adolescent and young-adult behaviors. The musician, songwriter, and filmmaker Amir Thompson, otherwise known as Questlove, grew up with *Soul Train* and apparently owns 600 episodes of the show. According to the *New York Times* writer Jazmine Hughes, "He has described the show as a 'sibling, a parent, a baby sitter, a friend, a textbook, a newscast, a business school and a church.' Ultimately culminating in a single role: a teacher."[19] Continuing the spiritual metaphor, Nelson George has commented that the "the scores of dancers who created the *Soul Train* tradition preached with their torsos, legs, and arms, speaking a human language that was as influential as any Sunday sermon."[20]

The Black, vernacular dance forms exhibited on *Soul Train*, to all of the many forms of musical styles showcased there—R&B, Soul, Gospel, Hip-Hop—was what 1950s and early 1960s television could not—was not ready to—accept in full. With every episode, it seemed, *Soul Train* made history by introducing new styles that added to the social dance lexicon. It is interesting that Questlove brings us back to *Soul Train* at the same time he brings us forward with his award-winning 2021 documentary *Summer of Soul (. . . Or, When the Revolution Could Not Be Televised)*. The film itself consists of "lost" footage from the 1969 Harlem Cultural Festival that Questlove rescued from near oblivion. The festival, filmed over the course of six weeks in Mount Morris Park, in Harlem, was just 100 miles south of Woodstock, but unlike that historical festival, this footage was never aired. Like many of the Black-based televised teen dance programs that struggled for air space, the Harlem Cultural Festival too faced huge obstacles in getting filmed—the festival producer Hal Tulchin was originally told that there "was not a market for broadcasting or distributing a Black cultural moment."[21] But like the dancing on the teen dance shows, the music at the Harlem Cultural Festival was thrilling and powerful for those who watched and experienced it, and it stands as a testament, and warning, to the ways that history can be so easily ignored and erased.[22] *Summer of Soul* does for us now what *Soul Train* did then, which was to bring Black musical forms and dance forms to the forefront. It reminds us, too, how social dance was and is deeply embedded in a much larger social and cultural history.

Notes

Introduction

1. The dance also resurfaced with the 2007 film remake of the musical *Hairspray*, which was based on Waters's 1998 film. The Madison was sometimes referred to as the Hully Gully. In the Godard film, a very young Anna Karina performs the dance with her two male outlaw friends in a Parisian café. As dance reconstructor Richard Powers points out, Karina replaces the typical side step in the Madison with a full stop in place. The step is punctuated with a clap of the hands. This version was often referred to as the French Madison. See Richard Powers, "The Hully Gully, the French Madison, Hot Chocolate and The Electric Slide," http://socialdance.stanford.edu/syllabi/Hully-Gully. htm. Also see Chapter 4 for more on the Madison.
2. Throughout the book I use the term "Black" when referring to teenagers, musicians, deejays, and performers and generally reserve "African American" for when it is possible to trace particular dances and dance forms to their specific racial/ethnic origins or background.
3. "The Madison," *Ebony*, July 1960, 72.
4. The popular poodle skirt consisted of a full, puffed-out circle of clothing, initially designed by Julie Lynn Charlot, an actress and opera singer, who in 1948 was inspired by a Dior design of the previous year. The skirt was originally made of felt and contained various appliqués, often of pet poodles. The skirts took hold with white teenage girls who found them irresistible for dancing. See "The Fun History of the Poodle Skirt," https://recollections.biz/blog/the-fun-history-of-the-poodle-skirt/.
5. Eric Foner, *Give Me Liberty! An American History*, Vol. 2 (New York: W. W. Norton, 2019), 938.
6. As Eric Foner explains, the civil rights movement didn't begin with the *Brown* decision; however, "the decision did ensure that when the movement resumed after waning in the early 1950s, it would have the backing of the federal courts." *Give Me Liberty*, 974. Also see Foner, *The Story of American Freedom* (New York: W. W. Norton, 1998), 275–276.
7. Maurice Isserman and Michael Kazin, *America Divided: The Civil War of the 1960s* (New York: Oxford University Press, 2004), 32.
8. For an excellent and riveting account of the incident at Central High School and the stories of the nine students attempting to enter the school, particularly the role of the young girls, see Rachel Devlin, *A Girl Stands at the Door: The Generation of Young Women Who Desegregated America's Schools* (New York: Basic Books, 2018), 201–218.
9. Mary L. Dudziak, *Cold War Civil Rights: Race and the Image of American Democracy* (Princeton, NJ: Princeton University Press, 2011), 115.

10. Alan Nadel, *Television in Black-and-White America: Race and National Identity* (Lawrence: University Press of Kansas, 2005), 14.

11. Raymond Williams, *Television: Technology and Cultural Form* (New York & London: Routledge, 2002), xiv.

12. Lynn Spigel, *Make Room for TV: Television and the Family Ideal in Postwar America* (Chicago and London: University of Chicago Press, 1992), 39.

13. Nadel, *Television in Black-and-White America*, 6.

14. Taylor Lorenz, "The Original Renegade," *New York Times*, February 13, 2020.

15. Gary Mullinax, "Radio Guided DJ to Stars," *News Journal Papers*, Wilmington, DE, January 26, 1986, as quoted in Matthew F. Delmont, *The Nicest Kids in Town: American Bandstand, Rock 'n' Roll, and the Struggle for Civil Rights in 1950s Philadelphia* (Berkeley: University of California Press, 2012), 173.

16. Delmont, *The Nicest Kids in Town*.

17. Brian Ward, *Just My Soul Responding: Rhythm and Blues, Black Consciousness, and Race Relations* (Berkeley: University of California Press, 1998), 47.

18. William Barlow, "Commercial and Noncommercial Radio," in *Split Image: African Americans in the Mass Media*, ed. Jannette L. Dates and William Barlow (Washington, DC: Howard University Press, 1990), 214.

19. *New York Times Magazine*, August 14, 2019. Morris's essay was in the ground-breaking "1619 Project" series of the magazine, initiated by Nikole Hannah-Jones, that reframed a conversation around the country's history with slavery. https://www.nytimes.com/interactive/2019/08/14/magazine/music-black-culture-appropriation.html.

20. Cultural critic Nelson George makes the point that such Black "self-sufficiency" was actually a radical concept at the end of the 1950s when the pull among civil rights or-ganizations was toward integration. The idea of Black self-sufficiency would become more pronounced in the 1960s, as explained in Chapter 6, when Black nationalists, among others, believed that economic ills, determined in part by racist housing and employment practices, might be alleviated by Black control. See George, *The Death of Rhythm & Blues* (New York: Penguin Books, 1998), 72. W. E. B. Du Bois, of course, had advocated such a stance in 1934 before his resignation from the NAACP, and then again in 1947 in a speech before the United Nations where he spoke "on behalf of the 'thirteen million American citizens of Negro descent.'" See Wilson Jeremiah Moses, *Afrotopia: The Roots of African American Popular History* (Cambridge: Cambridge University Press, 1998), 164.

21. As cultural critic George Lipsitz notes, "Consumption of mass popular cultural al-ways involved varied motivations and complex choices." "Against the Wind: Dialogic Aspects of Rock and Roll," in his *Time Passages: Collective Memory and American Popular Culture* (Minneapolis: University of Minnesota Press, 1990), 122. Also see Brian Ward, *Just My Soul Responding: Rhythm and Blues, Black Consciousness, and Race Relations* (Berkeley: University of California Press, 1998), 9.

22. Eric Lott, *Love and Theft: Blackface Minstrelsy and the American Working Class* (New York: Oxford University Press, 2013), 55.

23. Toni Morrison, *Playing in the Dark: Whiteness and the Literary Imagination* (New York: Vintage Books, 1993), 3–28.

24. Norman Mailer, "The White Negro: Superficial Reflections on the Hipster," in his *Advertisements for Myself* (London: A. Deutsch, 1961), 285.

25. Lott calls this process of "black mirroring" (by whites) as seeking "less to reproduce Blackness with any accuracy than to activate it for white purposes." Lott, *Black Mirror: The Cultural Contradictions of American Racism* (Cambridge, MA: Harvard University Press, 2017), 3.

26. Wini Breines, *Young, White, and Miserable: Growing Up Female in the Fifties* (Chicago: University of Chicago Press, 1992), 17.

27. Foner, *Give Me Liberty!*, 950.

28. Lipsitz, "Against the Wind," 122.

29. Guthrie Ramsey, *Race Music: Black Cultures from Bebop to Hip-Hop* (Berkeley: University of California Press, 2003), 4.

30. See Ward, *Just My Soul Responding*, 113.

Chapter 1

1. Louis Menand, *The Free World: Art and Thought in the Cold War* (New York: Farrar, Straus & Giroux, 2021), 94.

2. Ibid., 298–299.

3. Reebee Garofalo, "Crossing Over: 1939–1989," in *Split Image: African Americans in the Mass Media*, ed. Jannette L. Dates and William Barlow (Washington, DC: Howard University Press, 1990), 62.

4. Ibid.

5. On the reasons for the rise of a national audience for R&B music see ibid., 60; and William Barlow, "Commercial and Noncommercial Radio," in ibid., 208. Garofalo also proffers explanations for why the major record labels in a sense acceded the R&B market to the independents. Due to the shellac shortage during the war, which decreased the number of records sold and thus required belt tightening, the "majors" concentrated their efforts on the production of popular music, which was their main market. After the war, it was difficult for the major labels to recover the specialty markets (blues, jazz, gospel), so the independents (or "indies") gained the upper hand. The independents were also aided by the development of magnetic tape, which made it possible "for anyone to record anywhere." Ibid., 60, 62. Journalist Nick Tosches writes of the indies: "These small independent companies—mongrel labels they were called within the industry—were the breeding grounds of rock 'n' roll. None of them had any real ethnic or aesthetic identity. They all released whatever they thought might sell. Aladdin, Specialty, Mercury, Atlantic, Chess, and others all known for their rhythm-and-blues product all released hillbilly records on the side." See *Unsung Heroes of Rock 'n' Roll: The Birth of Rock in the Wild Years before Elvis* (New York: Da Capo Press, 1999), 5.

6. Garofolo, "Crossing Over," 65.

7. Barlow, "Commercial and Noncommercial Radio," 214.

8. William Barlow, "Cashing In: 1900–1939," in *Split Image*, 38, 51; Reebee Garofalo, *Rockin' Out: Popular Music in the U.S.A.* (Boston: Pearson Education Inc., 2014), 79; and Michael Bertrand, *Race, Rock, and Elvis* (Urbana and Chicago: University of Illinois Press, 2005), 46–47. It's important to keep in mind that the designation "race music" was not necessarily a pejorative. As Barlow notes, the terms itself may be traced to its use in the *Chicago Defender*, a Black newspaper, which Barlow contends "frequently used it as a progressive and positive connotation for African Americans" ("Cashing In," 38). At the same time, it is impossible to ignore the fact that the race-record business, managed primarily by white producers and managers, fostered "economic stratification and cultural bias." Black musicians were regularly paid less for their studio work and were routinely robbed of their royalties (ibid., 51). For more on race records see LeRoi Jones, *Blue People: Negro Music in White America* (New York: Harper Perennial, 1963, 2002), 99–103.

9. Menand, *The Free World*, 302.

10. Brian Ward, *Radio and the Struggle for Civil Rights in the South* (Gainesville: University Press of Florida, 2004), 6–7.

11. Brian Ward, *Just My Soul Responding: R&B, Black Consciousness, and Race Relations* (Berkeley: University of California Press, 1998), 37.

12. Charlie Gillett, *The Sound of the City: The Rise of Rock and Roll* (New York: Da Capo Press, 1996), 23. According to Gillett, there were essentially five styles of rock 'n' roll music, each emanating from a different part of the country. These were: northern band rock 'n' roll, New Orleans dance blues, Memphis country rock (sometimes referred to as rockabilly), Chicago R&B, and vocal group rock 'n' roll. All of these styles came together in the formation of what would become known as rock 'n' roll. All derived from the Black tradition and, as Gillett writes, "gave expression to moods of their audience that hitherto had not been represented in popular music." For some of the most authoritative sources on R&B and rock 'n' roll music, in addition to Gillett, see Garofalo, *Rockin' Out* and "Crossing Over"; Ward, *Just My Soul Responding*; Nelson George, *The Death of Rhythm & Blues* (New York: Penguin Books, 1988); Peter Guralnick, *Sweet Soul Music: R&B and the Southern Dream of Freedom* (New York: Harper & Row, 1986); and Robert Palmer, *Rock & Roll: An Unruly History* (New York: Harmony Books, 1995). For an interesting analysis of rock 'n' roll music as a "musical stream," or several elements—economic, artistic, politics—that all converge, see Philip H. Ennis, *The Seventh Stream: The Emergence of Rock 'n' Roll in American Popular Music* (Hanover, NH: Wesleyan University Press, 1992). According to Ennis, in considering the roots of rock 'n' roll music, "something does not come out of nothing, the new must come either from within one existing type of music or from the boundary of two or more different musics. The latter is the way rock 'n' roll began. Further, a new music is either the work of one or a small number of inspired artists or it comes from the pervasive and powerful presence of any anonymous cohort. In the case of rock 'n' roll, it was both."

13. Garofalo, "Crossing Over," 69. In what would eventually become rock 'n' roll, the horn section was greatly reduced, "first to a single saxophone, and then to no horns at all. The rhythmic base of the boogie-woogie structure had become even more dominant."

14. "Gospel: The Root of Popular Music," *The New Crisis* 106, no. 4 (July/August 1999): 60.

15. Michael Campbell, with James Brody, *Rock and Roll: An Introduction* (Belmont, CA: Thomson Schirmer 2008), 72. R&B, according to William Barlow, was "an amalgam of electrified urban blues, gospel vocal styles, and swing-band instrumental arrangements" (Barlow, *Voiceover: The Making of Black Radio* [Philadelphia, Temple University Press, 1999]), 100.

16. Ward, *Just My Soul*, 42.

17. Ibid.

18. Campbell, *Rock and Roll*, 82. According to New Orleans musicians, a "professor" was a skilled pianist.

19. Garofalo, *Rockin' Out*, 83. According to Campbell, "Professor Longhair was arguably one of the most important musical influence in New Orleans R&B, although he was virtually unknown outside of the city." Campbell, *Rock and Roll*, 82.

20. Garofalo, *Rockin' Out*, 83. As Michael Campbell notes, "By the end of the decade Latin-inspired rhythms were used increasingly as an alternative to rock and shuffle rhythms in a wide range of R&B styles. These were generally richer and more complex than the straightforward timekeeping of rock and roll." *Rock and Roll: An Introduction* (Belmont, CO: Thomson & Schirmer, 2008), n. 81.

21. George Lipsitz, "Land of a Thousand Dances," in *Recasting America: Culture and Politics in the Age of Cold War*, ed. Lary May (Chicago: University of Chicago Press, 1989), 269. As Lipsitz notes, "They [Cannibal and the Headhunters] originally learned to play music as folk artists in Mexican *mariachi* and *jarocho* bands, but like other brown, Black, white, red, and yellow youths all across America, they blended the traditional music of their community with the sounds they heard on records and radio, drawing inspiration from the diversity of urban life and the excitement of the city streets" (269). For more on Spanish influences on rock 'n' roll, see George Lipsitz, "Ain't Nobody Here but Us Chickens: Class Origins of Rock and Roll," Chapter 10 in *Class and Culture in Cold War America: "A Rainbow at Midnight"* (South Hadley, MA: Praeger Special Studies, 1982), 212.

22. Garofalo, *Rockin' Out*, 83–84.

23. *Just My Soul Responding*, 43.

24. Bertrand, *Race, Rock and Elvis*, 46–47. Historian Michael Bertrand, writing particularly of the role of the deejay in the American South, notes that "Since at the least the late 1940s, R&B and R&B-inspired deejays and entertainers had steadily become influential. Beyond the pale of traditional politics, these cultural arbiters exposed audiences to Black music and culture. They consistently encouraged emotions and activities inimical to southern racial etiquette and presented unorthodox images, sounds, and worldviews that increasingly appealed to receptive young people." For authoritative sources on the role of the radio deejay and the rise of R&B, see Willian Barlow, *Voiceover: The Making of Black Radio* (Philadelphia, Temple University Press, 1999); Arnold Passman, *The Deejays* (New York: Macmillan, 1971); Marc Fisher,

Something in the Air: Radio, Rock, and the Revolution That Shaped a Generation (New York, Random House, 2007); and Ward, *Radio and the Struggle for Civil Rights in the South.*

25. Garofalo, "Crossing Over," 65.
26. Barlow, *Voiceover*, 97.
27. George, *The Death of Rhythm & Blues*, 55.
28. Barlow, *Voiceover*, 97.
29. Ibid., 100.
30. Richard E. Stamz with Patrick Roberts, *Give 'Em Soul, Richard! Race, Radio, & Rhythm & Blues in Chicago* (Urbana and Chicago: University of Illinois Press, 2010), 61.
31. On Nat D. Williams and Hattie Leeper, see Barlow, *Voiceover*, 151–152; on Jocko Henderson, see John A. Jackson, *Big Beat Heat: Alan Freed and the Early Years of Rock & Roll* (New York: Schirmer Books, 1991), 187.
32. George, *The Death of Rhythm & Blues*, 3.
33. Ward, *Just My Soul*, 30. Ward notes that in 1949, a wealthy, Atlanta financier Jesse Blayton became the first Black man in the United States to own a radio station (WERD). However, by 1960, there were still only four Black-owned radio stations in the country and only fourteen a decade later. For more information on Black-owned radio stations, see Barlow, *Split Image*, 222.
34. On the fairly loose structure of local radio broadcasting in the early 1950, see Garofalo, "Crossing Over," 65. Well-known North Carolina deejay Hattie Leeper remarked in an interview of her broadcast on Charlotte's WGIV-Radio that "You played whatever you felt like playing, whatever you wanted to play, whatever your audience wanted to hear is what you played." WGIV was owned and run by white owner Francis Fitzgerald who was committed to Black-oriented radio; in fact, he was one of the few progressive white station owners who was devoted to reaching his Black constituents for political as well as financial reasons. The station was also known for its fully integrated staff. Ward, *Radio and the Struggle*, 236, 234–235.
35. Barlow, *Voiceover*, 204. Barlow has commented that Black radio deejays, talk-show hosts, and radio newscasters "helped mobilize people for demonstrations and marches, provided a forum for civil rights leaders such as Dr. Martin Luther King Jr., and, in the case of the DJs, boosted the morale of listeners by playing 'message music' on their shows" (10). He notes too that "By this time, radio had become the omnipresent mass medium in the Black community; a huge majority (over 90 percent) of African Americans owned radio receivers and listened to Black-formatted stations on a daily basis" (10).
36. Ibid., 204–205. Nat D. Williams, too, had an activist orientation; he wrote a weekly column for *the Memphis World* and hosted a public affairs TV program *Brown America Speaks.*
37. Ibid., 160.
38. Ibid., 159.
39. Ibid., 162–164. See Barlow for more on this WLAC trio. On the importance of Hoss Allen as a groundbreaking white deejay, more influential than Alan Freed, see Beverly Keel, "A Hoss of a Different Color: Rock and Roll Radio before Alan Freed,"

unpublished manuscript, Special Collections in Mass Media and Culture Serials Collection, University Libraries, University of Maryland. According to Keel, "Little Richard Penniman went into the studio for the first time in 1951 and recorded 'Every Hour.' The first time the 18-year old heard himself on the radio was when his family gathered around the radio in their Macon, Georgia home listening to WLAC" (5). In another part of Tennessee—Memphis—white deejay Dewey Phillips became notorious for his R&B-based radio shows, first on WDIA and then on WHBQ, which featured his show *Red, Hot, and Blue* that ran throughout the 1950s. It was Dewey Phillips to whom Sam Phillips rushed his demo of Elvis Presley's cover version of Arthur Crudup's "That's All Right Mama." Phillips was also the first individual to interview Presley on the air. Barlow, *Voiceover*, 178.

40. Barlow, *Voiceover*, 168–170.
41. Ibid., 171–172. For more on Hunter Hancock and LA-based disc jockey Al Jarvis, see Anthony Macias, "Bringing Music to the People: Race, Urban Culture, and Municipal Politics in Postwar Los Angeles," *American Quarterly* 56, no. 3 (September 2004): 704.
42. Interview with the author, August 18, 2014.
43. A Los Angeles city ordinance at the time forbade teenagers under the age of eighteen from participating in large gatherings without school-board permission. Log Angeles County, however (which included the town of El Monte), had no such restrictions; therefore the El Monte Legion Stadium became a very popular and hospitable place to present rock 'n' roll music and dance concerts. Matt Garcia, *A World of Its Own: Race, Labor, and Citrus in the Making of Greater Los Angeles, 1900–1970* (Chapel Hill: University of North Carolina Press, 2001), 199, 201; and Macias, "Bringing Music to the People," 720.
44. Gillett, *Sound of the City*, 13, 20. Gillett remarks of Freed that "he did play an incalculable role in developing the concept of an exciting music that could express the feeling of adolescence."
45. It is important to note, too, that in this early period of television, the networks and studios did not yet have the proper microphone capabilities that they would eventually have.
46. "'One Night on TV Is Worth Weeks at the Paramount': Musicians and Opportunity in Early Television, 1948–55," *Popular Music* 21, no. 3 (October 2002): 250–251.
47. Ibid., 273.
48. Garofalo, "Crossing Over," 60. These shows also developed from the practice on radio of broadcasting live music (and big bands) from actual ballrooms. "Radio," writes Garofalo, "was, in essence, their electronic ballroom; it provided very steady work."
49. Murray Forman, "One Night on TV," in his *One Night on TV Is Worth Weeks at the Paramount: Popular Music on Early Television* (Durham, NC: Duke University Press, 2012), 115.
50. Ibid., 155.
51. Ibid., 159. *The 950 Show* debuted in May 1945 with Joe Grady; by 1956 he had teamed up with Ed Hurst. No doubt this practice was influenced by the remote ballroom broadcasts that had occurred on radio as early as the 1930s. This trend was a throwback to famous deejay Martin Block's *Make Believe Ballroom* that, starting in 1935,

featured records, at first, and then live swing bands in the radio station studio, creating the illusion that Block was broadcasting from a ballroom. It became a tremendous success. See "Dance Band Revival: Jockey," *Metronome*, July 1951 (Special Collections in Mass Media and Culture Serials Collection, University Libraries, University of Maryland). Block got his idea from the famed local deejay Al Jarvis who, according to William Barlow, pioneered the "white swing and pop format on his show *The World's Largest Make-Believe Ballroom*, which debuted on KFWB in Los Angeles in 1932." Barlow, *Voiceover*, 308, n. 1.

52. Robin Seymour, interview with the author, July 1, 2011.

53. Brant Hart, interview with the author, September 14, 2020. This story was relayed to me in an interview with Brant Hart, who was a former North Carolina radio producer and a onetime assistant production manager for the news department at WSOC-TV in Charlotte, North Carolina, that aired a local teen dance program *Kilgo's Canteen*, hosted by Jimmy Kilgo. Hart recalled a radio interview aired in the early 1990s in which Kilgo interviewed Rockin' Ray Gooding who relayed this story. Also, according to Brant, WGIV was a very noteworthy station. "I think those folks probably did more to make a peaceful integration in Charlotte than anybody else. The station itself was owned by a white man [Francis Fitzgerald], who set up the station right after World War II. Over the years, he had both white and Black staff members. . . . When Mr. Fitzgerald saw that Charlotte was large enough to have a stage like Chicago and New York like the bigger markets, he decided to go in that direction." At another point in the interview, Hart recalled Gooding saying of the Black and white dance couples that "there was never any trouble. They were able to dance together like they'd been knowing each other all their lives." Hart also explained that the station operated from its actual transmitter site; the studio contained a small area, the size of a lobby, where kids could watch the shows as they aired.

54. Chattie Hattie Leeper Oral History Interview #2, J. Murrey Atkins Library Special Collections, Charlotte: University of North Carolina, December 12, 2006. In another interview in 2007, Hattie Leeper explained the Black and white teenage rage for R&B and rock 'n' roll music and how it guided her programming as a deejay:

> That was, I guess a feeling. It was a feeling. If I played a record by Aretha Franklin, a female, I would come back and play how I felt from the feeling I got from her and maybe do Ray Charles. I would go by my listeners' fan mail that they had sent me, requesting, "Would you play Ray Charles between two and two thirty? I'll be on my break from the phone company and we want to hear 'Baby What I Say'" by Ray Charles. And so, you would have an element of timeframes you would try to please the masses of people. Then at three when school was out, you got your teenagers and you want to play some fast music then for them, because they don't want to hear the blues, like that I may have been playing earlier at ten in the morning.

Chattie Hattie Leeper Oral History Interview #3, J. Murrey Atkins Library Special Collections, University of North Carolina at Charlotte, January 19, 2007.

55. Forman, *One Night on TV*, 159.

56. For more on the payola scandal, see John A. Jackson, *Big Beat Heat*, 238–267.

57. For more on the genesis of the sock hop and its use by radio deejays, see Ennis, *The Seventh Stream*, 154–160. Ennis uses as a case study the sock hops and dances of Detroit radio deejay Bill Randle. For sock hops by radio deejays in the Chicago area, see Robert Pruter, *Chicago Soul* (Urbana and Chicago: University of Illinois Press, 1991), 11–12.

58. Mark Opsasnick, *Capitol Rock* ([Philadelphia]: Xlibris Corporation, 2002), 71–72.

59. Interview with the author.

60. *One Night on TV*, 157.

61. Ibid., 118.

62. Ibid., 159."

63. See Forman, *Once Night on TV*, 156 and Jeff Martin, "TV Teen Club: Teen TV as Safe Harbor," in *Teen Television: Essays on Programming and Fandom*, ed. Sharon Marie Ross and Louisa Ellen Stein (Jefferson, NC: McFarland & Company, 2008), 30.

64. Dorothy Brandon, "Whiteman Contributes His Music at Dances of Town's Teen-Agers," *New York Herald Tribune*, February 6, 1949. Brandon was the editor of a section of the *Tribune* called "Today's Moderns."

65. Jeff Martin, "TV Teen Club," 33. .

66. "TV: The New Home for Deejays," *Billboard*, October 7, 1950.

67. "Jack Thayer," *Twin Cities Music Highlights*, Pavek Museum of Broadcasting, St. Louis Park, MN. http://twincitiesmusichighlights.net/radio—personalities/jack-thayer.

68. Another show, also titled *Bandstand Matinee*, was hosted by Sherman Butler, out of WMAL-TV, Washington, DC.

69. Dale Young, interview with the author, February 6, 2017.

70. June Bundy, "Who Picks Disks: D.J.'s Say They Do; Stations Say no," *Billboard*, November 10, 1956.

71. Matthew Delmont, *The Nicest Kids in Town: American Bandstand, Rock 'n' Roll, and the Struggle for Civil Rights in 1950s Philadelphia* (Berkeley: University of California Press, 2012), 35.

72. MacDonald, *Blacks and White TV*, 74.

73. Delmont, *Nicest Kids in Town*, 36.

74. Barlow, "Commercial Television," *Split Image*, 284. Acceptable "roles" for Black performers during the 1950s were as musicians, singers, and dancers. As Jannette L. Dates writes, "The dominant image of Black people on television in the fifties was that of 'the entertainer.'" She asserts that the Black performers who were ubiquitous on variety shows of the period "were employed with some degree of dignity." The idea, though, that Black people could only be safely presented on national television as performers also bespeaks the prejudicial and stereotypical attitudes and outlooks of white station owners, managers, and producers throughout TV's history.

75. "Television: Negro Performers Win Better Roles in TV Than Any Other Medium," *Ebony*, June 1, 1950, 22–24. Also see Dates, who argues that the belief among Black viewers that television was becoming more responsive to the visibility of Black expression "increased . . . because of Black-oriented publications. Black people involved with television even in minor ways were often featured in publications like *Ebony* magazine and the *Afro-American* newspaper. Unfortunately, the awesome breadth

and scope of original Black talent failed to penetrate the television medium, despite the emergence of an era of integration (between 1947 and 1965 that had resulted from the liberal momentum of the war years." Barlow, *Split Image*, 284.

76. Lynn Spigel, *Welcome to the Dreamhouse: Popular Media and Postwar Suburbs* (Durham, NC: Duke University Press, 2001), 36. Spigel refers to the widely cited remarks of NBC's then vice president Pat Weaver that television "would make the 'entire world into a small town, instantly available, with the leading actors on the world stage known on sight or by voice to all within it.'" As Spigel notes: "But for Weaver, this democratic utopian world was in fact a very small town, a place where different cultural practices were homogenized and channeled through a medium whose messages were truly American." Alan Nadel makes a similar point: "If television was the site of exemplary citizenship—the apotheosis of democracy—it was a new kind of democracy, one forging consensus by precluding controversy. And since television was *the* American activity, anything not suitable for broadcast, by implication, was un-American." *Television in Black and White America: Race and National Identity* (Lawrence: University Press of Kansas, 2005), 36. For more on Pat Weaver's remarks and their implications for the future of television see J. Fred MacDonald, *One Nation under Television: The Rise and Decline of Network TV* (Chicago: Nelson-Hall, 1994), 52–54.

77. Forman, *One Night on TV*, 249–250.

78. MacDonald, *One Nation under Television*, 9. Many Black organizations during the time banded together to protest the unfair and unequal representation of Black people on TV as well as the paucity of Blacks in positions of power and decision-making. Along with the NAACP, some of these organizations included the Television Authority Committee on Employment Opportunities for Negroes, Committee for the Negro in the Arts, Committee of Twelve, Harlem Committee on Unemployment in Television, and Coordinating Council for Negro Performers. MacDonald notes that in 1951 the Television Authority Committee wrote to the major networks and "challenged writers, directors and producers to employ Black specialty acts, integrate Black singers and dancers into chorus groups, use Black actors in the many dramatic role reflecting their participation in everyday life, and create new program appropriately utilizing Black talent." *Blacks and White TV*, 9–10. For an example of NAACP campaigns against discrimination in broadcasting see "Now a Negro Push on Radio-TV," *Broadcasting*, July 1, 1963, 27.

79. William H. Whyte, *The Organization Man* (New York: Simon & Schuster), 1956. A 1950s bestseller, Whyte's study analyzed the effects of corporate life on American men and scrutinized the burgeoning bureaucratization of the American workplace.

80. Alan Freed, of course, did make it to primetime TV with *Big Beat*—but not for long. Freed's *Big Beat* will be discussed in more detail in Chapter 2.

81. "WGR-TV Sends Apology to Negro Hustled Off Floor on 'Dance Party,'" unidentified newspaper clipping, ca. 1954, BRTC. WGR actually began as an NBC affiliate.

82. "WGR-TV Sends Apology to Negro Hustled Off Floor on 'Dance Party,'" *Variety*, ca. 1954. Apparently, the young man's father was a pullman car attendant in Toronto (where the show also broadcast) who threatened to have the Canadian Pacific

Railway union (which he belonged to) protest the station's actions. Clearly, the station managers feared such a reprisal.

83. Laurence W. Etling, "Pioneer Disc Jockey," *Popular Music & Society* 23, no. 3 (Fall 1999): 43.

84. Matthew F. Delmont, "Dancing around the 'Glaring Light of Television': Black Teen Dance Shows in the South," *Southern Spaces,* September 29, 2015, https://souther nspaces.org/2015/dancing-around-glaring-light-television-Black-teen-dance-shows-south/. Also see Thomas J. Porter and Art Peters, "Mitch Thomas Fired from TV Dance Party Job," *Philadelphia Tribune,* January 17, 1958. For more on Storer Broadcasting see Herbert Howard, *Multiple Ownership in Television Broadcasting* (New York: Arno Press, 1979), 142–144.

85. The kinescope was an early and rather crude form of videotaping.

86. Bud Buschardt, *The Sump'n Else Show* (Plano, TX: Entry Way Publishing, 2014), 29. Bud Buschardt, interview with the author, July 13, 2020. *The Sump'n Else Show* ran from 1965 to 1968 on WFAA-TV in the Dallas–Fort Worth area; even in 1965, then, this was pretty much still the standard way of filming the teen dance shows. Buschardt, who died in 2021, was an accomplished radio and TV professional. At WFAA-TV from 1963 to 1981, Buschardt was a producer, director, commercial and program writer, and audio specialist for *Music News Reports*. From 1981 to 1991, he served as producer, writer, and host of *The KVIL Oldies but Goodies Weekend Show* on Sundays; KVIL was the premier radio station in Dallas/Fort Worth. He also taught for many years in the Radio, Television and Film Department at the University of North Texas. Buschardt also boasted a personal collection consisting of over 300,000 photograph records, tapes, and compact discs.

87. Lee Woodward, interview with the author, August 27, 2014.

88. Steve Stephens, interview with the author, October 2, 2019.

89. Robert DuPree, "High Time of Oregon Rock," *Two Louies,* February 2003, 9. *High Time* debuted on KPTV-Channel 12, on August 12, 1957, in Portland, Oregon. This was the same day that on another Oregon channel *American Bandstand* premiered in syndicated form. The host of *High Time*, Gene Brendler, went on to become KPYV's public affairs director.

90. Philip Auslander, *Liveness: Performance in a Mediatized Culture* (London and New York: Routledge, 1999), 16. Auslander also discusses how in its early days television was compared to other forms of media including radio, film, and theater and often viewed "as a hybrid of existing forms." Auslander writes that "One analyst characterized television as a 'new and synthetic medium . . . radio with sight, movies with the zest of immediacy, theatre (intimate or spectactular) with all seats about six rows back and in the centre, tabloid opera and circus without peanut vendors'" (15).

91. Ibid., 15.

92. Lynn Spigel, "Television in the Family Circle," in *Logics of Television: Essays in Cultural Criticism*, ed. Patricia Mellencamp (Bloomington: Indiana University Press, 1990), 76.

93. Cecilia Tichi, *Electronic Hearth: Creating an American Television Culture* (New York: Oxford University Press, 1991).

94. Raymond Williams, *Television: Technology and Cultural Form* (Hanover, CT: Wesleyan University Press, 1974), 20–21.

95. Apparently both housewives and soldiers at army bases loved to watch *American Bandstand*.

96. *Television in Black and White*, 54.

97. "*Teen Time Dance Party*, with Jim Walton," Wied., *Variety*, February 5, 1958.

98. Carl Belz, *The Story of Rock* (New York: Harper/Colophon Books, 1969), 103.

99. Martin Esslin, "The Signs of Stage and Screen," in his *The Field of Drama* (London and New York: Metheun: 1987), 97.

100. Sally Banes and John F. Szwed, "From 'Messin' Around' to 'Funky Western Civilization': The Rise and Fall of Dance Instructions Songs," in *Dancing Many Drums: Excavacations in African American Dance*, ed. Thomas F. DeFrantz (Madison: University of Wisconsin Press, 2002), 169–205. This is a comprehensive essay on dance instruction songs with an emphasis on the 1960s.

101. Television, of course, also communicates stereotypical ideologies regarding class and gender, which will be explored in Chapter 5.

102. Lynn Spigel, *Make Room for TV: Television and the Family Ideal in Postwar America* (Chicago: University of Chicago Press, 1992), 44. Spigel explains that this type of advertising, to both Black and white viewers, reinforced "the middle-class suburban ideal."

103. John Fiske, *Reading Television* (London: Methuen, 1985), 86.

104. I am borrowing this phrase from what media scholar Alan Nadel has written about 1950s primetime television's "visual segregation." *Television in Black and White America: Race and National Identity* (Lawrence: University Press of Kansas, 2005), 137.

105. John Fiske, *Television Culture* (London: Taylor & Francis Group, 2010), 10.

106. George Lipsitz, *Time Passages, Collective Memory and American Popular Culture* (Minneapolis: University of Minnesota Press, 1990), 122.

107. John Fiske, *Reading Television* (London and New York: Methuen, 1985), 103. As Fiske explains, "[E]ach one of us holds mutually contradictory beliefs about our position in society, and we respond to our condition in different ways at the same time."

108. Robin D.G. Kelley, "Notes on Deconstructing 'The Folk,'" *American Historical Review* 97, no. 5 (December 1992): 1408, 1401. In this influential essay, Kelley lays out a very cogent analysis of how individuals relate to popular culture. He insists, along with other scholars such as Lawrence Levine and George Lipsitz, that audiences develop a dialogic relationship with the "texts" of mass-mediated culture. He writes of audiences, particularly those marginalized within the culture and within those cultural texts, that "they engage in a dialogue, a kind of conversation—informed by cultural memory and lived experience—with the voices, signs, and symbols created and disseminated ostensibly to 'entertain.'" Kelley's argument here serves as a counterpoint to that of Carl Belz, referred to earlier in this chapter, in refuting the idea that "folk" culture is necessarily untouched by commercial culture. Engagement in and with radio and film, as he argues (and by extension television), are not "antithetical" to the processes by which individuals, or performers, use their creativity and

create performances. The notion of a folk culture (or folk dance for my argument) also suggests a coming together of individuals of like-minded or homogeneous communities interested in the preservation of heritage and group traditions. But this was not the case with teenagers' involvement with the electronic medium of TV and the teen shows where they were essentially coming together because of the dancing and thus were making their own traditions. Social and collective bonds were created *as a result of* the dancing, and this was as true for Black teenagers, on the all-Black teen shows, as well as for the white dancers.

109. Robin D.G. Kelley, *Freedom Dreams: The Black Radical Imagination* (Boston: Beacon Press, 2002), 3–12.

110. Delmont, *The Nicest Kids in Town*, 44–45. Delmont notes that during *American Bandstand*'s earliest years, in 1952–1953 when it was hosted by Bob Horn, the show admitted Black teenagers, like white teenagers, on a first-come, first-served basis. By 1954, as the show's popularity increased, the exclusive "committee" of twelve white teenagers had greater sway over admittance procedures; a letter was required now to gain entry to the show, which favored suburban teenagers on the outskirts of Philadelphia while neglecting the Black teenagers who lived nearby and attended the local West Philadelphia High School. Delmont conducted an interview with the West Philadelphia teenager Walter Palmer who recounted organizing other local Black teenagers to challenge the prejudicial admission polices of *American Bandstand*, which by 1954 was, for all intents and purposes, segregated. (Palmer went on to become a noted community activist in Philadelphia.)

Chapter 2

1. *Red, Hot, and Blue* was hosted by Southern deejay Dewey Phillips, who was immortalized in the Broadway show *Memphis* in 2009. For more on Phillips, see Louis Cantor's *Dewey and Elvis: The Life and Times of a Rock 'n' Roll Deejay*. For more titles of shows from this period, and from the 1960s, see Jake Austen, *TV a-Go-Go: Rock on TV from American Bandstand to American Idol* (Chicago: Chicago Review Press), 36–48.

2. "Beat Generation," undated newspaper clipping, ca. 1956, n. pag. *American Bandstand* Clipping File, Billy Rose Theatre Collection, New York Public Library for the Performing Arts.

3. Tobias Wolff, *This Boy's Life: A Memoir* (New York: Grove Press, 1989), 135.

4. He actually refers here to the generation of white teen idols that included Fabian, Frankie Avalon, and Bobby Rydell. He admits that these singers could churn out commercially viable songs but that they had "no particular feel for the music's roots or subtleties." See Garofalo and Steve Waksman, *Rockin' Out: Popular Music in the USA* (Upper Saddle River, NJ: Pearson Education, 2008), 132–33.

5. Allen J. Matusow, *The Unraveling of America: A History of Liberalism in the 1960s* (New York: Harper & Row, 1984), 305.

6. Michael T. Bertrand, *Race, Rock, and Elvis* (Urbana: University of Illinois Press, 2005), 65–66.

7. George Lipsitz, *Time Passages: Collective Memory and American Popular Culture* (Minneapolis: University of Minnesota Press, 1989), 122–123.

8. Gay Morris, *A Game for Dancers: Performing Modernism in the Postwar Years: 1945–1960* (Middletown, CT: Wesleyan University Press, 2006), 88.

9. Brinkley, quoting from Daniel Bell's landmark Cold War–era book *The End of Ideology*, describes the consensus as "a worldview that sometimes seemed to rest on fear of what might happen if society embarked on any great crusades: a fear of class conflict, a fear of 'mass irrationality,' a fear of the dark passions that fanaticism could and had unleashed in the world.'" "The Illusion of Unity in Cold War Culture," in *Rethinking Cold War Culture*, ed. Peter J. Kuznick and James Gilbert (Washington, DC: Smithsonian Books, 2001), 62, 65.

10. "An Appeal to the World," quoted in Mary L. Dudziak, *Cold War Civil Rights: Race and the Image of American Democracy* (Princeton, NJ: Princeton University Press, 2000), 44. The petition was filed on October 23, 1947.

11. Alan Nadel, *Television in Black-and-White America: Race and National Identity* (Lawrence: University of Kansas Press, 2005), 35.

12. Ibid., 6. For more on this idea, also see Alan Nadel, *Containment Culture: American Narratives, Postmodernism, and the Atomic Age* (Durham, NC, and London: Duke University Press, 1995).

13. Of course, not all teenagers at all times have displayed subversive behaviors. Teenagers of the 1950s are often remembered, as youth historian Thomas Hine notes, as "golden and innocent." *The Rise and Fall of the American Teenager* (New York: Perennial/HarperCollins, 1992), 226. However, during the 1950s the idea of the teenager was tinged with subversiveness, particularly because of its association with juvenile delinquency. With the aid of movies and popular culture, teen culture had become associated with rebel culture. Marlon Brando in *The Wild One* (1953) and James Dean in *Rebel without a Cause* (1955) were favorite anti-heroes symbolizing a world of loud music, leather jackets, fast cars, and sex. For more on the history of the teenager see Grace Palladino, *Teenagers: An American History* (New York: Basic Books, 1996); and Jon Savage, *Teenage: The Creation of Youth Culture* (New York: Viking Press, 2007).

14. Andrea Carosso, *Cold War Narratives: American Culture in the 1950s* (New York: Peter Lang, 2012), 190.

15. James S. Coleman, *The Adolescent Society: The Social Life of the Teenager and Its Impact on Education* (New York: Free Press, 196), 97.

16. Carl Belz, *The Story of Rock* (New York: Harper/Colophon Books, 1969), 104.

17. J. Fred MacDonald, *Blacks and White TV: African Americans in Television since 1948* (Chicago: Nelson-Hall, 1992), 11.

18. John A. Jackson, *Big Beat Heat: Alan Freed and the Early Years of Rock & Roll* (New York: Schirmer Books, 1991), 122.

19. Ibid., 168.

20. Key texts on *American Bandstand* include John Jackson's *American Bandstand: Dick Clark and the Making of a Rock 'n' Roll Empire* (New York: Oxford University Press,

1997); and Matthew F. Delmont's *The Nicest Kids in Town: American Bandstand, Rock 'n' Roll, and the Struggle for Civil Rights in 1950s Philadelphia* (Berkeley: University of California Press, 2012).

21. Murray Forman, *One Night on TV Is Worth Weeks at the Paramount: Popular Music on Early Television* (Durham, NC: Duke University Press, 2012). See Chapter 1 for early precursors to *American Bandstand*.

22. Ibid., 26.

23. Delmont, *The Nicest Kids in Town*, 41.

24. Ibid., 2, 1, 137–143.

25. Ibid., *The Nicest Kids*, 41.

26. Jackson, *American Bandstand*, 17–19.

27. Lilla Anderson, "Backstage at Bandstand," April 17, 1958, *American Bandstand* Clipping file, Billy Rose Theatre Collection, New York Public Library for the Performing Arts.

28. Delmont, *The Nicest Kids*, 159.

29. Jackson, *American Bandstand*, 24.

30. Matthew Delmont makes the persuasive case that the discriminatory housing practices in Philadelphia were similar to the tactics used to keep Black teenagers from attending *American Bandstand*. *The Nicest Kids*, 48.

31. Ibid., 43.

32. Ibid., 44.

33. John W. Roberts, *From Hucklebuck to Hip Hop: Social Dance in the African American Community in Philadelphia* (Philadelphia: Odunde, 1995), 35.

34. Ibid., 36.

35. Ibid., 36.

36. Brenda Dixon Gottschild, *Digging the Africanist Presence in American Performance* (Westport, CT: Praeger, 1996), 26.

37. Yvonne Moten, transcript, "The Buddy Deane Show," Dancing Program 5: New Worlds, New Forms. Producer by Orlando Bagwell, Rhoda Grauer, and Susan Bellows (ArtHaus Musik, 1993). Accessed June 29, 2017, http://search.alexanderstreet.com/view/work/447170. On the TV broadcast, Moten also explained that "It felt very funny being segregated. I went to an all-white high school and I was used to that. But it still felt unnatural in some sense because you felt that we were all teenagers, we all had the same interests, and likes and dislikes, and problems, and you only saw whites dancing on certain days, and then there was an occasional day when black danced, and of course that was a highlight."

38. Dixon Gottschild, *Digging the Africanist Presence*, 24.

39. *Twist*, a film by Ron Mann. DVD: Home Vision Entertainment, 2002.

40. Matthew Delmont quotes Ray Smith, a former *Bandstand* dancer (who contributed research for one of Dick Clark's histories of the show), who states that Peatross told him that he learned the dance because "I watched this Black couple do it." "Dancing around the 'Glaring Light of Television': Black Teen Dance Shows in the South," *Southern Spaces*, September 29, 2015, https://southernspaces.org/2015/dancing-around-glaring-light-television-Black-teen-dance-shows-south/.

41. Mark Opsasnick, *Capitol Rock* ([Philadelphia]: Xlibris, 2002), 67–68.

42. Lawrence Laurent, "Youth Upholds TV DJs," *Washington Post*, October 23, 1960, Special Collection in Mass Media and Culture, University Libraries, University of Maryland.

43. Opsasnick, *Capitol Rock*, 68–69.

44. Antoinette Matlins, interview with the author, July 20, 2013.

45. See Chapter 5 for more on Antoinette Matlins and her career.

46. Flor, "Bandstand Matinee," *Variety*, undated newspaper clipping, [c. 1954]. *Bandstand Matinee* Clipping File, Billy Rose Theatre Collection, New York Public Library for the Performing Arts, n. pag.

47. Lynn Spigel, *Welcome to the Dreamhouse*: Popular Media and Postwar Suburbs (Durham, NC: Duke University Press, 2001), 35.

48. Louis Menand, "The Horror: Congress Investigates the Comics," *New Yorker*, March 31, 2008, 1–14. Accessed at www.newyorker.com/magazine/2008/03/31/the-horror.

49. Estes Kefauver, "Juvenile Delinquency (Motion Picture) Hearings before the Subcommittee to Investigate Juvenile Delinquency of the Committee on the Judiciary." Excerpt of transcript, 1955. Accessed at archive.org/stream/juveniledelinque955unit/juveniledelinque955unit_djvu.txtreaffirmed, n. pag.

50. *The Milt Grant Show*. *1950s Teen Dance TV Shows*, Vol. 1, The Video Beat 1950s & 1960s Rock 'n' Roll on Video, San Francisco, CA.

51. In his analysis, Dick Hebidge focuses primarily on working-class youth and subcultures. In this section, "The Sources of Style," he discusses how the media essentially takes working-class style (he is talking about the revival of British "Teddy Boy" culture of the 1970s) and reimagines it, or appropriates it, and gives it back to working-class youth audiences in a *new* form, "framed" by an overlay of ideological discourse. *Subculture: The Meaning of Style* (London: Methuen, 1979), 85. Of course, I am primarily discussing middle-class youth, but I think the same argument applies in the sense that these images of themselves, mediated now through TV, take on a new life.

52. "King of the 1956 Teenagers," *The Journal*, Friday, July 20, 1990, B1,4, unattributed newspaper article, WTTG-TV files, Special Collection in Mass Media and Culture Series Collection, University of Maryland.

53. Hebdige, *Subculture*, 80.

54. Hine, *The Rise and Fall of the American Teenager*, 247–248.

55. Tony Bonanno, interview with the author, June 29, 2013.

56. Hebdige, *Subculture*, 85. Again, discussing working-class subcultures, Hebdige makes the very interesting point that they "in part contest and in part agree with the dominant definitions of who and what they are, and there is a substantial amount of shared ideological ground not only between them and the adult working-class culture . . . but also between them and the dominant culture" (76). I believe the same holds true for this subculture of primarily white, middle-class youth. As I point out earlier in the chapter, they were resistant to yet also a part of the 1950s consensus culture.

57. For a highly entertaining and richly detailed account of *The Buddy Deane Show*, see John Waters, "Ladies and Gentlemen . . . The Nicest Kids in Town!," in *Crackpot: The*

Obsessions of John Waters (New York: Macmillan, 1986). Waters also describes the making of the Broadway production of *Hairspray* in "Finally, Footlights on the Fat Girls," *New York Times*, August 11, 2002.

58. Laura Wexler, "The Last Dance," *Style: Smart Living in Baltimore* 11, no. 5 (September/October 2003):132.

59. Orlando Bagwell, Rhoda Grauer, and Susan Bellow, prods., "Dancing New Worlds, New Forms," PBS *Dance* (ArtHaus Musick, 1993). Transcript. Accessed June 29, 2017, https://search.alexanderstreet.com/preview/work/bibliographic_entity|video_w ork|447170.

60. Laura Wexler, "The Last Dance," 133.

61. Antoinette Matlins, interview with the author, July 10, 2013.

62. Tony Warner, *Buddy's Top 20: The Story of Baltimore's Hottest TV Dance and the Guy Who Brought It to Life!* (Malvern, AR: Warner Marketing, 2003), 91.

63. Ibid.

64. Jessica Goldstein, "On Hairspray's 25th Anniversary, 'Buddy Deane' Committee Looks Back," *Washington Post*, January 20, 2013, 1–6, www.washingtonpost.com/entertainment/tv/buddy-deane -committee-looks-back/2013/01/17/a45a1cc2-5c23-11e2-88d0-c4cf65c3ad15_story.html.

65. Ibid., "On Hairspray's 25th Anniversary," 3.

66. John Fiske, *Television Culture* (London and New York: Methuen, 1987), 51.

67. This "one night only" practice, as such, was prevalent in many parts of the country in the postwar years. Dance historian Katrina Hazzard Gordon documents how most dance halls in Cleveland, for instance, usually set aside Monday evenings for Black social dancers. She notes that various Black groups rented a hall or club and charged a small admission fee to help cover costs. See *Jookin': The Rise of Social Dance Formations in African-American Culture* (Philadelphia: Temple University Press, 1990), 125–127,

68. Mickey Teague, interview with the author, November 23, 2013.

69. Donald Thoms, interview with Beverly Lindsay Johnson, 1988. *Teenarama*. Kendall Production Files: ACMA-AV005285, The Anacostia Museum and Center for African American History and Culture, Smithsonian Institution.

70. Teague, interview with the author.

71. Wexler, "The Last Dance," 133.

72. Ibid., 134.

73. "Pickets Protest TV Show," *The Afro-American*, June 30, 1962, n. pag.

74. Wexler, "The Last Dance," 166.

Chapter 3

1. Thomas DeFrantz, "Improvising Social Exchange: African American Social Dance," in *The Oxford Handbook of Critical Improvisation Studies*, vol. 1, ed. George E. Louis and Benjamin Piekut (New York: Oxford University Press, 2016), 330.

2. Several scholars have grappled with the concept of the racialization of space. Historian George Lipsitz has written that "the lived experience of race has a spatial dimension, and the lived experience of space has a racial dimension." He notes, too, that especially during the Jim Crow era "racial control rested openly upon spatial control." See "The Racialization of Space and the Spatialization of Race; Theorizing the Hidden Architecture of Landscape," *Landscape Journal* 6, no. 1 (2007): 12, 17. Gender historian LaKisha Simmons writes about the respatialization of Mardi Gras and how for many young Black women the event provided a space for "rethinking of the self and for constituting subjectivities momentarily free from the racism of Jim Crow." *Crescent City Girls: The Lives of Young Black Women in Segregated New Orleans* (Chapel Hill: University of North Carolina Press, 2015), 199.

3. Eustace Gay, "Pioneer in TV Field Doing Marvelous Job Furnishing Youth with Recreation," *Philadelphia Tribune*, February 11, 1956.

4. Alonzo Kittrels, "Back in the Day: *The Mitch Thomas Show* Was Must-Watch TV," *Philadelphia Tribune*, December 9, 2017. Kittrels (the director of administrative services at the *Philadelphia Tribune* (with whom I also had some personal communication), cites former social dancer Cliff Leatherberry whose aunt apparently drove him from Philadelphia to Wilmington to be on the show and "still remembers dancing his favorite dances such as the stroll, slop and cha-cha." Alonzo Kittrels, personal communication, July 2, 2019.

5. Kittrels, "Back in the Day."

6. Ibid.

7. "Disc Jockey's R&R Show Attracts," *Philadelphia Tribune*, September 11, 1956.

8. Kittrels, "Back in the Day."

9. Delores Lewis, "Philly Date Line," *Philadelphia Tribune*, December 7, 1957.

10. Matthew Delmont, "Dancing around the Glaring Light of Television: Black Teen Dance Shows in the South," *Southern Spaces*, September 29, 2015, https://southernspa ces.org/2015/dancing-around-glaring-light-television-Black-teen-dance-shows-south/.

11. *Black Philadelphia Memories*, dir. Trudi Brown (Philadelphia, WHYY-TV 12, 1999), television documentary.

12. Maxine Leeds Craig, *Ain't I a Beauty Queen: Black Women, Beauty, and the Politics of Race* (New York: Oxford University Press, 2002), 43.

13. Jelani Favors, "Building Black Institutions: Autonomy, Labor and HBCUs," Learning for Justice Podcast, www.learningforjustice.org/podcasts/teaching-hard-history/jim-crow-era/building-black-institutions-autonomy-labor-and-hbcus. For more on the history of Black institution building and W. E. B. Du Bois's thoughts on the subject, see Wilson Jeremiah Moses, *Afrotopia: The Roots of African American Popular History* (Cambridge: Cambridge University Press, 1998), 161–164.

14. Otis Givens, interview with the author, January 6, 2020.

15. Ibid.

16. Ibid.

17. Ibid.

18. "'Movin' N Grovin' [sic] Is New Dance Craze," *Philadelphia Tribune*, August 4, 1956. Also see "Hal Singer Starts New Dance Step," *Daily Defender*, July 30, 1956.

19. *Black Philadelphia Memories.*

20. Benita Brown, "'Boppin' at Miss Mattie's Place': African American Grassroots Culture in North Philadelphia from the Speakeasy to the Uptown Theater During the 1960s" (PhD diss., Temple University, 1999), 149.

21. See Sandra R. Lieb, *Mother of the Blues: A Study of Ma Rainey* (Amherst: University of Massachusetts Press, 1981), 26.

22. Matthew Delmont, *The Nicest Kids in Town: American Bandstand, Rock 'n' Roll, and the Struggle for Civil Rights in 1950s Philadelphia* (Berkeley: University of California Press, 2012), 172–173.

23. Art Peters, "Bosses Cite Low Rating of TV Show," *Philadelphia Tribune*, June 17, 1958; "Mitch Thomas, 72: TV Dance Show Host," [Wilmington] *News Journal*, February 13, 1999.

24. See *Teenage Frolics*, https://history.capitolbroadcasting.com/programs/entertainm ent-shows/teenage-frolics/.

25. Interview with the author, April 20, 2021. Yvonne Lewis-Holly ran for lieutenant governor of North Carolina in 2020.

26. Interview with the author, May 3, 2021. According to Fletcher, "I don't think that J. D. thought that his new position had tremendous symbolic significance. I know I didn't. When somebody would call and accuse me of contributing to the fall of southern civilization, I would tell them that J. D. was a good announcer, that was why he was hired, and that's why he would continue to announce us." Fred Fletcher and Chuck Holmes, *Tempus Fugit (Time Flies)* (self-pub: Fred Fletcher, 1990), 95–96.

27. Danny Hooley, "J. D. Lewis Jr., Black Broadcast Pioneer, Dies," *News and Observer* [Raleigh, NC], February 20, 2007.

28. The other Black radio program on the station at that time was the gospel show hosted by Sister Mabel Gary Philpot, a powerful and admired local community preacher and the first Black host/deejay of a regularly scheduled radio program. She later migrated to WRAL-TV where she garnered a large, multi-racial audience. "Sister Gary: This 'Powerful Preacher' was Raleigh's First Black Voice on the Radio," *[Raleigh] News & Observer*, February 20, 2022.

29. Interview with the author.

30. Interview with the author, April 30, 2021.

31. Ibid.

32. Interview with the author, August 9, 2021.

33. Ibid.

34. Interview with the author.

35. Interview with the author.

36. Interview with the author, November 19, 2021.

37. Interview with the author.

38. Interview with the author.

39. William Barlow, "Commercial and Noncommercial Radio," in *Split Image: African Americans in the Mass Media*, ed. Janette L. Dates and William Barlow (Washington, DC: Howard University Press, 1990), 210.

40. According to William Barlow, "In 1949 there were only four radio stations in the entire country with formats that appealed directly to Black consumers. By 1954 there

were no less than 200 stations in this category, and that number rose to 400 by 1956. However, Black ownership of radio properties lagged far behind these figures." "Commercial and Noncommercial Radio," 214, 212–213.

41. Patrice Gaines, "Dance Show Fans Bop Back in Time," *Washington Post*, August 2, 1998.

42. After Bob King, there was a rotation of hosts for *Teenarama*, including WOOK radio personality Leon Isaac Kennedy (who went on to become a popular actor in the 1970s).

43. "Dance Party: The *Teenarama* Story," press release, Kendall Production Records, Box 1, Folder 4, Administrative Records and Promotional Material, 1998–2002, Anacostia Community Museum, Smithsonian Institution. Also see: handdance.blinks.net.

44. "Dance Party: The *Teenarama* Story," press release.

45. *Teenarama*, "Research Narrative," Kendall Production Records, Box 1, Folder 4, Administrative Records and Promotional Material, 1998–2002, Anacostia Community Museum, Smithsonian Institution, 14.

46. Ibid.

47. Linda Wheeler, "Teen Dance the Years Away: With Vintage Ties and Tunes," *Washington Post*, February 19, 2001.

48. Laverne Parks, interview with the author, December 12, 2013.

49. Gaines, "Dance Show Fans Bop Back in Time," 1998.

50. Parks, interview with the author.

51. Ibid.

52. Virginia Vitzthum, "Dancing Together Apart: Filmmaker Beverly Lindsay Wants to Reprise *Teenarama* and the Heyday of Hand Dance in Segregated DC," *Washington City Paper*, November 13, 1992.

53. Gaines, "Dance Show Fans Bop Back in Time."

54. Yvonne Mills, interview with Beverly Lindsay-Johnson, 1998. *Teenarama*, ACMA AVOO5284, The Anacostia Community Museum, Smithsonian Institution.

55. Brian Ward, *Just My Soul Responding: Rhythm and Blues, Black Consciousness, and Race Relations* (Berkeley: University of California Press, 1998), 3.

56. Kevin Gaines, *Uplifting the Race: Black Leadership, Politics, and Culture in the Twentieth Century* (Chapel Hill and London: University of North Carolina Press, 1996), xiv. Gaines explains how ideas about racial uplift were attempts, by some, "to rehabilitate the image of black people through class distinctions." He notes, too, that historically uplift has had contested meanings: "On the one hand, a broader vision of uplift signifying collective social aspiration, advancement, and struggle had been the legacy of the emancipation era. On the other hand, black elites made uplift the basis for a racialized elite identity claiming Negro improvement through class stratification as race progress." *Uplifting the Race*, xiv, xv.

57. See Teresa Wiltz, "'The *Teenarama* Story': A Dance Floor Revolution," *Washington Post*, April 26, 2006. Also see "WOOK Says It Isn't Just One-Color TV," on criticism of the show when it was announced by members of the Black community. The reporter quotes Julius Hobson, the chairman of the Congress on Racial Equality, that "I object to foot tapping, dancing, and screaming and shouting. . . . If they play the traditional

type stuff they have a distorted idea of Negro interest." Unidentified newspaper clipping, ca. 1963, Kendall Production Records [*Teenarama*], The Anacostia Community Museum, The Smithsonian Institution. Kevin Gaines refers to this attitude as the "assimilationist cultural aesthetic," a belief held by many middle- and upper-class Black people "in response to pejorative minstrel-based constructions of blackness." *Uplifting the Race*, 76. Similar concerns were echoed by Washington, DC's Urban League, too, who worried that programs consisting entirely of Black performers or characters might do damage to the race by presenting stereotypical and demeaning images.

58. Robin D.G. Kelley, *Race Rebels: Culture, Politics, and the Black Working Class* (New York: Free Press, 1994), 50.

59. Mike Goodwin, interview with Beverly Lindsay-Johnson, 1998. *Teenarama*, ACMA AVOO5284, The Anacostia Community Museum, Smithsonian Institution.

60. *Teenarama*, "Research Narrative," 21.

61. Vitzthum, "Dancing Together Apart," 3.

62. Kelley, *Race Rebels*, 45.

63. Although Robin Kelley writes about the Black working-class in the early-to-mid-twentieth century, his argument may be applied to the kind of "congregation" taking place on the Black teen dance shows. He makes the important point that these "sensual pleasures of food, drink, and dancing" were not only about "escape." They were also about sharing "a common vernacular" that brought with it pleasure and common cause. *Race Rebels*, 47.

64. Katrina Hazzard-Gordon, *Jookin: The Rise of Social Dance Formations in African-American Culture* (Philadelphia: Temple University Press, 1990), xii.

65. James Sator, interview with the author, July 2, 2019.

66. Thomas Hine, The Rise and Fall of the American Teenager (New York: Perennial/HarperCollins, 1992), 247. Grace Palladino makes the point that "'The fact was, when middle-class parents condemned juvenile delinquency, they were usually referring to working-class teenage style." *Teenagers: An American History* (New York: Basic Books, 1996), 162.

67. Tony Bonanno, interview with the author, June 29, 2013.

68. Email correspondence with the author, May 16, 2022.

69. William Barlow, *Voiceover: The Making of Black Radio* (Philadelphia: Temple University Press, 1999), 103

70. Richard E. Stamz and Patrick A. Roberts, *Give 'Em Soul, Richard: Race, Radio, and R&B in Chicago* (Urbana and Chicago: University of Illinois Press, 2010), 59.

71. Ibid., 79.

72. Phyllis Stamz, interview with the author, August 27, 2019.

73. Ibid.

74. Stamz and Roberts, *Give 'Em Soul*, 63.

75. "Facts on Migration," undated report, Richard E. Stamz Papers, 1919–2010, The Center for Black Music Research, Columbia College, Chicago, Illinois.

76. Ibid.

77. Stamz and Roberts, *Give 'Em Soul*, 78.

78. Ibid.
79. *Teenarama*, "Research Narrative," 12.

Chapter 4

1. Jacqui Malone, *Steppin' on the Blues: The Visible Rhythms of Africa American Dance* (Urbana and Chicago: University of Illinois Press, 1996), 1.
2. Ibid., 14.
3. See Jurretta Heckscher, "Our National Poetry: The Afro-Chesapeake Inventions of American Dance," in *Ballroom, Boogie, Shimmy Sham, Shake: A Social and Popular Dance Reader*, ed. Julie Malnig (Urbana and Chicago: University of Illinois Press, 2009), 23.
4. Ibid. The "rhythmic complexity" of the music, as Jacqui Malone explains, also contributes to the articulation of different body parts—arms, hips, legs—as well as a lowered or crouched body stance to effectuate the movement. *Steppin' on the Blues*, 10. Also see Heckscher, "Our National Poetry," 23.
5. Malone, *Steppin' on the Blues*, 33.
6. Robert Farris Thompson, "An Aesthetic of the Cool," *African Arts* 7, no. 1 (Autumn 1973): 40–51. "Coolness," as Malone notes, "has to do with control, transcendental balance, and directing one's energy with a clear purpose in mind." *Steppin' on the Blues*, 18. What Robert Farris Thompson laid out so eloquently was the concept of an Africanist aesthetic principle of movement, rooted in cosmology and religion, with concomitant techniques of movement (what Dagel Caponi calls "a technology of stylization"), traces of which can still be located in many African-diasporic dances.
7. Heckscher, "Our National Poetry," 23.
8. Malone, *Steppin' on the Blues*, 18.
9. This kind of participatory dialogue, seen much more in Black communities, extended to the symbiotic relationship between studio dancers and their massive TV-viewing audience who were copying those moves and, in turn, bringing them to their school lunch rooms, church gyms, and local neighborhoods. In this somatic dialogue, if you will, there existed a dynamic interplay between the individual and the group—even if that group was virtual.
10. Marcel Mauss, "Techniques of the Body" (1935), in *Marcel Mauss: Techniques, Technology and Civilisation*, ed. Nathan Schlanger (New York: Berghahn Books, 2006).
11. Gena Dagel-Caponi, *Signifyin(g), Sanctifyin', and Slam Dunking: A Reader in African American Expressive Culture* (Amherst: University of Massachusetts Press, 1999), 6.
12. As Marya McQuirter asserts, "there exists an over-determined attitude on the part of many social dance historians regarding African Americans' relationship to and placement within dance." What gets overlooked, she contends, is "this crucial step of acculturation. The yawning lack of discussion about the process of moving from awkwardness to ballroom accomplishment implies an innate dance ability in African Americans." "Awkward Moves: Dance Lessons from the 1940s," in *Dancing*

Many Drums: Excavations in African American Dance, ed. Thomas. F. DeFrantz (Madison: University of Wisconsin Press, 2002), 91.

13. DeFrantz, "African American Dance: A Complex History," in *Dancing Many Drums*, 15.

14. Yvonne Daniels, "Rumba Then and Now," in *Ballroom, Boogie, Shimmy Sham, Shake: A Social and Popular Dance Reader*, ed. Julie Malnig (Urbana and Chicago: University of Illinois Press, 2009), 159.

15. Dagel-Caponi, *Signifyin(g), Sanctifyin', and Slam Dunking*, 8.

16. McQuirter, "Awkward Moves," 87.

17. Robin D.G. Kelley, *Race Rebels, Race Rebels: Culture, Politics, and the Black Working Class* (New York: Free Press, 1994), 47.

18. The Lindy, popular of course since the late 1920s, "had a long life and adapted to many kinds of music." Sally Sommer, "Social Dance," in *The Reader's Companion to American History*, ed. Eric Foner and John A. Garraty (New York: Houghton Mifflin, 1991), 264–265. Richard Powers describes how teenagers' version of the Lindy also mirrored rock 'n' roll's strong back beat. "Teen Dances of the 1950s," https://socialda nce.stanford.edu/Syllabi/teen_dances.htm.

19. Unlike the Lindy of the 1940s, this modified Lindy consisted of even beats in which the slows and quicks of swing were lost but which allowed for "little slides and shuffles to be slipped in between changes of weight." Carrie Stern, "Tube Dancing: Television, Rock and Roll, and Whiteness." Paper presented at the conference of the Congress on Research in Dance, November 17, 2011.

20. As Powers writes, "The tradition of executing one swing move after another was replaced by mostly dancing in place, holding one or both hands, with fewer swing moves." Powers also notes how there were literally hundreds of variations on the swing varying from city to city: "In one high school it might be low and smooth; in another, wide and angular." "Teen Dances."

21. Tony Warner, *Buddy's Top 20: The Story of Baltimore's Hottest TV Dance Show and the Guy Who Brought It to Life!* (Malvern, AR: Warner Marketing, 2003), 141.

22. Benita Brown, "'Boppin' at Miss Mattie's Place': African-American Grassroots Dance Culture in North Philadelphia from the Speakeasy to the Uptown Theater" (PhD diss., Temple University, 2000), 134.

23. For those in Philadelphia, the Bop succeeded the Boogie-woogie and Jitterbug. Brown quotes former dancer Jim Justice who noted that "the jitterbug required a lot of space; the boogie woogie needed somewhat less (space); the bop took very little room." What this meant, then, was that many couples could perform the bop side-by-side other couples on a fairly crowded dance floor (or TV studio). Brown, "'Boppin' at Miss Mattie's Place,'" 140.

24. Art Silva, *How to Dance the Bop!* (self-pub., ca. 1956), The Jerome Robbins Dance Division, The New York Public Library for the Performing Arts.

25. Marshall Stearns and Jean Stearns, *Jazz Dance: The Story of American Vernacular Dance* (New York: Schirmer Books, 1966), 65–67. This also describes what was done in Medicine Shows of the early twentieth century.

26. Brown, "'Boppin' at Miss Mattie's Place,'" 146.

27. In this dance, partners hold each other closely while the woman follows the lead of her male partner. According to Brown, "He takes her three steps backward and then moves forward. He may implement a spin, and after the spin he might lead her into a dip, guiding the woman to the floor where she could almost slide through his legs; but he holds her there for a beat. Again, the timing corresponds with the rhythm of the music. The woman holds tightly to her partner so that he will not drop her." " 'Boppin' at Miss Mattie's Place,'" 146–147.

28. *Swing, Bop and Hand Dance*, Exec. Dir. The National Hand Dance Association, Prod/ Dir. Beverly Lindsay-Johnson, WHUT-TV Howard University documentary, 1996, https://www.youtube.com/watch?v=VtEBmJ5_u0Q&t=1341s.

29. Ibid. Several regional variations of Hand Dance exist—Stepping in Chicago, the Shag in North and South Carolina, and the Philly Bop in Philadelphia; the DC Hand Dance is said to be distinguished by the "seamlessness between the dancers and the dance" and the level of communication between the dance partnership. Virginia Vitzthum, "Dancing Together, Apart: Filmmaker Beverly Lindsay Johnson Wants to Reprise *Teenarama* and the Heyday of Hand Dance in Segregated DC," *Washington City Paper*, November 13, 1998.

30. Sally Sommer, "Social Dance from the 1960s to the Present," in *The Oxford Encyclopedia of Dance* (New York: Oxford University Press, 2004), 631.

31. It is important to point out, too, that even with the group dances, there was, as Tim Wall notes, "the possibility for the more individualized dancing that was to be characteristic of the dances of the later 1960s. "Rocking Around the Clock: Teenage Dance Fads from 1955 to 1965," in *Ballroom, Boogie, Shimmy Sham, Shake: A Social and Popular Dance Reader*, ed. Julie Malnig (Urbana and Chicago: University of Illinois Press, 2009), 194.

32. Hazzard-Gordon, *Jookin': The Rise of Social Dance Formations in African American Culture* (Philadelphia: Temple University Press, 1990), 81.

33. Ibid., 71.

34. " 'Boppin' at Miss Mattie's Place,'" 100. Competition is always an element in the group and line dances, particularly in Black communities; even while performing as a group to the same steps, the aim is to improve on the dance and further individual innovations.

35. Band members Buddy Tate and Harry Edison had been members of The Count Basie Orchestra. The Bryant version was the top seller in the spring of 1960. Al Brown and the Tunetoppers were represented by General Artists and made a huge national tour of their number. They were the house band at hundreds of clubs across the country and at the same time opened for many R&B stars including the Isley Brothers, Clyde McPhatter, Chubby Checker, and Screamin' Jay Hawkins. Larry Benicewicz, "Remembering Al Brown," *Blues Art Journal* (August–October 2009). Ray Bryant, it should not be forgotten, performed with many jazz greats, among them Charlie Parker, Lester Young, and Sonny Rollins.

36. Adding to this mix of history and lineage, the deejay Buddy Young has been credited with bringing the song to Baltimore from the Midwest in the fall of 1959. Jacques Kelly, "Al Brown's Legacy Is the Madison," *Baltimore Sun*, April 4, 2009.

37. John Goodspeed, "A New Dance for the Nation: 'The Madison,'" *Baltimore Sun*, May 8, 1960.

38. Wall, "Rocking Around the Clock," 191.

39. See Doug Tracy who quotes from an article by Lucius E. Lee in the Black-owned weekly newspaper *The Ohio Sentinel* from June 16, 1960. According to the *Sentinel*, William (Bubbles) Holloway, "invented it," while inspired at a trip to New York City's Birdland club, and then took it back to Ohio where he went on tour with it. The article also lays claim to the idea that after a stint at the LVA social club, Count Basie incorporated the Madison into his regular stage show, which, according to journalist Larry Benicewicz, may explain "how the dance received press notices as far away as London." Tracy, "It's Madison Time! Another Columbus First?," ColumbusMusicHistory.com; Benicewicz, "Remembering Al Brown."

40. The Madison on *The Buddy Deane Show* to Al Brown and the Tunetoppers number, Summer 1960: https://www.youtube.com/watch?v=iT_QNC6o24E. The Madison performed to Ray Bryant's "Madison Time": https://www.youtube.com/watch?v=X25fkeP9PTU.

41. Benicewicz, "Remembering Al Brown."

42. The dance itself was essentially a two-step performed to a 4/4 rhythm as dancers, in parallel lines, all faced the same direction. As with the Bop, of course, there were regional variations and differences in step patterns between Black and white communities.

43. Warner, *Buddy's Top 20*, 204.

44. Wall, "Rocking Around the Clock," 194.

45. *Ebony*, "The Madison."

46. Benicewicz, "Remembering Al Brown."

47. "Demonstrating 'The Swivel,'" *The Cash Box*, Music, undated clipping, ca. 1960, The Buddy Deane Papers, Special Collections in Mass Media and Culture, University Libraries, University of Maryland. Another version similar to the Madison was known as the Hully-Gully, which appeared in the early 1960s; this was a line dance with a short sequence of steps (unlike the Madison) and dancers performing side by side. See Richard Powers, "The Hully Gully, French Madison, Hot Chocolate, and the Electric Slide," http://socialdance.stanford.edu/syllabi/Hully-Gully.htm. Robert Pruter states that in Chicago the dance was seen as early as 1959, in Black communities, as the Hully-Gully, and danced to the Olympics's "(Baby) Hully Gully" in 1959. Again, the lyrics of the song suggest various movements or pantomimes "that may have accompanied the sideways steps of the dance." *Chicago Soul* (Urbana and Chicago: University of Illinois Press, 1991), 196. The name of the dance also appears in Black juke joints of the early twentieth century.

48. Sally Banes and John Szwed, "From 'Messin' Around' to 'Funky Western Civilization': The Rise and Fall of Dance Instruction Songs," in *Dancing Many Drums*.

49. See an image of the album cover at https://www.discogs.com/Al-Browns-Tunetoppers-Madison-Dance-Party/master/1317983.

50. Banes and Szwed, "Dance Instruction Songs," 170, 181.

51. See Lisa Sagolla, *Rock 'n' Roll Dances of the 1950s* (Santa Barbara, CA: Greenwood, 2011), 67–68 for a close description of the step count. Chapter 2, "The Rock 'n' Roll Dance Floor," contains detailed descriptions of many of the era's dances. The Stroll song was often performed to "C. C. Rider," which itself had developed on the Black vaudeville circuit.

52. Katrina Hazzard-Gordon notes that post–World War II, a movement frequently seen in dancing down the center was the camel walk, "a step similar to the Ghanian Adowa, originally a funeral dance performed by the Ashanti people." Hazzard-Gordon also points out how the line and circle were structural survivals of West African forms and became secularized in contact with the secular European reels "in which women and faced each other in lines." She refers to the Madison as a "clear example of contemporary secular line formations." The Stroll could be said to be a hybrid of Black and European dance styles. *Jookin'*, 159; 210, fn. 60.

53. John Szwed and Morton Marks, "The Afro-American Transformation of European Set Dances and Suites," *Dance Research Journal* 20, no. 1 (Summer 1998): 29–36.

54. Szwed and Marks remark that "Long before the emergence of ragtime there were a considerable number of Afro-American orchestra directors and composers at work on dance music." Some of these individuals were also arrangers and composers as well as dance callers. Szwed and Marks also point out that ex-enslaved persons interviewed by the WPA, in the 1930s, reveal that the dances remembered from slavery tended to be those such as contredances, square dances, cotillions, and quadrilles. Travelers' accounts, too, from the turn of the twentieth century, "mention Black fiddlers playing and calling reels for white and Black audiences." "The Afro-American Transformation," 31, 32. In her essay "Afro-Chesapeake Inventions of American Dance," Jurretta Heckscher traces this argument back to the mid-eighteenth century and notes the beginning of a "genuine creolization of African and European expressive movement systems," which would emerge more full-blown in the nineteenth century, including more extensive heterosexual partnering and even a more erect posture. But, as she notes, "What is European has been added without obscuring or diminishing what is African, which persists like the generative rhythm at the dance's core." "Our National Poetry," 27.

55. See Banes and Szwed, "Dance Instruction Songs," 195.

56. Ibid., 183.

57. Matthew Delmont, *The Nicest Kids in Town: American Bandstand, Rock 'n' Roll, and the Struggle for Civil Rights in the 1950s* (Berkeley: University of California Press, 2016), 169, 172–173.

58. "Willie and the Hand Jive, by the Late, Great, Johnny Otis," *Open Culture*, January 20, 2012.

59. Ihsan Taylor, "Johnny Otis, 'Godfather of Rhythm and Blues,' Dies at 90," *New York Times*, January 19, 2012. Otis produced the hit recording "Hound Dog" for Big Mama Thornton in 1952, which was then made famous by Elvis Presley.

60. Otis was also a disc jockey and had his own show on KFOX, Long Beach, California, in 1955. See George Lipsitz, *Midnight at the Barrelhouse: The Johnny Otis Story* (Minneapolis: University of Minnesota Press, 2010), xiii, 53, 57.

61. Tim Londergan, "Bo Didley/Willie and the Hand Jive: Bo Diddley, Johnny Otis, and Eric Clapton," *Tim's Cover Story*, November 16, 2015. https://timscoverstory.wordpr ess.com/2015/11/16/bo-diddleywillie-and-the-hand-jive-bo-diddley-johnny-otis-and-eric-clapton/.

62. Malone, *Steppin' on the Blues*, 15.

63. According to his biographer, historian George Lipsitz, Johnny Otis's inspiration for the song was a chain gang song he had heard while he was on tour with his band in the early 1950s. *Midnight at the Barrelhouse*, 68. For another rendition of the Hand Jive, see the jazzy, theatricalized sequence in the 1959 Columbia Pictures film *Juke Box Rhythm* featuring Johnny Otis and band members along with professional jazz dancers Gil and Nikky Brady. The film was directed by Harold Bruce Belfer, who started out as a dance director in 1930s Hollywood.

64. "Studio Party, 1957," *Big Beat Legends*, DVD, www.thevideobeat.com. The Susie Q was performed to rockabilly singer and rhythm guitarist Dale Hawkins's song of the same name in 1957. It was a line dance considered similar in orientation to the Big Apple from the late 1930s. The Walk was a type of line dance performed to an eponymous song by blues singer Jimmy McCracklin in 1958. On *American Bandstand*, the dance was performed in a Conga line, as dancers moved their hips and torso from side to side as they traveled around the floor. (See Sagolla, *Rock 'n' Roll Dances of the 1950s*, 70.) Robert Pruter, on the other hand, contends that Black dancers in Chicago were performing something called the Walk in the early 1950s, well before McCracklin's hit song. As he notes, "partners would hold onto each other, side by side, and stroll across the floor in a slow walk tempo." According to Pruter, the first song performed for the Walk was the Spaniels' "Play It Cool" in 1954. *Chicago Soul* (Urbana and Chicago: University of Illinois Press, 1991), 207, 208.

65. David Garcia, "Embodying Music/Disciplining Dance/The Mambo Body in Havana and New York City," in *Ballroom Boogie, Shimmy Sham, Shake a Social and Popular Dance Reader*, ed. Julie Malnig (Urbana and Chicago: University of Illinois Press, 2009),166.

66. Sagolla, *Rock 'n' Roll Dances of the 1950s*, 70; Garcia, "Embodying Music," 168–169.

67. Although Clark recorded these songs with the Kool Gents, a top vocal group in Chicago, when the singles were released a year later, they were simply under the name of Dee Clark. Pruter, *Chicago Soul*, 28–29. Even though Dee Clark made appearances on *American Bandstand*, the Chalypso-oriented song that became most popular on the show was "La De Dah," recorded in 1957 by the Black doo-wop duo Billy and Lillie (Billie Ford and Lillie Bryant); not that surprisingly, the number was issued on the Swan record label with whom Dick Clark had part interest. John A. Jackson, *American Bandstand: Dick Clark and the Making of a Rock 'n' Roll Empire* (New York: Oxford University Press, 1997), 210–211. "La De Dah," written by record producer Bob Crewe and producer Frank Slay (who later went on to write for The Four Seasons), hit the top ten *Billboard* chart at #9. Billy Ford started out as a trumpeter and bandleader, originally of Billy Ford and the Thunderbirds. Lillie Bryant sang in church and then appeared at the Apollo Theatre amateur nights. The Spaniels recording in 1960 of "I Know" "featured a light Latin-beat, dubbed 'chalypso,' typical of many R&B tunes of

the days. The song lasted six weeks and went to number twenty-three on Billboard's R&B chart, and Vee Jay put out the group's second LP." Robert Pruter, *Doowop: The Chicago Scene* (Urbana and Chicago: University of Illinois Press, 1991), 111.

68. Clay Cole, *Sh-Boom! The Explosion of Rock 'N' Roll 1953–1968* (Garden City, NY: Morgan James Publishing: 2009), 126.

69. See "Alas, Chicken's Dead," *Detroit Free Press*, April 20, 1958, for a variation of this dance on *Detroit Bandstand*.

70. https://www.youtube.com/watch?v=9zSJHKMYDXQ&list=RDkHVRIf9B xms&index=24.

71. *Twist*, a film by Ron Mann (DVD: Home Vision Entertainment, 2002).

72. Ibid.

73. A former member of Ballard's "Midnighters," Lawson Smith, offers his explanation of how the movements may have come about. See interview with Tom Meros: https://www.youtube.com/watch?v=-7eXm91EVms.

74. Dance historian Sally Sommer makes this point when she notes of Black vernacular styles that, "given the exchanges of song and movement that always occur between singers and their audiences, it is easy to understand how twisting got transformed into a singular dance when the right song arrived." "Twentieth-Century Social Dance since 1960," in *The Oxford Encyclopedia of Dance*, 632.

75. *Jookin*, 83.

76. In "Ballin' the Jack," the early twentieth-century song with dance lyrics, dancers are exhorted to "twis around and twis around with all your might," which translated into a rotating the pelvis in a circular motion. Stearns and Stearns, *Jazz Dance*, 99. One of the best extended treatments of the history of the Twist as a musical composition is Jim Dawson, *The Twist: The Story of a Song That Changed the World* (Winchester, MA: Faber and Faber, 1995).

77. In Black vernacular dance, these movements were also alternately referred to as the Grind and Snake Hip, "a flow of undulating rhythm from chest to heels." See Stearns and Stearns, *Jazz Dance*, 107. Also see Banes and Szwed, "From Messin' Around,'" 177–178; and Dawson, *The Twist*, 107.

78. Wall, "Rocking Around the Clock," 194.

79. Chubby Checker is well known for describing what he felt he taught dancers to do: "I showed people my concept of what the Twist was to me. You remove your hands from your partner, putting out a cigarette with both feet, wiping off your bottom with a towel to the beat of the music. People understood that." *Twist* (documentary).

80. Lipsitz, *Barrelhouse*, 59.

81. *Twist* (documentary).

82. Brian Ward, *Just My Soul Responding: Rhythm and Blues, Black Consciousness and Race Relations* (London: Routledge, 1998), 481, n. 107.

83. In a Zoom class on dances of the 1960s, Toni Basil suggests that the dancer should let the changes in tempo and rhythm guide the improvisational movement.

84. Cynthia J. Novack, "Looking at Movement as Culture: Contact Improvisation to Disco," *The Drama Review* 32, no. 4 (Winter 1988): 106.

85. The Mashed Potato was introduced nationally by James Brown and his band in 1960 with "Do the Mashed Potatoes" but was then popularized by the R&B singer Dee Dee Sharp's "Mashed Potato Time" in 1962; "Twine Time," by Alvin Williams, was a dance initially performed by Black teenagers at Chicago's Dunbar High School. See Pruter, *Chicago Soul*, 202–203.

86. Sommer, "Social Dance," in *Oxford Encyclopedia*, 632.

87. Pruter, *Chicago Soul*, 188. The Stearns note that "As the dances multiplied, the quality deteriorated. Many such new 'dances' . . . were simply charades, pantomimes with band-and-arm gestures and little body or footwork." *Jazz Dance*, 5; Reebee Garafolo is dismissive in his contention that Chubby Checker followed up the Twist "with a series of short-lived faddish dance records like the 'Hucklebuck,' the 'Pony,' and the 'Fly.'" "Crossing Over," 85. Charlie Gillett, too, dismisses many of these dances and blames the teen dance shows for their decline and "homogenization." *Sound of the City*, 208. Of course, Gillett fails to take into more serious account the role of the local teen dance shows in fostering regional and citywide variations across the country. Robert Pruter makes the valid point that the Stearnses, in particular, fail to make a distinction between dances performed in the white community and those in the Black community, the latter of which maintained their "high quality" during the 1960s. *Chicago Soul*, 190.

88. Dance teachers, among them Arthur Murray, in his numerous dance manuals, also attempted to codify rock 'n' roll dance in easy-to-retain and memorize steps and sequences for the commercial ballroom-dance studio world. Some of the dance manuals include Arthur Murray's *How to Become a Good Dancer* (New York: Simon & Schuster, 1959); and John G. Youmans's *Social Dance* (Pacific Palisades, CA: Goodyear Publishing Co., 1969). Thomas DeFrantz argues how codification became aa particularly European American phenomenon. For more on this, see *Uprooted: The Journey of Jazz Dance* (TV documentary, Dir. Khadifa Wong, Prod. Lisa Donmall-Reeve, On the Rocks Film, 2020).

89. Weingarten, *Station to Station*, 62.

90. Garofalo, "Crossing Over," 85.

91. Banes and Szwed, "Dance Instruction Songs," 188.

Chapter 5

1. Peter Guralnick, *The Last Train to Memphis: The Rise of Elvis Presley* (Boston: Little Brown & Co., 1994), 370. Nat Williams was the first Black deejay in Memphis. He was also host of the Palace Theatre's famed Beale Street Amateur Night and director of Booker T. Washington's high school talent show. He was also a nationally syndicated columnist/journalist. He made stars of the likes of B. B. King, Rufus Thomas, and Bobby "Blue" Bland. Guralnick, *The Last Train to Memphis*, 369.

2. As Frith notes, "Girl culture, indeed, starts and finishes in the bedroom" (228). A few years later, Iain Chambers designated a photo of a young, sweatered girl, sitting on

the floor handling her record covers, as "Bedroom girl" (43). Such images, though, appeared even before the 1950s. Rachel Devlin refers to a magazine cover of *Woman's Home Companion* published right after the end of the war, featuring the "Sub-Deb" girl who "in a sweater sits next to a haphazard stack of records, clutching one of them to her chest." Frith, *Sound Effects: Youth, Leisure, and the Politics of Rock 'n' Roll* (New York: Pantheon, 1988), 228; Chambers, *Urban Rhythms: Pop Music and Popular Music* (New York: St. Martin's Press, 1985), 43. Devlin, *Relative Intimacy: Fathers, Daughters, and Postwar American Culture* (Chapel Hill: University of North Carolina Press, 2005), 93.

3. Frith, *Sound Effects*, 226.
4. Kearney, "Producing Girls: Rethinking the Study of Female Youth Culture," in *Delinquents and Debutantes: Twentieth-Century American Girls' Cultures*, ed. Sherrie A. Inness (New York: New York University Press, 1998), 285. For a theorization of girls' "bedroom culture," see Catherine Driscoll, *Girls: Feminine Adolescence in Popular Culture and Cultural Theory* (New York: Columbia University Press, 2002), 257–263.
5. Savage, "Sex, Rock, and Identity," in *Facing the Music: A Pantheon Guide to Popular Music*, ed. Simon Frith (New York: Pantheon Books, 1988), 143.
6. Breines, in Joanne J. Meyerowitz, *Not June Cleaver: Women and Gender in Postwar America, 1945–1960* (Philadelphia: Temple University Press, 1994), 384.
7. LaKisha Simmons, *Crescent City Girls: The Lives of Young Black Women in Segregated New Orleans* (Chapel Hill: University of North Carolina Press, 2015), 177.
8. Lawrence Laurent, "Youth Upholds TV DJs," *Washington Post*, October 23, 1960.
9. Devlin, "Female Juvenile Delinquency and the Problems of Sexuality Authority in America, 1945–1965," in *Delinquents and Debutantes*, 85.
10. *Where the Girls Are: Growing Up Female with the Mass Media* (New York: Times Books, 1994), 85.
11. As Amanda Littauer has written, "It is critical to focus more closely on women and girls not simply as a matter of inclusion but because of the highly gendered nature of mid-century sexual values." *Bad Girls: Young Women, Sex, and Rebellion before the Sixties* (Chapel Hill: University of North Carolina Press, 2015), 7.
12. Branstetter, womeninrockproject.org/introduction.
13. In her excellent work *Black Diamond Queens: African American Women and Rock and Roll* (Durham, NC: Duke University Press, 2020), Maureen Mahon takes stock of the reasons why African American women have not been seen as a central part of rock 'n' roll history. One of these has to do with the nature of genre. Citing Jacqueline Warwick's book on girl groups of the 1960s, Mahon writes that "a process of making gendered distinctions between masculine, authentic rock and feminine, commercial pop has diminished the creative contributions of women and underplayed the commercial motivations of male performers" Another reason, Mahon contends, has to do with the undervaluing of vocalists in rock criticism, "which prioritizes instrumentalists, songwriters, and producers as the significant creative forces in the field." See pp. 3–9. Also see Jacqueline Warwick, *Girls Groups, Girl Culture: Popular Music and Identity in the 1960s* (New York: Routledge, 2007).

14. Susan Cahn, *Sexual Reckonings: Southern Girls in a Troubling Age* (Cambridge, MA: Harvard University Press, 2007), 12.

15. Ibid.

16. Devlin, *Relative Intimacy*, 13. Kelly Schrum, too, in points out the development of the popularization of female teen culture: "From the early twentieth century until mid-century, professionals defined adolescence while advertisers, media, educators, parents, and girls experimented with the related but distinct concept of the 'teenager.'" *Some Wore Bobby Sox: The Emergence of Teenage Girls' Culture, 1920–1945* (New York: Palgrave, 2004), 20.

17. According to a description in the Estelle Ellis Papers at the National Museum of American History at the Smithsonian Institution, Ellis was the first to commission market research reports "to establish teenage girls and working women as distinct and economically powerful markets." Archives Center, Estelle Ellis Papers, ACO423 (423-FA) (1941–2004).

18. Cahn, *Sexual Reckonings*, 243.

19. Ibid., 259. .

20. Kelly Schrum points out that the number of Black students grew more slowly particularly in rural areas and in the South. As she also points out, "High school had a dramatic effect on students because it provided a place for constant peer interaction without parental supervision. In classrooms and through extracurricular activities, high school students discovered an unprecedented opportunity to develop friendships and peer culture free from adult control. Peer culture played a new, central role in shaping the experience of adolescence, especially for girls, by promoting conformity and age-specific norms and allowing for the development and dissemination of teenage culture." *Some Wore Bobby Sox*, 13, 14. In another work, Schrum notes, "the proportion of fourteen-to-seventeen-year olds who attended high school grew from 11 percent in 1990 ... to almost 80 percent in 1940. Enrollment for girls roughly equaled that of boys." "Teena Means Business: Teenage Girls Culture and *Seventeen* Magazines, 1944–1950," in *Delinquents and Debutantes*, 136. Here, Schrum is quoting from Paula Fass, *The Damned and the Beautiful*, 124; 407–408.

21. Inness, "Introduction," in *Delinquents and Debutantes*, 6, 11.

22. Cahn, *Sexual Reckonings*, 259.

23. Wini Breines, *Young, White and Miserable: Growing Up Female in the 1950s* (Chicago: University of Chicago Press, 1992), 87.

24. Cahn, *Sexual Reckonings*, 260.

25. Amanda Littauer, *Young Women, Sex, and Rebellion before the Sixties* (Chapel Hill: University of North Carolina Press, 2016), 7.

26. Here Devlin cites the work of Lynn Weiner in *From Working Girl to Working Mother: The Female Labor Force in the United States, 1820–1980* (Chapel Hill: University of North Carolina Press, 1985). Devlin herself notes that "What is interesting about the entrance of older, white, middle-class women into the workforce in the late 1940s and 1950s is that their greatest growth was among white, middle-class wives who worked for their own personal satisfaction and to raise their family's overall standard of living." She also notes how married women's work helped support

the lifestyles of their daughters and freed them from work as in the 1940s; these expenses included "an extra telephone line, more clothes, another car, entertainment, etc." *Relative Intimacy*, 199, fn. 47.

27. The "domestic-containment" analysis was proffered by historian Elaine Tyler May. Joanne Meyerowitz, though, is wary of what she calls this "conservatism-and constraints approach" to analyzing women of the 1950s; she asserts that "an unrelenting focus on women's subordination" "tends to downplay women's agency and to portray women primarily as victims." I agree with her but also believe that the abundant *representations* of women in the 1950s—despite how women actually *behaved*—were continual reminders to women and girls of their expected roles. It is true, as Meyerowitz argues, that historians today "read" mass cultural products not as monolithic message-makers but as contradictory and ambivalent, and which can be read differently by different readers. Nonetheless, the power of these images cannot be denied, as Betty Friedan powerfully argued in *The Feminine Mystique* (1963). The prevailing cultural attitudes, transmitted by the media, emphasized women's place within the home and domestic life. Rachel Devlin, too, critiques Tyler May's thesis; she doesn't deny its force, however, but argues rather that it wasn't the sole ideology of the period: "The staid familial containment of the 1950s was constantly in danger of collapsing under the weight of its contradictory imperatives and the ongoing rebellions these imperatives engendered." See Tyler May, *Homeward Bound: American Families in the Cold War Era* (New York: Basic Books, 2008), 14; Meyerowitz, "Introduction," in *Not June Cleaver*, 4; and Devlin, "Female Juvenile Delinquency," in *Delinquents and Debutantes*, 86.

28. Breines, "Introduction," in *Young, White, and Miserable*, 17.

29. Ibid., 11.

30. Cahn, *Sexual Reckonings*, 242. Also see Schrum, "Teena Means Business," 136–137.

31. Cahn, *Sexual Reckonings*, 266.

32. See Simmons, *Crescent City Girls*, 185; and Breines, *Young, White, and Miserable*, 96.

33. Simmons, *Crescent City Girls*, 182. Cahn refers to a 1950 sociological study of Black beauticians and their customers noting that *True Confessions* and *Love Story* were extremely popular with Black women and girls.

34. Beverly Lindsay-Johnson, interview with the author, August 19, 2020.

35. Rachel Devlin, *A Girl Stands at the Door: The Generation of Young Women Who Desegregated America's Schools* (New York: Basic Books, 2018), xxi.

36. Ibid., xxi.

37. Simmons, *Crescent City Girls*, 4.

38. Quoted in Maxine Leeds Craig, *Ain't I a Beauty Queen? Black Women, Beauty, and the Politics of Race* (New York: Oxford University Press, 2002), 31.

39. Ibid., For more on what Craig calls the "gendered discourse of race and respectability," see ibid., 30–37.

40. Rachel Devlin, drawing on the work of historians of Black women including Darlene Clark Hine, Deborah Gray White, and Nell Irvin Painter, points out that "Black girls and women were both sexually vulnerable and viewed as sexually dangerous." Devlin notes that, particularly in the South, Black girls were often

seen as sexually threatening (to white boys) as much as Black boys were viewed as sexually threatening to white girls. As she explains, "sexualized stereotypes also followed Black girls when they desegregated schools." *A Girl Stands at the Door*, xxii, xxiii.

41. Margo Jefferson, *Negroland: A Memoir* (New York: Pantheon, 2015), 165.
42. Ibid., 123. *The Girl Can't Help It* (1956), starring Jayne Mansfield, featured Little Richard performing the title song written by Bobby Troup.
43. "King of Rock 'N' Roll: Fats Domino Hailed as New Idol of Teen-agers," *Ebony* 12, no. 4 (February 1957): 26.
44. Ibid.
45. Shaw, quoted in Philip H. Ennis, *The Seventh Stream: The Emergence of Rock 'n' Roll in American Popular Music* (Middleton, CT: Wesleyan University Press, 1992), 238.
46. Guralnick, *Last Train to Memphis*, 369.
47. Ibid., *The Last Train to Memphis*, 370.
48. Shayla Thiel-Stern, *From the Dance Hall to Facebook: Teen Girls, Mass Media, and Moral Panic in the United States, 1905–2010* (Amherst: University of Massachusetts Press, 2014), 118. Susan Cahn also offers an intriguing analysis of the possible reasons for the perpetuation of the image of the screaming female fan. She is typically depicted as unhinged and uncontrolled, as opposed to conscious of her behavior (and her desires). As Cahn writes, "Stories about crazed female fans tended to focus on pre-adolescent eleven- to thirteen-year-olds, thus locating the phenomenon among pubescent girls typically too young to be aware of sexual arousal and their erotic agency." *Sexual Reckonings*, 260.
49. Breines, *Young, White, and Miserable*, 96. According to Breines, "For girls who lived through it, just hearing the word 'popularity,' is enough to generate a cold sweat." *Young, White, and Miserable*, 111.
50. As Jacqueline Jones points out, the images of working women in *Ebony* were a natural outgrowth of the fact that Black women had for long, unlike their white counterparts, combined paid labor with domestic concerns. She also describes Ebony's stance as "aggressively integrationist," and that it had long been a strong advocate for civil rights. *Labor of Love, Labor of Sorrow: Black Women, Work, and the Family from Slavery to the Present* (New York: Perseus Books, 2009), 222, 223. For a very good analysis of *Ebony* magazine in relation to Betty Friedan's *The Feminine Mystique*, see ibid., 221–227.
51. See Dwight Macdonald, "Profiles: A Caste, A Culture, A Market-1," *New Yorker*, November 22, 1958. This was part one of a fascinating two-part series by Macdonald on the advertising guru of the time Eugene Gilbert. Also see Devlin, *Relative Intimacy*, 82, on how teenagers of this era might exercise a sense of "cultural power" through their consumerism.
52. Schrum, *Some Wore Bobby Sox*, 20.
53. Cahn, *Sexual Reckonings*, 218–219.
54. Ibid., 222.
55. Lee Woodward, interview with the author, August 27, 2014. Woodward was the host of *Oklahoma Dance Party*.

56. Richard E. Stamz Papers, Subseries 2: Radio and Television, 1932–2006, Box 29, Center for Black Music Research, Columbia College, Chicago, Illinois. Cue sheets from Saturday, January 21, 1956. The models were hired from the Crest Charm and Model School on South Parkway in Chicago. Since Stamz's show was not strictly a teen dance show, it featured fashion designs geared toward slightly older girls and women; the show advertised dresses which could be worn for day-into-evening wear, bouffant dresses for "evening frolics," and a multi-purpose dress with "the little girl look with 1/4 inch length sleeves, scoop neckline and low gathered waist."

57. Patrick A. Roberts, *Give 'Em Soul, Richard!: Race, Radio, and Rhythm and Blues in Chicago* (Urbana and Chicago: University of Illinois Press, 2010), 77.

58. Craig, *Ain't I a Beauty Queen*, 7.

59. Ibid., 46. LaKisha Simmons notes how racist ideologies of the time also saw Black women and girls "as always an object of someone else's pleasure." *Crescent City Girls*, 176. Rachel Devlin, writing about the young Black girls responsible for desegregating public schools, explains that "while some of the most sensational anti–civil rights propaganda of the fifties and sixties deployed images of Black men with white women, when it came to school desegregation the record shows that judges and lawyers spoke more about the innate promiscuity of Black girls." *A Girl Stands at the Door*, xxii.

60. Craig, *Ain't I a Beauty Queen*, 8. Importantly, as Craig notes of the period of the civil rights era, "Beauty contests, explicit attempts to rebuild a lost Black culture and implicit acts of self-love, played parts in the rearticulation of race during those years." The beauty pageants, seen in many Black schools, were born out of the Black middle class "and reflected the biases characteristic of this class" (16, 19). Later in the civil rights movement, there were attempts to integrate white beauty contests when integrationist and assimilationist efforts were underway.

61. Cahn, *Sexual Reckonings*, 218.

62. Craig, *Ain't I a Beauty Queen*, 19. For more on Black modeling agencies see Malia McAndrew, "Selling Black Beauty: African American Modeling Agencies and Charm Schools in Postwar America," *OAH Magazine of History* 24, no. 1 (January 2010): 29–32. As McAndrew notes, the Black modeling and charm schools, despite attempting to change the image of Black women, often at the same time reinforced traditional white, middle-class conceptions of beauty and behavior. "Moreover," she notes, "they uncritically accepted popular thinking that tied women's social worth to their physical appearance" (29).

63. Mulvey, "Visual Pleasure and Cinema," in *Visual Pleasure and Narrative Cinema* (London: Koenig Books, 1974).

64. Beth L. Bailey, *From Front Porch to Back Seat: Courtship in Twentieth-Century America* (Baltimore: Johns Hopkins University Press, 1989), 59.

65. Breines, *Young, White and Miserable*, 105.

66. Ibid., 106.

67. The well-known developmental psychologist quoted here is David Elkind, author of "Egocentrism in Adolescence," *Child Development* 48, no. 4 (1967): 1025–1034. Also see Jennifer Senior, "A High School We Can't Escape," *New York Times*, August 5, 2018.

68. *Bandstand Days*. Part of Gipson's yearning to "be seen" on the teen shows can be said to be, too, a kind of "movie star fantasy"—of being recognized and then swept away in a world of make-believe. In Gipson's comment is also a kind of dismissal of the family, or at least a break away from the family, with its ordinariness as well as its inherent restrictions: As Breines writes, "For this generation, the weakening hold of the family magnified the contradictions created by passive romance fantasies of being discovered (the way movie stars were by Hollywood) and chosen." *Young, White, and Miserable*, 106.

69. Beverly Lindsay-Johnson, interview with the author, August 19, 2020.

70. Yvonne Mills, interview with the author, August 24, 2020. Mills is also the president of *Teenarama* Inc., a promotional and civic-oriented organization in DC.

71. Breines, *Young, White, and Miserable*, 113.

72. James Coleman, "The Adolescent Culture," Chapter 2 in *The Adolescent Society: The Social Life of The Teenager and Its Impact on Education* (New York: Free Press of Glencoe, 1961), 11.

73. Sheryl Garratt, "Teenage Dreams," in *On Records: Rock, Pop, and the Written Word*, ed. Simon Frith and Andrew Goodwin (London: Taylor & Francis Group, 2000), 342.

74. Schrum, *Some Wore Bobby Sox*, 126; 127. Although Schrum refers specifically to the 1940s, the trends she identifies lasted well into the 1950s. She also notes a tradition dating back to the 1940s of girls, as evidenced in the yearbook pages, with interests in musical careers or avocations—"seniors who wanted to be crooners, orchestra leaders, or 'boogie-woogie' piano players."

75. Garratt, "Teenage Dreams," 344.

76. Douglas, *Where the Girls Are*, 88.

77. Interview with the author, August 19, 2020.

78. Garratt, "Teenage Dreams," 49.

79. James Sullivan, "Guitarist Link Wray Dies," *Rolling Stone*, November 21, 2005. "Rumble" was Wray's signature number, notable for its "highly stylized instrumental swagger" sometimes dubbed "raunchy." Wray was actually one of the first electric guitar innovators. In the mid-1950s, Link's group, The Wraymen, were regular guests on *The Milt Grant Show*. As Sullivan notes, " 'Rumble,' despite the radio bans, eventually reached Number Sixteen on the national pop charts."

80. Interview with the author, August 11, 2020.

81. Ibid.

82. Interview with the author, July 10, 2013.

83. Interview with the author, August 11, 2020. Wollensak was a very popular brand of audiovisual products in the 1950s and 1960s.

84. Ibid.

85. Link Wray's big hit was "Rumble," in 1957.

86. Interview with the author.

87. In our August 11 interview, Matlins explained that she had read, years later, that Vernon Wray's son had died in an automobile accident, which, she said, may have explained his disappearance. In 2010, the Smithsonian's National Museum of the American Indian featured the Wray Brothers in an exhibition entitled "Up

Where We Belong: Native Musicians in Pop Culture" (the brothers, Link, Doug, and Vernon, were part Shawnee). In an interview with the *American Indian News Service*, Sherry Wray, Vernon's daughter and executor of the family's music estate, describes the brothers' musical accomplishments and how Link, in particular, was an inspiration for many rock icons, among them Jimi Hendrix, Bob Dylan, and Pete Townshend. For more on the brothers' musical backgrounds and their efforts to establish a foothold in the recording business, see John O'Connor, "Mystic Chords," *Oxford American: A Magazine of the South*, November 20, 2018.

88. Interview with the author, August 11, 2020.
89. According to Robin Seymour, "In '63 there, every recording artist that ever recorded with Motown was on my show first." Interview with the author, July 1, 2011.
90. *Swingin' Time* actually went by various names during its long run (it lasted until 1971). It began as *Teen Town* and then ended as *The Lively Spot*. See Gordon Castelonero, *TV Land Detroit* (Ann Arbor: University of Michigan Press, 2007), 137–144. Some of the early Detroit teen-bandstand shows included *Detroit Bandstand*, *Ed McKenzie's Saturday Party*, and *Club 1270*.
91. Robin Seymour, interview with the author, July 21, 2011.
92. Leslie Tipton Russell, interview with the author, June 5, 2013.
93. Robin Seymour, interview with the author.
94. "Dick Clark: The Black Music Connection and More," April 25, 2012, https://michiganchronicle.com/2012/04/25/dick-clark-the-Black-music-connection-and-more.
95. Leslie Tipton Russell, interview with the author.
96. Toni Morrison, *Playing in the Dark: Whiteness and the Literary Imagination* (New York: Vintage Books, 1993), 15–19.
97. Kobena Mercer, "1968: Periodizing Politics and History," in his *Welcome to the Jungle: New Positions in Black Cultural Studies* (New York: Routledge, 2013), 58. As Antoinette Matlins relayed to me, "When I was a kid, you know, women were expected to get married and have husbands, have children, cook, and clean. You know, our world after high school didn't look all that attractive, quite frankly." Interview with the author.
98. Pete Daniel, *Lost Revolutions: The South in the 1950s* (Chapel Hill: University of North Carolina Press: 2000), 67.
99. For middle-class society, this was also a class issue, as young girls were seen as venturing into a male world of Black as well as working-class men. Also see Wini Breines, "Postwar White Girls' Dark Others," in *The Other Fifties: Interrogating Midcentury American Icons*, ed. Joel Foreman (Urbana and Chicago: University of Illinois Press), 71. I am in agreement with her analysis that girls were "active agents in the rejection of racial and gendered meanings of a femininity meant to confine them."
100. This could also be said of the white male Beats.
101. For more on DC Hand Dance see Chapter 4. Also see the documentary film *Swing, Bop and Hand Dance*, Exec. Dir. The National Hand Dance Association, Prod/Dir. Beverly Lindsay-Johnson, WHUT-TV Howard University documentary, 1996;

and Kim L. Frazier, *D.C. Hand Dance: Capitol City Swing* (Kearney, NE: Morris Publishing/Scriptural Foundations, 2000).

102. Peg Desonier, interview with the author, November 10, 2020.

103. Ibid.

104. Desonier watched *Teenarama* all the time but at a friend's house (since at home she couldn't access the UHF band).

105. Desonier was actually a dance major at the University of Maryland; she dropped out of college after two years, but then at age forty-six she completed her undergraduate degree, followed by law school. She is now a retired criminal defense lawyer.

106. According to George Lipsitz's biography, Otis has said that "I was never viewed as a white kid. . . . It was unheard of. There wouldn't be such a thing, a white kid wouldn't be playing with Black bands. Besides, there were lighter skinned Black youngsters than myself playing in the bands." Derek Richardson, "R&B's Johnny Otis Back Again," *San Francisco Chronicle*, June 26, 1983, 45, cited in Lipsitz, *Midnight at the Barrelhouse: The Johnny Otis Story* (Minneapolis: University of Minnesota Press, 2010), xviii.

107. *Rock Baby Rock It* is now something of an international cult favorite. It is viewed as a prototype of the 1950s "teen exploitation" movie. *Rock Baby Rock It* featured several up-and-coming R&B musicians, among them Don Coates and the Bon-Aires, Preacher Smith and the Deacons, and the doo-wop group The 5 Stars. *Hot Rod Gang* featured Gene Vincent, the originator of "Be-Bop-a-Lula."

108. Kay Wheeler. Interview with the author, August 18, 2020.

109. Interview with the author.

110. Ibid.

111. Ibid.

112. Julie Burns, "The King & Kay," *Vintage Rock*, April 2020, pocketmags.com/us/onlinereader/html5_reader/false/195-455.

113. Ibid.

114. Ibid.

115. Cahn, *Sexual Reckonings*, 249.

116. Interview with the author.

117. As music critic Nelson George astutely points out, it was a performance that was "sexy in the aggressive early manner associated by whites with Black males." Quoted in Breines, *Young, White and Miserable*, 158.

118. Interview with the author. During her career, too, at the height of Presley's fame, Wheeler became the West Coast editor of *Cool* magazine, which eventually merged with *Hep Cats* (one of the first magazine devoted to teen and rock stars and aimed toward working-class teenagers). She also wrote feature stories about rock 'n' roll.

119. Ibid.

120. Ibid.

121. Ibid.

122. In an interview with musicologist Leah Branstetter, Wheeler remarks that she pretty much developed her own style and own routine but that "the movie never got my best performance, because the song they selected for me to dance to was not a Black

R&B song, and I had to try to make it fit the rockabilly song of Johnny Carroll." "Interview with Kay Wheeler," www.womeninrockproject.org, February 20, 2012. For the film clip, see www.kaywheeler.com.

123. Wheeler suggests that director Alex Romero may have seen *Rock Baby Rock It*.

124. Nelson George, *The Death of Rhythm & Blues* (New York: Penguin, 2014), 67.

125. Breines, *Young, White, and Miserable*, 155.

126. Thiel-Stern, *From the Dance Hall to Facebook*, 119.

127. Ibid.

128. Mary Wilson, "Supreme Glamour," Zoom presentation, National Arts Club, New York City, December 1, 2020.

Chapter 6

1. Allen J. Matusaw notes how Title II of the 1964 Civil Rights Acts "outlawing discrimination in such places of public accommodation as restaurants, motels, theaters, and gas stations" was actually adhered to in most cities across the country, including the South. Rural areas, however, experienced the most opposition, "where significant resistance lingered for years and where even in the long arm of the Justice Department seldom reached." His contention, though, is that the South's adapting to desegregationist measures "confirmed the liberal faith that law, at least sometimes, could help change custom." *The Unraveling of America: A History of Liberalism in the 1960s* (New York: Harper & Row, 1984), 187. Eventually, though, many in the more radical arm of the civil rights movement came to believe that this was *not* the case. For more on civil rights in the 1960s and, in particular, the rise of the Black Power movement, see Eric Foner, *The Story of American Freedom* (New York: W. W. Norton, 1998); Maurice Isserman and Michael Kazin, *America Divided: The Civil War of the 1960s* (New York: Oxford University Press, 2004). Also see Renee C. Romano and Leigh Raiford, *The Civil Rights Movement in American Memory* (Athens: University of Georgia Press, 2006). On the civil rights movement of the 1950s and 1960s in relation to the Cold War see Mary L. Dudziak, *Cold War Civil Rights: Race and the Image of American Democracy* (Princeton, NJ: Princeton University Press, 2000); and Thomas Borstelmann, *The Cold War and the Color Line: American Race Relations in the Global Arena* (Cambridge, MA: Harvard University Press, 2001). For history of the 1960s and the rise of the New Left see Andrew Jamison and Rony Eyerman, *Seeds of the Sixties* (Berkeley: University of California Press, 1994).

2. Foner, *The Story of American Freedom*, 289. The quote within the quote here is from the Port Huron Statement, the guiding document of the Students for a Democratic Society (SDS).

3. Isserman and Kazin, *America Divided*, 20.

4. Telephone conversation with the author, August 14, 2021.

5. According to J. Fred MacDonald, "In its formative first decade, [the 1950s] the TV industry veered from honesty to duplicity in its depiction of African Americans. . . . In

the second period, which was particularly touched by the civil rights movement of the 1960s, television slowly, but undeniably, evolved toward a fairer treatment of blacks, yet even here, TV was not without significant failings." *Blacks and White TV: African Americans in Television since 1948*, 2nd ed. (Chicago: Nelson-Hall, 1992), xvii–xviii.

6. Julian Bond, "The Media and the Movement: Looking Back from the Southern Front," in *Media, Culture, and the Modern African American Freedom Struggle*, ed. Brian Ward (Gainesville: University Press of Florida, 2001), 27.

7. Elijah Wald, *How the Beatles Destroyed Rock 'N' Roll: An Alternative History of American Popular Music* (New York: Oxford University Press, 2009), 231.

8. Ibid.

9. Reebee Garofalo, *Rockin' Out: Popular Music in the U.S.A.* (Boston: Pearson Education, Inc., 2014), 164.

10. Wald, *How the Beatles Destroyed Rock 'N' Roll*, 250.

11. Another trend that musicologists point out was the increasing separation of Black-based styles of music from "rock" music with its attention to instrumentation and electronic experimentation. In the 1950s, as Wald points out, Black and white styles seemed to develop in tandem, "whether it was Little Richard and Jerry Lewis, the Drifters and the Belmonts, Hank Ballard and Joey Dee, Ray Charles and Bobby Darin, or the Crystals and the Shangri-Las." The Beatles were not shy about paying homage to their Black rock 'n' roll predecessors—Little Richard, James Brown, Muddy Waters—but there is a terrible irony here; as Garofalo notes, "the Beatles eclipsed all other talent so quickly and completely that many lost sight of the fact that, prior to their arrival, the most exciting developments in popular music had been in African American music." *How the Beatles Destroyed Rock 'N' Roll*, 239; *Rockin' Out*, 164.

12. Bud Buschardt with Sam Sauls, *The Sump'n Else Show* (Plano, TX: Entry Way Publishing, 2014), 12.

13. The original idea for the T.A.M.I. show was to serve as the anchor for a series of yearly concerts with awards ceremonies for music scholarships to benefit teenagers internationally. This never materialized; however, the concert itself became a milestone in music history and music filmmaking. After its live, debut concert (which ran over two nights), the T.A.M.I. show film appeared at thirty-three Los Angeles theaters in November 1964. In December, it was released nationally. It debuted in the UK with the title Teen Age Command Performance in 1965. It was a concert and film of many "firsts," including performances by eventual dance stars Michael Stewart (of *A Chorus Line*), Emmy Award–winning choreographer Anita Mann, and actress Teri Garr. The show's choreographer, the British dancer David Winters (who played A-Rab in the Broadway and film productions of *West Side Story* and Baby John in the musical version), would later go on to choreograph for several televised dance shows, among them *Shindig!* and *Hullabaloo*, discussed in this chapter.

14. Steve Binder Interview, Archive of American Television, Television Academy Foundation. https://interviews.televisionacademy.com/interviews/steve-binder.

15. In many respects, "jazz dance" is a misnomer, as the kind of dance performed on these teen dance shows of the 1960s was certainly not authentic jazz dance but rather a kind of theatrical or commercial dance typically seen on musical theater stages. The

"jazz dancers" on the shows were mostly trained and skilled in ballet technique along with modern dance. What was termed jazz dance by most professionals of the time (even the dancers themselves) was in essence modern and ballet dance and dance steps performed to jazz music, which then got *interpreted* as jazz dance. For the sake of clarity, though, and to avoid confusion, in this chapter I refer to this style of theatrical dance as jazz dance, as it was the commonly accepted parlance of the time. I am grateful to former dancer and professor of dance Karen W. Hubbard (quoted later in this chapter) for her insights on this subject. Hubbard has described much of the dancing on the shows as ballet "infused with vernacular glosses." Interview with the author, September 23, 2021; October 22, 2021.

16. Steve Binder interview.

17. The assistant choreographer, Toni Basil, became well known for her popular dance choreography on television and film and garnered a #1 hit single "Mickey" (and its cheerleader-driven video) in 1982. Some of her greatest fame came with the hip-hop group The Lockers, featuring LA-based dancer Don "Campbellock" Campbell, the originator of the locking style of hip-hop dance. See Don Waller, Liner Notes, "The T.A.M.I. Show Collector's Edition" DVD (Dick Clark Productions, Inc., 2009); and Toni Basil, interview with the author, August 23, 2020.

18. "Toni Basil Reflects: James Brown on the T.A.M.I. Show," Prod. by Toni Basil and Grip Reality, Inc., Toni Basil, 2015; www.tonibasil.net/streetdance.html.

19. Basil notes that she got this information directly from Bobbi Bennett, a member of The Flames who was also a songwriter, choreographer, and dancer in The James Brown Revue. He was inducted into The Rock and Roll Hall of Fame in 2012. "Toni Basil Reflects." Director Steve Binder, too, recalls how powerful the performance was. He said the relationship between the Flames and James Brown was "perfection" and that the entire act was "a rush on your brain." *The T.A.M.I. Show Collector's Edition* DVD (Dick Clark Productions, Inc., 2009).

20. Interview with Don Waller, *T.A.M.I.* DVD.

21. At the heart of the controversy was a Chrysler Plymouth executive (Chrysler was the advertising sponsor of the show), Doyle Lott, who wanted the segment edited out of the broadcast. According to Binder, "Doyle Lott was a racist. He didn't want Belafonte because Belafonte was Black, and he didn't want a Black star on the show with Petula." Binder refused to edit the tape, and NBC backed him up. Lott was fired as a result of the incident. See Interview with Steve Binder, Archive of American Television; and Robert E. Dallos, "Incident at TV Taping Irks Belafonte," *New York Times*, March 7, 1968.

22. Jake Austen, *TV a-Go-Go: Rock on TV from American Bandstand to American Idol* (Chicago: Chicago Review Press, 2005), 38.

23. Simon Frith, "Look! Hear! The Uneasy Relationship of Music and Television," *Popular Music* 21, no. 3 (October 2002): 285.

24. Ibid.

25. Austen, *TV a-Go-Go*, 38.

26. Anita Mann Interview, Archive of American Television, Television Academy Foundation, https://interviews.televisionacademy.com/interviews/anita-mann.

27. The Shindig Band feature the great percussionist Billy Preston. The final number also usually included the Blossoms (with Darlene Love) and The Wellingtons, a trio of male singers who often alternated with the white doo-wop group The Eligibles.

28. *Shindig* Retrospective (1991), https://www.youtube.com/watch?v=KdO4TP21Xys.

29. The first season lasted from January to May 1964, with repeats through August of that year. The second season ran from September 1965 to April 1966 and was reduced to a thirty-minute show. Directing credits were shared by Steve Binder and Bill Davis.

30. As Aniko Bodroghkozy notes, TV executives worried that viewing was down in the thirty-five to over-fifty group. Thus, the rock 'n' roll shows had to appeal to the teenage market (which was definitely on the rise) and to older viewers who, while they might not do some of these dances themselves, could be entertained by known, professional performers." *Groove Tube: Sixties Television and the Youth Rebellion* (Durham, NC: Duke University Press, 2001), 64–65.

31. In another nod, it seems, to older viewers, Paul Anka introduced his number "Feed the Birds," from *Mary Poppins*, by saying that "The same kids that are buying the single records are also buying albums too. And one of the bestsellers in that category is the cast album from *Mary Poppins*." Anka's rendition also includes a lovely dance number spotlighting McKechnie. See https://www.youtube.com/watch?v=F4J68ZyLNGg.

32. Toni Basil, interview with the author, August 23, 2020. Of the dancers who got their professional start on *Hullabaloo* were Donna McKechnie and Michael Bennett, of *A Chorus Line* fame. McKechnie went on to create the Tony Award–winning role of Cassie in *A Chorus Line*, in 1976, which was directed by Bennett.

33. Basil describes the relationship between social and professional dance when she discusses *Shindig!* guest Jackie Wilson, who performed the social dance the Twine: "What he was doing was the Twine, but basic Twine is step-touch just to move across; but then people raised the level, and all of a sudden that step-cross was leaping. It was like a chiasma. You just raised the level." Toni Basil, interview with the author.

34. Hubbard had had professional training in ballet as well as contemporary and traditional jazz dance while growing up in Columbus, Ohio. Her mentor was jazz dancer great Pepsi Bethel. When in New York in 1965, taking class at the June Taylor Dance studio, she was spotted by noted Hollywood choreographer Joe Cassini. As Hubbard said, "Right place at the right time with the right skills. And I remember Joe Cassini, the choreographer. He said, 'Let me see you do a pirouette.' And I did it like on Broadway, in the street." On the summer tour was Patrick Adiarte, the Filipino-American dancer who also became a hit on *Hullabaloo*. After the summer tour, the company went on to Las Vegas, but at that point Hubbard dropped out to attend college at Kent State University. Interview with the author, September 23, 2021. Hubbard, now a professor of dance at the University of North Carolina–Charlotte, was a member of the Karamu Concert Dancers, a modern dance company based in Cleveland, Ohio; she appeared in the 1976 production of *Hello Dolly!* on Broadway with Pearl Bailey in the starring role.

35. Norma Coates, "Excitement Is Made, Not Born: Jack Good, Television, and Rock and Roll," *Journal of Popular Music Studies* 25, no. 3 (September 2013): 318.

36. Jack Austen makes the point that by focusing on the crowd's excitement, the shows made TV viewers "feel like they were part of the action." *TV a-Go-Go*, 38.

37. Jackson, *American Bandstand*, 232. Jackson notes how *American Bandstand* also lost its sense of immediacy and community in part as a result of being taped, now, "up to a month or more in advance of its broadcast date." *American Bandstand*, 231.

38. For an interview with Peter Menefee, "Peter Menefee: A Dancer's Life," see https://www.youtube.com/watch?v=cK4RsR_5Sjg. Menefee was a featured dancer in touring companies of *West Side Story*, playing Baby John. In the interview, he recounts his audition process for *West Side Story* choreographer Jerome Robbins. Toni Basil reports that she choreographed the pilot for *Where the Action Is*. Correspondence with the author, August 25, 2021.

39. Austen, *TV a-Go-Go*, 40.

40. Interview with the author, January 24, 2017. Vilarino, an avid social dancer during the 1960s, danced on all the major local, LA-based shows including *Shivaree*, *Shebang*, and *The Lloyd Thaxton Show*.

41. The host of the show was the popular and affable deejay Sam Riddle. For more details on *Hollywood A Go-Go* see Austen, *TV a-Go-Go*, 43; and Marc Weingarten, *Station to Station: The History of Rock 'n' Roll on Television* (New York: Pocket Books, 2000), 134–135.

42. Al Burton began in Los Angeles as a writer of "Tele-Teen Reporter," a news show about teenagers for KLAC-TV. He was known for producing several Teen-Age Fairs, which featured musical performers by major rock 'n' roll groups and sold teenage parapher-nalia. He is known today for his collaborations with Norman Lear on several sitcoms and variety specials. Richard Sandemir, "Al Burton, 91, Dies; Sitcom Producer with an Eye for Youth Culture," *New York Times*, November 4, 2019.

43. Jim Freyler, www.gazzarridancers.com.

44. Apparently during the British Invasion, "singles from Los Angeles occu-pied the No. 1 spot for 20 weeks, compared to just one for New York." Clay Cole, *Sh-Boom: The Explosion of Rock 'N' Roll, 1953–1968* (New York: Morgan James Publishing, 2009), 249.

45. Bud Buschardt with Sam Sauls, *The Sump'n Else Show* (Plano, TX: Entry Way Publishing, 2014), 68. Ron Chapman went by the name of Irving Harrigan, profes-sionally, for his early disk jockey years. For more on Chapman's career see https://www.wfaa.com/video/news/local/d-fw-radio-legend-ron-chapman-dies-at-85/287-f9ada308-22a9-4fb7-83aa-98679da212d6.

46. *American Bandstand* was an inspiration, as was *The Lloyd Thaxton Show*, which had aired on WFAA in its syndicated form. The show aired in syndication from 1963 to 1968.

47. Buschardt, *The Sump'n Else Show*, 114.

48. Email correspondence with the author, August 18, 2021. According to Buschardt, "Local and national promotions were of great value to the show. 'The Little Group' was very active in beauty pageants, talent shows, fashion shows, theater and other personal appearances. Those appearances kept the show out in front of various and

numerous groups." *The Sump'n Else Show*, 122. The dancers were also trained in how to lip-sync custom jingles that got them in and out of commercial breaks.

49. Interview with the author, August 17, 2021.

50. Many of the televised teen dance shows of the 1960s employed dance teachers or coaches for the teenagers or required that they have some sort of dance training and background. According to the director (and eventually producer) for Houston's *The Larry Kane Show* Kerry Richards, Kane worked with the local Jerry Roe Dance Studio that taught the show's teenagers the latest dance styles. Richards notes how one of the teachers, Don Stewart, "was in charge of the placement of the kids when they would dance . . . he would constantly rotate everybody around so they would get seen more." Interview with the author, September 1, 2020. A former dancer and "regular" on the show, Glenn Pitts, had nine months of ballroom dance classes before coming onto the show. He recalled that dance director Jerry Roe "required that dancers be proficient in six steps in five dances to be accepted for the show." Email correspondence with the author, September 6, 2020.

51. TV director Jim Rowley mentioned how *The Sump'n Else Show* was the seeding ground for the musicians England Dan and John Ford Coley (then known as Dan Seals, the younger brother of Jim Seals of the 1970s rock duo Seals and Crofts). The two of them became friends at W. W. Samuell High School in Dallas. Seals eventually became a well-known country artist. Interview with the author, August 17, 2021.

52. Bud Buschardt, interview with the author.

53. Interview with the author, August 4, 2021. Tommy Johnson also served as director on later episodes of *The!!!! Beat*. Although the show developed in Nashville, Hoss Allen appealed to WFAA's Dallas–Fort Worth studios because he wanted the live show to air in color, and WFAA was the closest city that had the best equipment and technology. For episodes of *The!!!! Beat* see *The!!!! Beat*, Legendary R&B and Soul Shows from 1966, vol. 2, DVD, Bear Family Records (Holste-Oldendorf, Germany), https://www.bear-family.com/.

54. These included Otis Redding, Percy Sledge, Joe Tex, Sam and Dave, Carla Thomas, Patti LaBelle and The Bluebelles, and Etta James. James, who appeared on the show in 1966 (vol. #1, show 2), gives a stirring performance belting out "Only Time Will Tell." Overlooked earlier on in her career, James became a sensation after recordings done at the Fame studios in Muscle Shoals, Alabama. See https://www.youtube.com/watch?v=kFf22WIFC0Y&t=430s.

55. Weingarten, *Station to Station*, 138.

56. Rowley was also responsible for the animated logo that appears at the start of each show—the big, colorful punctuation marks that became a part of the show's signature televisual style.

57. Marc Weingarten suggests that *The!!!! Beat* may have been a little too unpolished "for affiliates who had grown comfortable with well-mannered *American Bandstand* knockoffs." *Station to Station*, 138–139. Jake Austen has documented two other local, Black-based R&B-based shows—*Night Train*, which also aired on WLAC, from 1964 to 1965, just prior to *The!!!! Beat*, and *Soul Time USA*, which aired out of San Diego in the late 1960s and early 1970s. Austen has described *Night Train*, primarily a

music show, as "a low-budget soulful version of *Shindig.*" *Night Train* was also white-produced. Austen suggests that these locally produced music shows functioned like an underground chitlin circuit for Black audiences. *TV a-Go-Go*, 94–95. For filmed episodes of *Night Train*, see *Night Train*, DVD, The Video Beat (www.thevideob eat.com).

58. Cynthia Novack, *Sharing the Dance: Contact Improvisation and American Culture* (Madison: University of Wisconsin Press, 1990), 38.

59. See this statement by music critic Wesley Morris in his essay "Why Is Everyone Always Stealing Black Music?," cited in the Introduction.

60. George Lipsitz, "Against the Wind," in *Time Passages: Collective Memory and American Popular Culture* (Minneapolis: University of Minnesota Press, 199), 122.

61. The actors were Brittany Snow and Vanessa Lengies.

62. Novack, *Sharing the Dance*, 34–35.

63. Michael Omi and Howard Winant, *Racial Formation in the United States* (New York: Routledge, 2015), 165.

64. Thomas DeFrantz, "Improvising Social Exchange: African American Social Dance," in *The Oxford Handbook of Improvisation Studies*, vol. 1, ed. George E. Lewis and Benjamin Piekut (New York: Oxford University Press: 2016), 331.

65. Interview with the author, April 20, 2021.

66. Jiiko Ozimba and Beverly Lindsay-Johnson, interview with the author, September 14, 2021.

Epilogue: Soul Train

1. Sally Sommer, "Social Dance," in *The Reader's Companion to American History*, edited by Eric Foner and John A. Garraty (Boston: Houghton Mifflin, 1991), 265.

2. *Soul Train* first aired in Chicago, at WCIU-TV, in 1970. It appeared daily on weekdays at 4:30 P.M.

3. Eric Foner, *The Story of American Freedom* (New York: W. W. Norton, 1998), 284.

4. Isserman and Kazin, *America Divided: The Civil War of the 1960s* (New York: Oxford University Press, 2004), 43.

5. Ibid.

6. Reebee Garofalo, with Steve Waksman, *Rockin' Out: Popular Music in the U.S.A.* (Upper Saddle River, NJ: Pearson Publishing, 2014), 72.

7. Peter Guralnick, *Sweet Soul Music: Rhythm and Blues and the Southern Dream of Freedom* (New York: Harper & Row, 1986), 12. Increasingly, this brand of Black music showed up on the televised teen dance programs. As John A. Jackson notes, after *American Bandstand*'s move to Los Angeles, in 1965, the number of Black musical acts, including soul and Motown performers, formed at least 35 percent of the musical talent on the show. *American Bandstand: Dick Clark and the Making of a Rock 'N' Roll Empire* (New York: Oxford University Press, 1997), 244. The same held true for many of the local TV dance shows.

8. Of James Brown's powerful and influential music, Reebee Garofalo has written that "In taking every instrument to the limit of its rhythmic capabilities, Brown carried the Africanization of popular music to its logical extreme, and strongly echoed the cultural nationalism developing in some segments of the African American community." *Rockin' Out*, 174, 175.

9. Ibid., 172.

10. Ibid., 174.

11. See Christopher Lehman, *A Critical History of Soul Train on Television* (Jefferson, NC: McFarland & Co., 2008); Ericka Blount Danois, *Love, Peace, and Soul: Behind the Scenes of America's Favorite Dance Show "Soul Train": Classic Moments* (Milwaukee: Backbeat Books, 2013); Nelson George, *The Hippest Trip in America: Soul Train and the Evolution of Culture and Style* (New York: William Morrow, 2014); and Questlove, *Soul Train: The Music, Dance, and Style of a Generation* (New York: HarperCollins, 2013).

12. Lehman, *A Critical History of Soul Train*, 55. For more on the dancers, see Danois, *Love, Peace, and Soul*, 33–54.

13. Don Campbell, who as a Los Angeles teenager became known for his renditions of the Funky Chicken at local clubs, later teamed up with choreographer Toni Basil who got the idea to form a group called the Campbellock Lockers (eventually known as the Lockers). The group went on to considerable success in clubs and on television. Members were Greg Campbellock Jr., Bill "Slim the Robot" Williams, Leo "Fluky Luke" Williamson, Adolfo "Shabba Doo" Quinones, and Fred "Mr. Penguin" Berry. Danois, 35, 42–43, 52.

14. The dancers were later referred to as the Soul Train Dancers after Cornelius signed a few of the original Soul Train Gang dancers to a record label where they were billed as the "Soul Train Gang." Lehman, *A Critical History of Soul Train*, 110.

15. George, *The Hippest Trip in America*, 31.

16. Ibid., 15.

17. Marc Weingarten, *Station to Station: The History of Rock 'n' Roll on Television* (New York: Picket Books, 2009), 239.

18. George, *The Hippest Trip*, xi.

19. Jazmine Hughes, "The Passion of Questlove," *New York Times Magazine*, October 12, 2021.

20. George, *The Hippest Trip*, 32.

21. "FridayFilms: Summer of Soul Explores the Modern Problem of Public Secrets," *New Light*, Oklahoma Contemporary (gallery): https://oklahomacontemporary.org/new-light/2021/08/fridayfilms-summer-of-soul-explores-the-modern-problem-of-public-secrets?gclid=EAIaIQobChMI_pbRt9C—AIVhd7ICh2BHwHTEAAYAyAA EgLHVvD_BwE.

22. *Summer of Soul* won Best Documentary Feature at the 2022 Academy Awards ceremony. "Ironically," as journalist Alan Light writes (before *Summer of Soul* won the Academy Award), "the only concert documentary to win an Academy award was 'Woodstock' in 1971, a film that cast a strong shadow on 'Summer of Soul.'" "'Summer of Soul' Reclaims a Concert Documentary Tradition," *New York Times*, March 1, 2022.

Research Centers and Collections Consulted

Anacostia Museum and Center for African American History and Culture, Smithsonian Institution, Washington, DC (Kendall Production Files, *Teenarama Dance Party*)

Behind the Veil Project, African American Life in the Jim Crow South Records, Duke University, Durham, NC

Billy Rose Theatre Collection, New York Public Library for the Performing Arts

Capitol Broadcasting Company Archives (WRAL-TV), Raleigh, NC

Center for Black Music Research, Columbia College, Chicago (Richard E. Stamz Papers)

Federation of North Carolina Historical Societies, Archives and History, Raleigh, NC

Historical Society of Washington, DC

Iowa State University Archives, Ames, IA

Jerome Robbins Dance Division, New York Public Library for the Performing Arts

Library of Congress, Motion Picture Collection, Washington, DC

Martin Luther King Research Center, Washington, DC, Public Library (Washingtoniana & Black Studies Collection)

Maryland Historical Society, Special Collections, Baltimore

Moorland-Spingarn Research Center, Howard University, Washington, DC (Black Life and Culture in the 1950s)

Murrey Atkins Library Special Collections, University of North Carolina (UNC) Charlotte Library (Chattie Hattie Leeper Oral Interviews)

Museum of Broadcast Communications, Chicago

Museum of Pop Culture (formerly the Experience Music Project), Seattle, WA

National Capital Radio & Television Museum, Bowie, MD

National Museum of American History, Smithsonian Institution, Washington, DC (The Estelle Ellis Papers)

Paley Center for Media, New York City

Peabody Awards Collection. University of Georgia Libraries, Athens, GA

Ray & Pat Browne Popular Library for Popular Culture Studies, Bowling Green State University, Bowling Green, OH

Rock and Roll Hall of Fame, Library & Archives, Cleveland, OH

Schlesinger Library, Radcliffe College, Dorothy Height Collection, Cambridge, MA (Black Women's Sororities and YWCAs)

Schomburg Center for Research in Black Culture, New York Public Library, Archives Division (Catherine Clarke Civil Rights Collection; Ralph Bunche Papers; Nat King Cole Papers)

Smith College, YWCA National Papers, Northampton, MA

Special Collections in Mass Media and Culture, Serials Collection, University of Maryland Libraries, Baltimore

Television Academy Foundation, Archive of American Television, Los Angeles

Temple University Urban Archives, Philadelphia

UCLA Digital Archive, Manuscripts Division, Los Angeles
UCLA Film & Television Archive, Los Angeles
Washington, DC, Historical Society, Kiplinger Collection
Wilson Library, University of North Carolina (UNC) Chapel Hill Library (J. D. Lewis
Family Papers)

Selected Bibliography

Auslander, Philip. *Liveness: Performance in a Mediatized Culture*. London and New York: Routledge, 1999.

Banes, Sally, and John Szwed. "From 'Messin' Around' to 'Funky Western Civilization': The Rise and Fall of Dance Instruction Songs." In *Dancing Many Drums: Excavations in African American Dance*, edited by Thomas F. DeFrantz, 169–205. Madison: University of Wisconsin Press, 2002.

Barlow, William. "Commercial and Noncommercial Radio." In *Split Image: African Americans in the Mass Media*, edited by Jannette L. Dates and William Barlow, 189–264. Washington, DC: Howard University Press, 1990.

Barlow, William. *Voiceover: The Making of Black Radio*. Philadelphia: Temple University Press, 1999.

Bertrand, Michael. *Race, Rock, and Elvis*. Urbana and Chicago: University of Illinois Press, 2005.

Bodroghkozy, Aniko. *Equal Time: Television and the Civil Rights Movement*. Urbana and Chicago: University of Illinois Press, 2013.

Breines, Wini. *Young, White and Miserable: Growing Up Female in the 1950s*. Chicago: University of Chicago Press, 1992.

Brown, Benita. "'Boppin' at Miss Mattie's Place': African American Grassroots Culture in North Philadelphia from the Speakeasy to the Uptown Theater during the 1960s." PhD diss., Temple University, 1999.

Cahn, Susan. *Sexual Reckonings: Southern Girls in a Troubling Age*. Cambridge, MA: Harvard University Press, 2007.

Chambers, Iain. *Urban Rhythms: Pop Music and Popular Culture*. London: Macmillan, 1985.

Delmont, Matthew. *The Nicest Kids in Town: American Bandstand, Rock 'n' Roll, and the Struggle for Civil Rights in 1950s Philadelphia*. Berkeley: University of California Press, 2012.

Devlin, Rachel. *A Girl Stands at the Door: The Generation of Young Women Who Desegregated America's Schools*. New York: Basic Books, 2018.

Devlin, Rachel. *Relative Intimacy: Fathers, Adolescent Daughters, and Postwar American Culture*. Chapel Hill and London: University of North Carolina Press, 2005.

Douglas, Susan. *Where the Girls Are: Growing Up Female with the Mass Media*. New York: Times Books, 1994.

Driscoll, Catherine. *Girls: Feminine Adolescence in Popular Culture and Cultural Theory*. New York: Columbia University Press, 2002.

Dudziak, Mary L. *Cold War Civil Rights: Race and the Image of American Democracy*. Princeton, NJ: Princeton University Press, 2000.

Ennis, Philip S. *The Seventh Stream: The Emergence of Rock 'n' Roll in American Popular Music*. Hanover, NH: Wesleyan University Press, 1992.

Foner, Eric. *The Story of American Freedom*. New York: W. W. Norton, 1998.

Forman, Murray. *One Night on TV Is Worth Weeks at the Paramount: Popular Music on Early Television*. Durham, NC: Duke University Press, 2012.

Garcia, Matt. *A World of Its Own: Race, Labor, and Citrus in the Making of Greater Los Angeles, 1900–1970*. Chapel Hill: University of North Carolina Press, 2001.

Garofalo, Reebee. "Crossing Over: 1939–1989." In *Split Image: African Americans in the Mass Media*, edited by William Barlow and Jannette L. Dates, 57–121. Washington, DC: Howard University Press, 1990.

George, Nelson. *The Death of Rhythm & Blues*. New York: Penguin Books, 1988.

Gillett, Charlie. *The Sound of the City: The Rise of Rock and Roll*. New York: Da Capo Press, 1996.

Guralnick, Peter. *The Last Train to Memphis: The Rise of Elvis Presley*. Boston: Little Brown, 1994.

Guralnick, Peter. *Sweet Soul Music: R&B and the Southern Dream of Freedom*. New York: Harper & Row, 1986.

Hazzard-Gordon, Katrina. *Jookin: The Rise of Social Dance Formations in African-American Culture*. Philadelphia: Temple University Press, 1990.

Hebdige, Dick. *Subculture: The Meaning of Style*. London: Methuen, 2003.

Jackoway, Elizabeth, and C. Fred Williams, eds. *Understanding the Little Rock Crisis: An Exercise in Remembrance and Reconciliation*. Fayetteville: University of Arkansas Press, 1999.

Jackson, John A. *American Bandstand: Dick Clark and the Making of a Rock 'n' Roll Empire*. New York: Oxford University Press, 1997.

Jackson, John A. *Big Beat Heat: Alan Freed and the Early Years of Rock & Roll*. New York: Schirmer Books, 1991.

Jones, Jacqueline. *Labor of Love, Labor of Sorrow: Black Women, Work, and the Family from Slavery to the Present*. New York: Perseus Books, 2009.

Jones, Leroi. *Blue People: Negro Music in White America*. New York: HarperPerennial, 2002.

Keil, Charles. *Urban Blues*. Chicago and London: University of Chicago Press, 1991.

Kelley, Robin D. G. *Freedom Dreams: The Black Radical Imagination*. Boston: Beacon Press, 2002.

Kelley, Robin D. G. *Race Rebels: Culture, Politics, and the Black Working Class*. New York: Free Press, 1994.

Leeds Craig, Maxine. *Ain't I a Beauty Queen: Black Women, Beauty, and the Politics of Race*. New York: Oxford University Press, 2002.

Lipsitz, George. "Against the Wind: Dialogic Aspects of Rock and Roll." In *Time Passages: Collective Memory and American Popular Culture*, 99–132. Minneapolis: University of Minnesota Press, 1990.

Lipsitz, George. *Class and Culture in Cold War America: "A Rainbow at Midnight."* South Hadley, MA: Praeger Special Studies, 1982.

Lipsitz, George. "Land of a Thousand Dances." In *Recasting America: Culture and Politics in the Age of Cold War*, edited by Lary May, 267–284. Chicago: University of Chicago Press, 1989.

MacDonald, J. Fred. *Blacks and White TV: African Americans in Television since 1948*. Chicago: Nelson-Hall, 1992.

MacDonald, J. Fred. *One Nation under Television: The Rise and Decline of Network TV*. Chicago: Nelson-Hall, 1994.

Macias, Antony. "Bringing Music to the People: Race, Urban Culture, and Municipal Politics in Postwar Los Angeles." *American Quarterly* 36, no. 3 (September 2004): 693–717.

Malone, Jacqui. *Steppin' on the Blues: The Visible Rhythms of African American Dance.* Urbana and Chicago: University of Illinois Press, 1996.

Meyerowitz, Joanne. "A Reassessment of Postwar Mass Culture, 1946–1958." In *Not June Cleaver: Women and Gender in Postwar America, 1945–1960*, edited by Joanne Meyerowitz, 229–262. Philadelphia: Temple University Press, 1994.

Morrison, Toni. *Playing in the Dark: Whiteness and the Literary Imagination.* New York: Vintage Books, 1993.

Nadel, Alan. *Containment Culture: American Narratives, Postmodernism, and the Atomic Age.* Durham, NC, and London: Duke University Press, 1995.

Nadel, Alan. *Television in Black and White America: Race and National Identity.* Lawrence: University Press of Kansas, 2005.

Pruter, Robert. *Chicago Soul.* Urbana and Chicago: University of Illinois Press, 1991.

Ramsey, Guthrie P. *Race Music: Black Cultures from Bebop to Hip-Hop.* Berkeley: University of California Press, 2003.

Roberts, John W. *From Hucklebuck to Hip Hop: Social Dance in the African American Community in Philadelphia.* Philadelphia: Odunde, 1995.

Schrum, Kelly. *Some Wore Bobby Sox: The Emergence of Teenage Girls' Culture, 1920–1945.* New York: Palgrave, 2004.

Simmons, LaKisha. *Crescent City Girls: The Lives of Young Black Women in Segregated New Orleans.* Chapel Hill: University of North Carolina Press, 2015.

Spigel, Lynn. *Make Room for TV: Television and the Family Ideal in Postwar America.* Chicago: University of Chicago Press, 1992.

Spigel, Lynn. *Welcome to the Dreamhouse: Popular Media and Postwar Suburbs.* Durham, NC: Duke University Press, 2001.

Stamz, Richard E., with Patrick Roberts. *Give 'Em Soul, Richard!: Race, Radio, & Rhythm & Blues in Chicago.* Urbana and Chicago: University of Illinois Press, 2010.

Torres, Sasha. *Black, White, and in Color: Television and Black Civil Rights.* Princeton, NJ: Princeton University Press, 2003.

Ward, Brian. *Just My Soul Responding: R&B, Black Consciousness, and Race Relations.* Berkeley: University of California Press, 1998.

Ward, Brian. *Radio and the Struggle for Civil Rights in the South.* Gainesville: University Press of Florida, 2004.

Williams, Raymond. *Television: Technology and Cultural Form.* Hanover, NH: Wesleyan University Press, 1992.

Index

For the benefit of digital users, indexed terms that span two pages (e.g., 52–53) may, on occasion, appear on only one of those pages.
Figures are indicated by *f* following the page number